PITT SERIES IN POLICY AND INSTITUTIONAL STUDIES

Turn to
page 77

IMAGERY AND IDEOLOGY

IN U.S. POLICY TOWARD LIBYA,

1969–1982 ➤ *Mahmoud G. ElWarfally*

UNIVERSITY OF PITTSBURGH PRESS

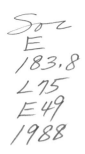
Published by the University of Pittsburgh Press,
Pittsburgh, Pa. 15260
Copyright © 1988, University of Pittsburgh Press
All rights reserved
Feffer and Simons, Inc., London
Manufactured in the United States of America

Library of Congress Cataloging in Publication Data

ElWarfally, Mahmoud G., 1952–
  Imagery and ideology in U.S. policy toward Libya, 1969–1982.

  (Pitt series in policy and institutional studies)
  Bibliography: p. 197.
  Includes index.
    1. United States—Foreign relations—Libya.   2. Libya—Foreign
relations—United States.   3. United States—Foreign relations—
1945–   4. Libya—Politics and government—1969–
I. Title.   II. Title: Imagery and ideology in US policy toward Libya.
III. Series.
E183.8.L75E49   1988   327.730612   87–35807
ISBN 0–8229–3580–5

CONTENTS

PART IV. U.S. POLICY TOWARD LIBYA DURING THE REAGAN ADMINISTRATION

TABLES

FIGURES

IMAGERY AND IDEOLOGY IN U.S. POLICY TOWARD LIBYA, 1969–1982

INTRODUCTION

Those who study how foreign policy decisions are made have often assumed that decision makers are rational actors who analyze problems with a cost-benefit formula. According to this theory, if all relevant information is available, problems can be broken down into logical components. Costs and potential outcomes can be rationally weighed, so that decision makers can choose the best course of action.

This mode of analysis has come under heavy criticism from various scholars, particularly cybernetic theorists and students of bureaucratic and organizational decision making. Of special importance is the cybernetic theory developed by John Steinbruner because of its resemblance to, or use of, some of the cognitive process theories developed by Noam Chomsky, Ulric Neisser, Leon Festinger, Robert Abelson, and others. Steinbruner questions the assumption that decision makers analyze all the components of a problem and, on the basis of full information, perform cost-benefit calculations. To him, decision-making behavior can be explained without resorting to elaborate mechanisms. He argues that decision makers are like tennis players moving to meet a ball with their racquets—selecting, without rational calculation, one pattern of response from hundreds of possibilities. Thus, according to this theory, for cybernetic decision makers the decisional process is a simple one that does not require much calculation. In other words, the sequence of decisional behavior is related less to an intellectual analysis of the problem at hand than to *past experience* from which there emerges an almost *intuitive* approach to problem solving. Steinbruner asserts what cognitive theory scholars have argued for before, namely, that "a great deal of information processing is conducted apparently prior and certainly independently of conscious direction and . . . in this activity the mind routinely performs logical operations of considerable power."[1]

This hidden cognitive dimension of the human personality is still the focus of study for many scholars and theorists, although there is no consensus as to what this cognitive dimension is. A panoply of concepts have been used: Milton Rokeach focuses on "belief systems," Michael Brecher talks about the decision maker's "view," Philip Burgess discusses "elite images" and "strategic images," Alexander George examines "operational codes," Winham deals with the decision maker's "image of a situation," Robert Axelrod is concerned with "cognitive maps," and Robert Jervis prefers the "evoked set."[2] Whatever terminology is used, the point of departure for all theorists is that individuals are affected by their cognitive systems, consciously or unconsciously, in different degrees, in their perception of the physical environment and their behavior within that environment—social, economic, and political. In this study, I use the concepts of *image* and *belief* synonymously in describing the workings of the cognitive dimension.[3]

As we interact with reality, beliefs and images become the lenses through which we interpret the stimuli of the situation. They affect our responses to it. Because every situation is complex by nature, to cope with the confusion of physical and social reality we tend to form a simplified yet well-structured set of beliefs and images about this reality.[4] These beliefs and images are ingrained in our minds to such a degree that reality itself becomes a succession of images. This is the notion that Joseph Jastrow was trying to articulate when he argued sixty years ago that "the mind is a belief-seeking rather than a fact-seeking apparatus."[5] Beliefs, nonetheless, differ in their impact on our conception of reality and our behavior toward it. They also differ in their receptivity to change and modification.

Most theorists agree that beliefs are divided into primary and secondary categories. Alexander George, for instance, distinguishes between what he calls "philosophical" and "instrumental" beliefs. The former, to which he assigns more importance, are reserved for the nature of politics and political conflict and the image of the opponent, whereas the latter govern the individual's approach to action.[6] Milton Rokeach talks about three types: "primitive" beliefs, which everyone is assumed to have formed early in life; "intermediate" beliefs, concerned with positive and negative authority and on which we depend "to fill out a map of our world"; and finally, "peripheral" beliefs, derived from the first two types, which differ from one person to another.[7]

Primary beliefs differ from secondary ones in their receptivity to change and their effect on our perception of reality, or definition of a situation, and our behavior toward it. For example, primary beliefs have been found to be much less changeable than secondary, derivative beliefs because of the rigidity of the mechanisms with which people react to information that contradicts primary beliefs.[8] Robert Jervis cites some of these mechanisms.[9] The simplest is to reject contradictory information automatically. Eunice Cooper and Marie Jahoda suggest that prejudiced people usually "evade the issue psychologically by simply not understanding the message."[10]

Rokeach describes the difference between the open and the closed mind:

> The extent to which information about the world is coerced into the system depends upon the degree to which the total belief-disbelief system is closed or open. At the closed extreme, it is the new information that must be tampered with, by narrowing it out, altering it, or containing it within isolated bounds. . . . At the open extreme, it is the other way around: new information is assimilated as is.[11]

In the first case the belief system is left intact, whereas in the second, change might occur. However, it will be minor and gradual because, in Jervis's words, "People change as little of their attitudes structure as possible. If they must change something they will first alter those beliefs that are the least important, that are supported by the least information, and that are tied to fewest other beliefs."[12] This rigidity of belief is called by cognitive process theorists "cognitive consistency." This is "the strong tendency for people to see and to assimilate incoming information to pre-existing images."[13]

Despite differences in terminology, theorists stress the same point: that information contradictory to our belief structure creates a condition of psychological pressure. To escape it, we strive to retain and preserve consistency either by rejecting, ignoring, or assimilating that information. Fritz Heider, Robert Abelson, and Milton Rosenberg discuss this issue in terms of the "balance" or "imbalance" within the belief structure. To them a balanced structure is one in which "all relations among good elements [that is, those that are positively valued] are positive (or null), all relations among 'bad elements' [those negatively valued] are positive (or null), and all relations among good and bad elements are negative (or null)."[14] For example, we tend to see that countries we like do things we like, and to see our enemies pursuing policies that would harm our interests. T. M. Newcomb discussed the same issue, using the terms "symmetry" and "asymmetry." He argues that human communication is crucial to regaining and maintaining symmetry in one's belief structure.[15]

Referring to relations that may exist between pairs of cognitive elements, Leon Festinger presents the same argument in terms of "consonance" and "dissonance."[16] Articulating the same thesis, Osgood and Tannenbaum present what they call "congruity hypothesis," the essence of which was developed by Heider, Newcomb, and Festinger before them.[17]

Because of the strong resistance to change inherent in image and belief structures, we develop prejudices and preestablished images (stereotypes) of other peoples and nations. A Nazi leader was said to give the following answer, when criticized for permitting the performance of an operetta written by a Jew: "A Jew could not have written something so beautiful; he must have stolen it from a Christian."[18] In the same vein, Max Planck argued that "a new scientific truth does not triumph by convincing its opponents and making them see the light, but rather because its opponents eventually die, and a new generation grows up that is familiar with it."[19]

Foreign policy officials and decision makers are certainly no exception to this cognitive pattern. Cognitive-process theorists place a strong emphasis on the psychological environment in which foreign policy decisions are made. Some even argue that international conflict is basically not a conflict between states, but between distorted images of states.[20] One might argue that this emphasis on images and beliefs could reduce the analysis to one variable, and produce a simplistic and distorted analysis because of the exclusion of other variables. For example, Ole R. Holsti and David Singer voice their concern over using cognitive perspectives in a "somewhat simplistic manner . . . assuming, for example, that beliefs constitute a set of decision rules that are mechanically applied by policy makers."[21]

I will argue that images and beliefs can have two kinds of impact on decision making. The first is a diagnostic impact—namely, the initial effect of the decision maker's images and beliefs on how a situation is perceived. This is the definition-of-the-situation stage, or what Alexander George calls the "information processing stage."[22] At this point, the impact of preestablished images and beliefs is overwhelming, simply because they determine our boundaries of comprehension and construct a frame of reference, a world view. Information is filtered through this frame, thereby given meaning, and that meaning is usually consistent with preestablished beliefs and images. Hence, the decision maker's policy preferences are usually also congruent with preestablished beliefs and images.

The second dimension of decision making is choosing the decision itself. At this stage, the analysis should be more careful and more sensitive to other variables that might be at work and may influence the selection of one decision over another. Although many studies, such as that of Burgess about Sweden and Norway, and Nazli Choucri on nonaligned nations, argue that the images of officials are translated into their states' foreign policies, we should not take this finding as an axiom without proof. It would also seem logical that "knowledge of higher-level elements [such as a preference for liberal or conservative policy] permits the observer to infer lower-level phenomena [such as specific policy preferences],"[23] but we should regard this idea only as a hypothesis requiring empirical research to establish its accuracy.

In *Cognitive Beliefs and Decision-Making Behavior,* Alexander George suggests two ways of assessing the impact of beliefs on decisional choices. First is to determine the "congruence" between the content of beliefs and the content of decisions. Consistency may be determined deductively:

> From the actor's operational code beliefs, the investigator deduces what implications they have for decision. If the characteristics of the decision are consistent with the actor's beliefs, there is at least a presumption that the beliefs may have played a causal role in this particular instance of decision-making.[24]

Determining a causal link between the decision makers' images and actions, or policy choices, entails a methodological assumption that should be examined carefully. Such consistency cannot be proved by any general law or nomothetic frame. However, some support can be provided for the cognitive balance theories discussed above.[25] Consistency between beliefs and actions may sometimes be observed repeatedly over a period of time. Stephen Walker's study of the impact of Henry Kissinger's beliefs on his bargaining with the North Vietnamese is a good illustration of a repeated consistency between belief and action.[26]

This study will assume that beliefs and images are central to choosing decisions, that through them decision makers define a situation, and that presumably their decision patterns will follow an expected course. I will attempt to answer these questions: Can we ascertain prevailing image of a situation in leaders' minds? Can we determine its potential effect on behavior or policy?

In any political system there are shared beliefs or "shared images."[27] But especially in a pluralistic system, there may also be considerable variation in those images, which in turn has significant implications for variations in decision making. Holsti properly contends, "This is precisely the reason for focusing on the individual policy maker, rather than assuming a homogeneity of beliefs among [decision makers]."[28] This inquiry will attempt to do it the hard way by trying to find the dominant image among decision makers in a pluralistic system—specifically U.S. officials' prevailing image of Libya.

After inferring the prevailing U.S. official image of Libya at specific times, I will discuss how much congruence exists between that image and U.S. policy toward Libya during those periods. Using deductive logic and the premises of cognitive-balance theory, I will try to construct some patterns of policy that can be inferred from various images. The researcher's task in the next step will be to compare the prevailing image with actual policy conduct, to discover the degree of congruence between the two. Should such congruence be established, it will bè reasonable to assume that actual policy conduct was affected—at least partially—by that prevailing image. This method will be discussed further in the next chapter.

But this study's most important task is to discover the priority of beliefs within the belief structure of U.S. officials regarding Libya. In other words, decision makers share certain beliefs or images that constitute primary concerns for them, through which they respond to the environmental stimuli of a situation. Jervis calls these beliefs the "evoked set" which "may be strong enough to lead the person to ignore information that is not relevant to his immediate concerns, even if in retrospect it seems clear that the message merited serious attention."[29] Translating this statement into foreign policy terminology, decision makers of state A (the United States, in this case) in their dealing with state B (Libya) will be most concerned with B's conduct only as it touches the area of their primary interest. This does not mean that A ignores other aspects of B's conduct, only that the intensity of A's image of B will be most affected when B's behavior is perceived as affecting A's most important concerns.

In this study, U.S. objectives and interests in the Middle East will be used as a general frame for U.S. concerns in the region. It will be my essential goal to discover which of these objectives most concerns the United States in the context of U.S.-Libyan relations. Thus, the study will be divided into four parts. The first will discuss methodology and U.S. objectives in the middle East. The second part will be devoted to Libya's conduct vis-à-vis U.S. objectives and the U.S. image of and policy toward Libya in 1969–1976. The third part will discuss Libya's policy toward U.S. objectives in 1977–1980 and the U.S. image of and policy toward Libya during that period. The fourth part deals with U.S.-Libyan relations during the first two years of the Reagan administration. A conclusion and an epilogue complete the study.

watch the Simpsons

Tur to page 153

PART I ➤ IMAGES, PATTERNS OF POLICY, AND U.S. OBJECTIVES IN THE MIDDLE EAST

1 ➤ METHODOLOGY

Most scholars who discuss how perceptions affect foreign policy behavior define image as a "picture in the mind,"[1] a model,"[2] or a "mental construction"[3] through which reality is viewed. To some it represents the product of the belief system.[4] To others, it is a subpart of the belief system.[5] In this study *image* is thought of as the mental whole of the behavior unit, through which the stimuli of the environment are received, interpreted, evaluated, and responded to. It reflects the learning process of the behavior unit, through past experience (as represented by its belief system) and present experience (illustrating the accumulative nature of knowledge that reasserts past experience, modifies it, and sometimes changes it).

This study is not concerned with why a certain type of image was prevalent in a certain foreign policy situation. Rather, it is concerned with the prevalence of certain images among American officials at given times and how congruent those images were with the American policy toward Libya at those times. The reason for using the *prevailing image* instead of merely the term *image* is that different and sometimes conflicting images of the same entity could exist in the same situation. The term *national image*,[6] as Holsti uses it, is too broad because it may include the images of the people of the country, too. Therefore this study will use the term *prevailing official image* to describe U.S. officials' image of Libya or its leadership in any period of time under study.

The prevailing official image will be inferred from the publicly available statements that include the U.S. view or policy toward Libya. The study will focus exclusively on the public statements of both the White House (the president) and State Department officials.

TYPES OF IMAGES

After inferring a nation's prevailing official image of another nation at any period of time, the next step is to classify it. In this study I will attempt to develop some of Richard Cottam's ideal patterns of images by adding some other ideal types, namely, *agitator, affiliate with the enemy, proxy, responsible moderate,* and *friend.* In developing and operationalizing these images, I have built on Cottam's framework. Ideal patterns are constructs of different combinations of the following possible responses to various foreign policy situations: perceptions of threat, of opportunity, of differences in power capability, and differences in culture from one's own nation.[7]

IDENTIFYING CHARACTERISTICS

The following dimensions were used by Cottam to identify and systematize typical image patterns:

Motivation is defined as a compound of factors that predispose a nation to move in a certain decisional direction in its foreign policy.

Capability is defined as a nation's tangible sources of power; variations among the capabilities of nations will be seen in terms of intangible factors such as the quality of government and the will to act. Culture will include the level of industrialization, technology, commercialization, and military development.

Decisional style and *locus of decision making* refer to the process through which decisions are made in a nation. Variations will be between a highly rational, elaborately orchestrated style and an ad hoc, incremental style of decision making, and between a monolithic, hierarchical structure and a highly differentiated one that is difficult to coordinate.

IDEAL PATTERNS OF IMAGES

To study the United States' prevailing official image of Libya, I will use the following ideal patterns of images as referents intended to gauge and determine what type of image existed at a certain time. But it should be pointed out that these patterns represent absolute pure cases; real images may approach them, but never be identical with them.

Enemy   David Finlay defines political enemies as "those who are in the 'opposition' or those who oppose 'our' power aspirations and ends, particularly when 'they' are outsiders or act in bad faith and employ 'dirty' tactics."[8] Cottam emphasizes another characteristic of an enemy state: it is comparable in capability and culture to one's own state. Cottam's definition of enemy is the one to be used in this study. Operational indicators are as follows:

1. *Motivation.* "The enemy is by prevailing value standards adjudged to be simply motivated, evil, and highly aggressive."

2. *Capability.* "Enemy capability is a derivative of the will, determination, and realism of the government and people of the threatened state. If their natural good will and faith persist, the enemy's capability is much enhanced, since the enemy will take full advantage of such weakness. But when confronted with a single minded will and determination to resist, the enemy will be exposed for what it is—a paper tiger."

3. *Style and Decisional Locus.* "The enemy is monolithic in its decisional structure and highly rational in its decisional process. It knows exactly what it wants and will use negotiations as a cover for achieving his objectives. Any indication of willingness to compromise is simply a pose. The surface appearance is a charade designed to deceive wishful thinkers. The public of the Enemy is disregarded in governmental decisions."[9]

Proxy   When a state perceives a threat from another state that is considered inferior in both capability and culture, but because of its intense friendly relations with an enemy (inferred from both actual conduct and the verbal statements), that state is considered a proxy. The perceived capabilities of the proxy state will be greater because of its perceived ability to mobilize the enemy's influence in its bargaining vis-à-vis the perceiver state. Consequently, the intensity of threat resulting from the proxy state's behavior will be larger than that perceived in the next two ideal patterns. Operational indicators are as follows:

1. *Motivation.* The proxy's motivations are assumed to reflect the enemy's motivations and they are described as evil and immoral. Its leaders are depicted as "puppets" of the enemy and an extension of the enemy's commitment to aggression, disruption, and expansion. The

proxy will use unlawful means to achieve its immoral objectives. Describing the leaders of the proxy state and their policies as disruptive, subversive, terrorist, aggressive reflects the perceiver state's perception of the enemy. Therefore, confronting or punishing this proxy is not only justifiable but also good and moral.

2. *Capability*. The proxy's capabilities are viewed as derived from the enemy's capability and from other states' weakness and lack of determination to stop the proxy's misconduct. However, it is only a "paper tiger." If confronted with solid will and determination, the proxy's real fragile structure and inherent weakness will be revealed.[10]

3. *Style and Decisional Locus*. The proxy's elite, viewed as surrogates of the enemy, will be described as "despotic, and deceitful, and able to formulate and hatch the most devious conspiracies."[11] Their decisional locus will be seen as monolithic and as part of the enemy's decisional structure. By contrast, the opposition elite will be described as "champions of democracy," rational and moderate responsible elements who follow an incremental diversified rational process of decision making.

Affiliate of the Enemy   Another image is that of the state friendly to the enemy. If a threat is perceived from a state which is inferior in both capability and culture to one's own but engages in friendly relations with the enemy, and if its policies may result in the expansion of the enemy's influence, it seems more threatening than the next category, the agitator state. That is because there is always a potential that this state may mobilize the power of the enemy in its bargaining vis-à-vis the perceiver state. Thus it appears to have more capability and its threat will seem more intense. Operational indicators are as follows:

1. *Motivation*. The ruling elite's declared intentions will be suspect, due to their friendly relations with enemy. Their claims of neutrality and self-independence will be questioned. There will be some doubt about whether the radical elite's policies stem from their extreme fanaticism or they really serve the enemy's ends. The stronger the elite's relations with the enemy, the more they will be described as puppets, surrogates, and dupes. This is true even if their policies are congruent with the enemy's by accident. The cooperative elite who call for disengagement with the enemy and cooperation with the perceiver state will be described as moderate, responsible modernizers who could serve their country more effectively.

2. *Capability*. The affiliate of the enemy will be perceived to be more capable than is empirically indicated. That is because the affiliate could influence the enemy's bargaining leverage vis-à-vis the perceiver state, even if unintentionally. The more intense the affiliate's relations with the enemy, the more its capabilities will be overestimated or even attributed to the enemy. But until the affiliate actually mobilizes the enemy's influence, it will be seen as technologically deficient because of the inferiority of its culture.

3. *Style and Decisional Locus*. Decisions of the affiliate's ruling elite will be seen as monolithic, reflecting the leaders' authoritarian will. Those leaders could be described even as agents of the enemy because their decisions serve the enemy more than their own country, even if unintentionally. The public and its interests will be seen as ignored. The cooperative members of the elite are seen as capable of putting the country back onto the right path because they are moderate and responsible.

Agitator   The agitator state is perceived as inferior in both capability and culture. Yet it is less threatening because it is viewed as incapable of carrying out its rhetorical threats. The agitator state, because of its purported inferiority, has little bargaining leverage with the perceiver state because of its inability to mobilize the influence of a third party that is similar to the perceiver in capability and culture. Thus, the agitator regime will be looked at with disdain and its leaders will be viewed as immature and irrational. Operational indicators are as follows:

1. *Motivation*. The agitator state's ruling elite who are unwilling to cooperate with the perceiver will be seen as erratic, irresponsible, pursuing radical policies that stem mainly from their fanatic ideas and extreme thinking, and not susceptible to compromise because of their lack of flexibility and rigid thinking. However, elites who call for cooperation with the perceiver state will be seen as responsible, moderate, and rational, and the real agents of modernization. The motives of the first group are judged to be immoral and evil whereas the motives of the second group are described as moral and good.

2. *Capability*. The agitator state will be perceived as incompetent and its leaders immature and unable to handle advanced technology and the complications of modern administration. Its capability will also be discounted because of its inability to influence a third power that is similar in

capability and culture to the perceiver state. If it could do so, it would be seen as more threatening and more capable.

3. *Decisional Style and Locus*. The ruling elite of the agitator state will be described as xenophobic, authoritarian, and highly individualistic. Decisions will be seen as reflections of the fanatic ideas of the leaders and their erratic personalities. If the cooperating elite were in power, their decisions would be seen as rational, incremental, and directed toward the modernization and the good of their society. The repressive measures taken by the agitators are described as undemocratic and obstacles to modernization, while if the same measures were taken by the cooperating elite, they would be either ignored or described as necessary for modernization.

Complex This pattern represents a detached, differentiated view in which reality is seen in all its complexity. A state has a complex image of another state when there is no external threat, or a state poses a threat that is considered insignificant. Operational indicators are as follows:

1. *Motivation*. "Motivational complexity will be granted governments in this situation. There will be little tendency to ascribe judgment of good or bad to the policy thrust associated with motivation. Defense is likely to be perceived as a significant aspect of motivation."

2. *Capability*. "Judgment will be made on the basis of empirical estimates of industrial and resource base, armed forces, training, and equipment rather than estimates of aggressive will and cunning from power advantage drives."

3. *Style and Decisional Locus*. "A highly diversified process will be seen with decisions made incrementally rather than coldly rationally in accordance with a pre-ordained plan."[12]

Ally This image is applicable when a state is viewed as comparable in both culture and capability to the perceiver, and as offering an opportunity. It is mainly a derivative image that results from an enemy threat. The more intense the threat, the more valuable the ally becomes as a "reflection of opportunity." Operational indicators are as follows:

1. Motivation. "Defensive, relatively simple, and generally benign, [the ally's] imperial activity will be justified in defensive reasons. It is a self-image projection of beneficent motivation to the ally."

2. *Capability*. "A favorite estimate of capability will be made. Na-

tional morale and quality of government will be praised. However, the ally is prone to grant good will to an enemy and this counters the favorable judgment."

3. *Style and Decisional Locus*. "The decisional process will be seen as diversified and incremental. Support for those leaders favoring the alliance will be substantial. The elements who oppose it are traitors or dupes of traitors."[13]

Friend   Like the ally, the friend represents an opportunity perceived in a state viewed as inferior in both capability and culture. But, unlike the responsible moderate, the friend is seen as more capable economically, politically, and militarily. The friend is also seen as moderate and responsible, but unlike the next category, it shares the perceiver's world view on most issues. Therefore, the friend offers a greater opportunity because of its commitment toward the perceiver and the "stability" of its foreign policy, even if the friend is not formally allied with the perceiver. Operational indicators are as follows:

1. *Motivation*. The cooperative ruling elite are perceived as modernizers of their country. Their foreign policy is geared toward stability, self-defense, and peace. Opposition elements whose objectives are instability and the control of power, are depicted as motivated by evil. They are agitators suspected of being agents of the enemy.

2. *Capability*. Though the friend is perceived as inferior in both capability and culture, it is more capable than the responsible moderate state. For it possesses capabilities—economic, military, or political prestige—that are deemed important for the achievement of either regional or domestic objectives. Because of its stability and strong commitment toward the perceiver state, it is characterized as a strong, *dependable friend* that could be relied upon to further the perceiver's objectives. The friend's technical capabilities, although not very efficient, are seen as improving and much higher than those of the responsible moderate state.

3. *Style and Decisional Locus*. The friend's decisional process is depicted as rational, diversified, moderate, and aimed at stability and progress. Repressive measures, when they take place, are justified as necessary steps against the extremism and radicalism that are trying to destabilize the regime. Those extreme elements are usually depicted as agents of a foreign power.

Responsible Moderate   When a state perceives an opportunity from a state it considers inferior in both capability and culture, it tends to see through imperialistic lenses.[14] Cottam clarifies this perception by arguing:

> If a people perceives a serious threat from a great enemy and perceives the probability of that enemy's expanding its influence into a third country [and] when in response to this threat an opportunity is perceived to gain a controlling influence in the threatened third country, thus obviating the threat, that third country will be seen in a way that conforms to the imperial ideal typical image. Most frequently in our era, such third countries will be of the variety called "underdeveloped" [read: culturally inferior].[15]

The perceiver state's policy will aim at assuring the continuity of the opportunity. Thus foreign aid programs will not only help weak states in which opportunity is perceived but also protect the existence of that opportunity, or channels of influence. Operational indicators are as follows:

1. *Motivation*. The ruling elite will be described as moderate, responsible, Western-oriented, and devoted to modernizing their country. The derogatory term *wog* (Western oriented gentleman) fits the description of this elite very acccurately.[16] Groups who oppose cooperation with the perceiver state are usually described as irresponsible factions who might be working as surrogates of a foreign state. On some minor issues the modern, responsible elite may differ in their world view from that of the perceiver state. Nevertheless, this difference does not affect their basic orientation toward the perceiver and consequently does not affect their policies which are seen as conducive to the achievement of the perceiver's objectives. In sum, it does not affect the opportunity offered by the perceiver state.

2. *Capability*. The responsible moderate's capabilities are downplayed because its administrative and technical skills are well below the level required to modernize the country. Thus, financial, economic, and military aid programs are necessary to help this *dependent friend,* not only to avoid socioeconomic instability but also to protect against external sources of destabilization. In sum, the responsible moderate is a very weak friend that should be helped to stay in power so as to help preserve an opportunity.

3. *Style and Decisional Locus*. The decisional style of the moderate-responsible elite is seen as rational. Leaders are described as constructive people trying to build their society, though lacking trained staff capable of running the country more efficiently. Opposition groups are seen as extremists desiring to rule on behalf of external powers that seek to impose their control on that country.

The scheme of images developed in figure 1 is consistent with the theory of cognitive consistency, as developed by Abelson, Rosenberg, Osgood, and Tannenbaum, which argues that people's belief structures tend toward consistency. In a consistent structure, "all relations among good elements [those that are positively valued] are positive (or null), all relations among bad elements [i.e., those that are negatively valued] are positive (or null)."[17] Fritz Heider uses a similar theoretical approach. Using the concepts of sentiment (like versus dislike), unit formation (separate entities comprising a unit when they are perceived as belonging together), and the balanced state (a situation in which the perceived units and the experienced sentiments coexist without stress), Heider argues that similarity creates a tendency toward liking or disliking (we tend to like those who are similar to us and dislike those who are similar to our enemies). That is because "if several parts, or traits, or aspects, of a person are considered, the tendency exists to see them all as positive, or all as negative."[18]

Essential to the previous theories is the tendency to dichotomize experience between good and bad, positive and negative, like and dislike, and so between threat and opportunity.

Let us take a closer look at the scheme of ideal patterns of images. Two remarks become obvious. First, it is divided among three different sentiments: positive, associated with the perception of another state as offering an opportunity; negative, associated with the perception of threat; and neutral or detached, associated with the perception of complexity—when perceptions of both opportunity and threat are absent. Second, there is a hierarchical order of intensity associated with perceptions of threat and opportunity resulting from the perceived conduct of the target state and its perceived ability to behave in a certain manner. This hierarchy of intensity gives the scheme an ordinal character which adds a certain degree of complexity (congruent with reality), although the scheme is basically dichotomous.

On the negative perception side the *enemy* pattern is given a first degree

Turn to pg. 101

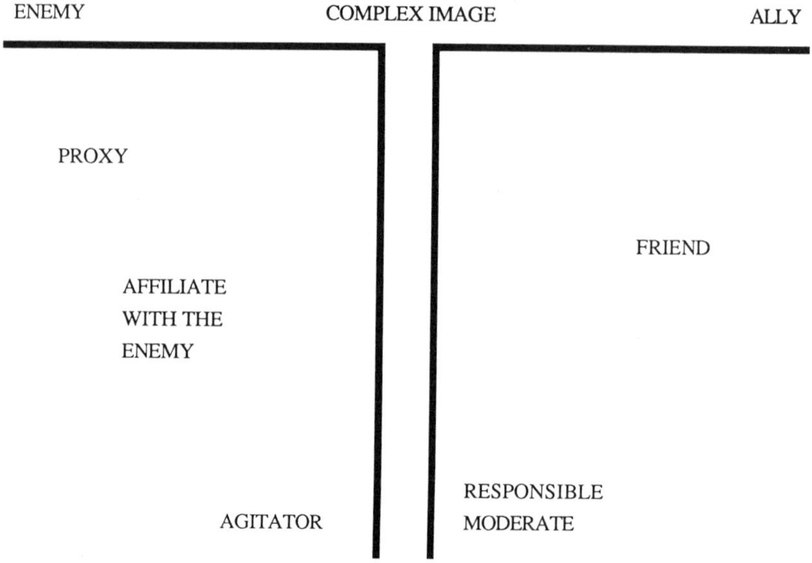

ENEMY	COMPLEX IMAGE	ALLY

PROXY

FRIEND

AFFILIATE
WITH THE
ENEMY

RESPONSIBLE
MODERATE

AGITATOR

Negative: Perception of Threat	Neutral	Positive: Perception of Opportunity
The higher the point on the map, the greater the intensity of threat, because of a state's perceived increase in capability and its ability to mobilize a third power for bargaining leverage.	The closer the point to the center, the more detached, neutral, and complex the image: a state is seen from various sides and is perceived as neither nostile nor friendly.	The higher the point on the map, the greater the perception of opportunity, because of a state's perceived increase in capability and potential usefulness as an ally against a common enemy.

FIGURE 1.   Ideal Patterns of Images

of intensity, the *proxy* state a second degree of intensity, the *affiliate with the enemy* a third degree of intensity, and a fourth degree of intensity is assigned to the *agitator* state. On the positive side, a first degree of intensity will be assigned to the *ally* state, a second degree to the *friend*, and a third degree to the *responsible moderate* state. A zero intensity will be assigned to the *neutral* or *complex* perception.

TECHNIQUE USED IN CONTENT ANALYSIS

Step 1 entails using the operational indicators of each ideal image as a guide, so we can analyze public statements issued by U.S. officials

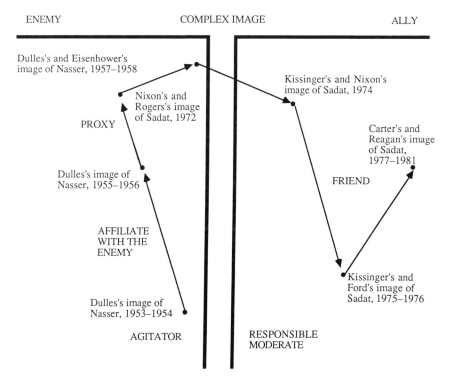

FIGURE 2.   Illustrative Example: U.S. Images of Egypt, 1953–1981

regarding Libya to find out which of the indicators best applies to each statement.

Step 2 involves determining what sentiment can be inferred (negative, positive, or neutral) from each statement and what degree of intensity the statement conveys.

Step 3 is to analyze all the publicly available U.S. statements regarding Libya. The empirical evidence will converge or cluster around one particular image more than others. That image will be considered the prevailing official U.S. image of Libya at a certain time.

Step 4 is to map the image along the scheme of ideal typical images, as exemplified in figure 1. Figure 2 illustrates the mapping of the prevailing U.S. image of Egypt at different periods in recent history.

The second essential task of this study is to compare the prevailing official U.S. image of Libya in a certain period of time with its policy toward that country during that period to find out how consistent the U.S. image of Libya has been with its policy toward that country. But before we turn to the scheme to be used in classifying the types of policies that one state may pursue toward another at different times, some points should be clarified. Many of the studies dealing with image use both verbal behavior and foreign policy to determine the prevailing image one state has of another in a certain situation. To them, the prevailing image becomes the implemented image, or the image that becomes policy.

This study, as the introductory chapter explains, will use a slightly different technique that focuses on verbal behavior as the sole basis for inferring image. Actual foreign policy behavior will be used as a control device to which image will be compared to ascertain the consistency between the two. In other words, the prevailing image, in this study, will be the most often stated image. Whether or not it is the one that became policy will be established by comparing the image with behavior. If an incongruity is detected, the following possible explanations will be explored.

1. That the officials responsible for formulating and executing U.S. policy toward Libya were not those whose statements constituted the prevailing image (the publicly stated one), or they did not express their image publicly and, hence, it did not emerge as the prevailing image.

2. That the officials who held the prevailing image were the same officials who formulated and executed the policy toward Libya, but in initiating the policy they were exposed to other factors of influence, domestic and international, that created a deviation of policy from their image (the effect of pressure groups, for example); or that some new developments took place that did not exist when they expressed their image, and hence influenced the path of policy according to the new situation.

In this study, no effort will be made to distinguish between the White House image of Libya and that of the U.S. Department of State. The documents from both sources will be treated as a unified source of data, from which images will be inferred.

IDEAL PATTERNS OF POLICY

As mentioned before, the second essential focus of this study will be the congruence between the prevailing official U.S. image of Libya and the actual U.S. policies toward that country during various periods in recent history. The following ideal policy patterns have been developed which, theoretically, should correspond to the scheme of image patterns discussed above. It should be pointed out that inferring those ideal types of policy from ideal images is based on the logical rules of deduction and heavily premised on assumptions of consistency, as discussed in the introductory chapter.

ANTAGONISM

This policy pattern should take place as a reaction to a perceived threat—when one state's prevailing image of another state falls within the enemy-complex-agitator triangle in the image scheme. This pattern of behavior includes using whatever economic, political, or military measures a government deems appropriate as pressure or punishment to deter the antagonist from initiating certain policies or to force it to change its policies. Three types of antagonistic policies can be distinguished.

Confrontation   When a threat is perceived from a country with equal capability and culture, it will be viewed in enemy terms, and the prevailing image held by the threatened country should approach the enemy pole in the image scheme. If the threat is the result of factors that are considered irreconcilable, such as conflicting ideologies and contradictory objectives, then the threatened country will become convinced that the enemy will block the pursuit of its objectives. Thus, every expansion of the enemy's influence will be seen as a decline in the threatened country's influence. (It will appear to be a zero-sum game, although not in reality.) Hence the expected policy pattern is total confrontation. Reconciliation, if it occurs, will be regarded as temporary and superficial. If the two countries can neither reconcile their contradictions nor eliminate each other (because of the equality and quality of their capabilities), then the logical conclusion is a relationship that resembles acute competition; each party tries to outrace the other in every aspect of life.

Intervention   This type of policy is assumed to reflect an increase in the intensity of threat perceived from a country inferior in capability and culture from one's own. This could result from that country's conduct toward some interests or objectives that are considered vital to the perceiver, or because its conduct is so unacceptable that the perceiver believes that the time has come to put an end to it. All this hostile conduct is perceived as indicating a strong affiliation or a proxy relationship with the perceiver's enemy. And finally, intervention may serve as a signal to another power that is perceived as supporting the proxy's misconduct. This type of policy may take the form of overt or covert intervention.

Overt intervention can take the course of direct military action to punish a regime or send it a signal that it should give up the policies it is pursuing. Also, it may take the form of military intervention in some areas considered as vulnerable and which could enable the enemy to expand its influence. Examples may be found in the U.S. "gunboat policy" intervention in Lebanon, July 15, 1968.

Covert intervention usually takes the form of subversion and plotting to overthrow a regime. Internal dissident elements, particularly within the military, are usually used as a spearhead to implement this form of intervention. (Mossadegh in 1953, Syria in 1957, Chile in 1973, are some examples of U.S. covert intervention against these regimes.)

Pressure   This type of policy may take place under the following conditions: (1) if a threat is perceived from a country that is regarded as inferior in capability and culture; (2) if a country is perceived as affiliated with the perceiver's enemy; (3) if its conduct was directed against certain of the perceiver's objectives; (4) if action has just been initiated and could perhaps be changed by pressure rather than by actual intervention, which could push it further in its unacceptable conduct; or (5) if that intervention, even if successful, is feared to result in the emergence of leaders that are more hostile to the perceiver. Pressure may take several forms.

Military pressure could take the form of embargoes on arms shipments and other military equipment. Supplying the adversaries of the target regime with arms, under the justification of protecting them against the regime's threats, is another form of military pressure. A third course may include the conduct of military maneuvers near the territorial zones of that regime ("showing the flag") as a warning sign to the regime to cease its undesirable actions.

Political pressure may take the form of isolating the regime internationally through convincing or pressuring other parties not to cooperate with that regime. It may also take the form of lowering the level of diplomatic representation with the regime, or even the total breakdown of diplomatic relations. Voting against the regime in international forums and carrying out a campaign of misinformation (propaganda) are other kinds of political pressure.

Economic pressure involves economic sanctions and attempts to influence other countries to follow the same course against the regime. (Iran and Poland are cases in point, when the United States tried to convince its Western allies to follow its pattern of economic pressure against these regimes.) Also, economic pressure could be applied against a regime through international economic organizations (as with the United States' actions against Egypt through the World Bank in 1956). Finally, the cancellation of mutual trade and foreign aid agreements that are usually beneficial to Third World regimes is another form of economic pressure.

Marginal Pressure   This type of policy is pursued when a regime's policies are viewed as representing more threat than opportunity. The target state's rigid and irresponsible policies are viewed as stemming from its leaders' extreme fanaticism and not from a foreign power. Consequently, the "stick" is used more often than the "carrot" as a way of applying some pressure against that regime to deter it from moving any further in that direction. The pressure is called marginal because it is intended as a warning, not as a punishment. Marginal pressure may involve any form of interaction between the two countries. For instance, it may take the form of delaying or suspending arms delivery to the target regime, or using strong language to protest or condemn the policies of that regime. At the same time, some forms of economic cooperation and trade continue to exist ("carrots"), and also some intense political contacts may be used to persuade the regime to turn away from policies that are deemed undesirable.

CONCILIATION

This policy pattern presumably prevails when one nation's prevailing image of another is complex. It involves taking sometimes contradictory measures toward a target regime whose conduct represents neither opportunity nor threat, and offers a potential opportunity. Thus, the two forms listed below reflect these variations in image.

Indifference   This type of policy takes place when a regime's policies are viewed as representing neither threat nor opportunity. Its neutral role is attributed to some factors such as the regime's insignificance (in terms of its capabilities) as a regional actor, or the insignificance of the region itself. The regime's pursuit of low-profile foreign policy is another factor. States such as Togo, Fiji, Lesotho, and Mauritius are only some examples of this type of country. The conduct of these regimes does not concern the superpowers except for the fact that they are members of the world community and occupy seats in the UN. Thus, some forms of economic assistance to these countries may exist but more as a response to their needs rather than their foreign policies.

Rapprochement   This type of policy prevails when the target regime changes the direction of its conduct that had represented some form of threat. Consequently, it offers a potential opportunity. Nevertheless, the regime is not completely trusted because of the changing character of its policies, or because more time is needed to judge its foreign policy line. Thus, the policy initiated toward this regime is characterized by cautious cooperation. Some of the regime's needs (economic, military) are to be responded to favorably, while others (usually requests for military equipment of the more sophisticated type) are to be delayed or turned down politely. But the point is to use the "carrot" more often than the "stick" as a way of encouraging the regime to move more responsively toward U.S. policies and objectives.

FRIENDSHIP

This policy pattern presumably prevails when the prevailing image is within the responsible moderate–friend area in the moderate-complex-ally triangle. For Cottam, the imperial pattern is followed to deal with situations in which perception of opportunity is more important than perception of threat and one people perceives another as culturally inferior, measured in terms of commercial development, industrialization, and technology.[19] Using this as a defining criterion, I would argue that the relations between any one of the superpowers and any Third World country would be of the imperialistic type if the opportunity is perceived to be large enough to promote a superpower's objectives vis-à-vis another superpower. Logically, the superpowers' policies would promote and strengthen that opportunity. The larger the opportunity, the more a superpower's policies will promote that situation. Two forms of friendship policy can be distinguished.

Cooperation   This policy pattern is expected to be pursued when one state's prevailing image of another falls within the responsible moderate orbit. This type includes those Third World countries that pursue a friendly policy that promotes U.S. objectives and policies in their region. Nevertheless, because of their low capabilities, they cannot affect the course of events in their region. Thus, U.S. policy toward them would be of the cooperative type, entailing military and economic foreign aid. The importance of these regimes may increase unexpectedly, and consequently a friendly U.S. policy may accelerate its cooperative tone as the United States' need of that regime and the regime's response to the United States both increase. For instance, Jordan would be considered a less important actor without the existence of the Arab-Israeli conflict.

Protectionism   This form of friendly policy is expected to be pursued when the prevailing U.S. image of another state falls within the "friend" orbit. This type includes those Third World regimes that pursue policies conducive to the U.S. policies and objectives in their region and possess capabilities that can affect the regional strategic balance. Therefore, the survival of these regimes is considered vital to U.S. interests and, hence, U.S. policy would be to protect their security and survival. Economic, military, and political cooperation is intense in this type of policy, in terms of the kind of military equipment sold to those regimes, the size of trade, and the political support given to those regimes.

To clarify both types of the friendship policy pattern, one could compare U.S. policies toward Saudi Arabia with its policies toward Tunis. Both regimes are considered by the United States as friends, but, whereas Saudi Arabia's policies toward Israel, the Soviets, and the flow of oil, are regarded as promoting and facilitating U.S. objectives, Tunis's conduct does not reach the Saudi level (because of its lack of significant assets—oil in this case—and because its policies toward the Soviets are less hostile than the Saudis').

ALLIANCE

This policy pattern is presumably pursued when one state sees opportunities in the conduct and attitude of another state regarded as equal or comparable in capability or culture. The prevailing image of the other state lies within the responsible moderate–complex–ally triangle. The more a threat is seen from an enemy, the more acute the need for an ally. The more friendly a country's policies are toward the United States (as theoretically they should be), the closer the image approaches the ally pole because of the benefit of countering the enemy collectively. The policy of alliance reflects the conviction that the ally is indispensable to the threatened country, and, by the same token, any threat against it is a threat against one's own state. Economic, military, political coordination take place between the allies, especially in times of intensive threat. Any difference in policies, if they arise, should be solved through dialogue because they are differences between brothers in the same family (see figure 3).

Before concluding this chapter, we should keep two points in mind: first, the ideal policy patterns (including the types of policy within each pattern which serve as indications of variation within each pattern) should be viewed only as hypothetical categories for examining and measuring real policy in a systematic manner.

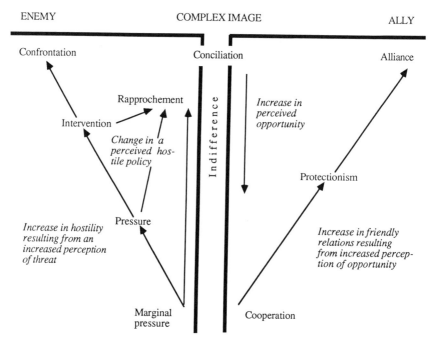

FIGURE 3.   Typical Patterns of Foreign Policy Relations

Second, the types of policy within each pattern are intended to be congruent with the changes in the perceptions of threat and opportunity in a temporal sequence. For example, with the increase in the perception of threat, the policy line should move from the indifference type (assuming that it is the starting point) to the marginal pressure type. With more intensity there should be a change in the pattern of policy itself from conciliation into antagonism. With more intensity of threat, there should be a change of policy in the antagonism category from pressure to intervention or confrontation. And the same sequence applies to the changes from conciliation to friendship as a result of increased perception of opportunity.

This is not to assume that the policies move up and down in fixed lines, because different lines of policy may be pursued at the same time. Also, it is conceivable to assume a change of policy and image from the friend–responsible moderate category to the enemy-antagonist category, without passing through the conciliation-complex category. (This happens when a sharp shift of the regime's policy takes place that results in a shift of the U.S. image from opportunity to threat, that is, a crisis.) An example of this might be a Marxist coup d'état in a friendly regime.

But it is hard to conceive of change in image and policy from the antagonist-enemy category to the friend–responsible moderate category without passing through the middle category (conciliation-complex) because regaining trust takes time.

2 ➤ THE UNITED STATES' OBJECTIVES
IN THE MIDDLE EAST

The basic assumption of this study is that both the U.S. image of and policy toward the revolutionary regime in the Socialist People's Libyan Arab Jamahira, or Libya, will be a function of that revolutionary regime's conduct, as perceived by the U.S. officials, in relation to U.S. objectives in the Middle East, simply because those objectives reflect the "evoked set" of U.S. images in that region. The policies of the Libyan regime vis-à-vis U.S. objectives will be dealt with as factors that presumably affect the U.S. image of and policy toward that regime.

This study seeks to discover the most important factor that affects the U.S. image of and policy toward Libya and consequently which of the United State's objectives or interests is most important in the Libyan-American relationship.

The objectives that are generally accepted as the pillars of U.S. foreign policy in the Middle East since the early 1950s, are as follows: (1) to maintain access to oil sources in the region (mainly Arab sources); (2) to preserve and enhance the security and well-being of Israel; (3) to minimize the influence and presence of the Soviet Union in the region. (This objective calls for containing the Soviet Union and also avoiding a direct superpower confrontation that could escalate into a nuclear conflict.) (4) A fourth objective, which is regime-related, could be added: to confront Libya's external revolutionary activities that could adversely affect the stability of regimes friendly to the United States in the Middle East and worldwide.

OIL

It was the vast reserves of oil and Britain's endeavor to monopolize them at the end of World War I that first attracted the U.S. oil companies to the Middle East. By 1928 several American firms managed to join a European group in operating the Turkish (later the Iraq) Petroleum Company. Since then, access to Middle Eastern oil has become one of the key objectives of U.S. policy in the region. The following factors make this objective even more crucial not only to the welfare and well-being of the American people, but also the well-being of its allies in Europe and Japan.

First, Western Europe depends on the Middle East and North Africa for about 85 percent of its oil needs, and Japan for about 90 percent. Second, United States imports only about 37 percent of its oil from the Middle East; nevertheless, in the 1970s, U.S. demand continued to rise at a 4 percent yearly rate which meant that according to official projections, that U.S. imports were going to rise from 9 million barrels per day in 1977 to 25 million barrels per day in 1985.[1] (Table 1 shows this growing trend, 1947–1977.) Third, this fact was coupled with some official projections that the Soviet Union would become a major importer of oil by the end of the 1980s,[2] and, fourth, the fact that the American oil corporations have dominated the international market added to the importance of this national objective. (See table 2.)

Although official projections about the growing trend of U.S. oil imports did not prove to be accurate (as tables 3 and 4 show), Middle Eastern oil is still considered the main source of imports for the United States' Western European allies and continues to be a profitable source of investment for U.S. corporations.

Thus, any events that could interrupt oil supplies to the United States or its allies would logically be considered a serious threat to all Western economies, as the 1973 embargo demonstrated. Obviously, the United States would view the conduct of the Libyan regime's oil policies in light of this objective.

ISRAEL

Since President Truman decided to work for Israel's establishment as a state, its security and well-being have been considered as inseparable

TABLE 1.   U.S. Trade in Crude Oil, 1947–1977 (thousands b/d)

	Exports	Imports		Exports	Imports
1947	126	268	1963	5	1,132
1948	116	353	1964	3	1,203
1949	90	422	1965	3	1,238
1950	96	488	1966	5	1,225
1951	79	490	1967	74	1,129
1952	74	575	1968	5	1,293
1953	55	649	1969	3	1,468
1954	38	658	1970	14	1,323
1955	33	781	1971	1	1,680
1956	79	937	1972	—[a]	2,222
1957	137	1,022	1973	2	3,244
1958	11	953	1974	3	3,422
1959	8	964	1975	6	4,165
1960	8	1,019	1976	2	7,300
1961	8	1,047	1977	—	9,699
1962	5	1,126			

Source: International Economic Report of the President, January 1977, as quoted in *Congressional Quarterly*, September 1977, p. 132.

a. Less than 500 barrels per day.

from the objectives of U.S. foreign policy in the Middle East. As Secretary of State Henry Kissinger put it on November 12, 1973,

> It has been a constant American policy, supported in every administration and carrying wide bipartisan support, that the existence of Israel will be supported by the U.S. This has been our policy in the absence of any formal arrangement, and it has never been challenged, no matter which administration was in office.[3]

President Carter went even further on May 13, 1977, to assert, "It's absolutely crucial that no one in our country or around the world ever doubt that our No. 1 commitment in the Middle East is to protect the right of Israel to exist, to exist permanently, and to exist in peace. It's a special relationship."[4]

This commitment, which became a de facto alliance, originated in concern for "the terrible plight of Jewish refugees from Hitler's

TABLE 2.   U.S. Direct Investment in the Middle East, 1971–1975 (in percent)

	1971	1973	1974	1975
Total Middle East investment as a percentage of total U.S. investment abroad	1.7	—	1.4	2.7
Total investment in oil as a percentage of total U.S. investment in the Middle East	6.0	7.8	5.4	10.6

Source: Survey of Current Business, November 1972, August 1974, October 1975, and August 1976.

TABLE 3.   U.S. Crude Oil Imports from Major Middle Eastern Oil-Exporting Countries, 1977–1982 (millions of barrels)

	1977	1978	1979	1980	1981	1982
Algeria	198	231	222	167	95	33
Iran	193	202	108	3	—	13
Iraq	27	23	32	10	—	1
Kuwait	15	2	2	10	—	1
Libya	**257**	**233**	**234**	**200**	**116**	**8**
Nigeria	412	332	390	308	223	186
Qatar	24	23	11	8	3	3
Saudi Arabia	501	417	492	458	406	194
United Arab Emirates	122	141	103	63	28	30

Source: Derived from Statistical Abstract of the United States 1984, 104th ed. (U.S. Department of Commerce, Bureau of the Census), p. 580.

genocide" and has been sustained by considerable public support. Israel is perceived as being an extension of Western democracy in a sea of what are seen as aggressive authoritarian Arab regimes. Israel also has a very influential U.S. lobby. In addition, Jewish voters are a very important bloc and can affect elections in key states. Due to these internal factors, the United States became Israel's chief arms supplier and protector in international forums. Over a twenty-year period, starting with the first

TABLE 4.   U.S. Dependence on Petroleum Imports, 1977–1982 (million b/d average)

	1977	1978	1979	1980	1981	1982
Arab Countries	3.18	2.96	3.05	2.55	1.85	.84
All OPEC	6.19	5.75	5.63	4.29	3.32	2.10
All Nations	8.56	8.00	7.99	6.37	5.40	4.23

Source: The World Almanac and Book of Facts, 1984 (New York: Newspaper Enterprise Associates, Inc.), p. 132.

shipment of arms, September 26, 1962, U.S. assistance to Israel has totaled $14,255 billion—an amount that has never been matched in the history of U.S. assistance to its other allies and friends. (See table 5.) Despite periodic tensions that may characterize the relations between these two countries, the basic commitment still stands firm. Therefore, it is natural to assume that hostile or friendly conduct by any other Middle Eastern regime in relation to this objective would be seen by U.S. officials as a source of threat or opportunity for one of this country's long-standing objectives in that area.

THE SOVIET UNION

One of the first reasons for the U.S. commitment to the region after World War II was prompted by the perception of a Soviet threat against America's, friends in the Middle East. The extension of Soviet control into Eastern Europe, viewed by U.S. officials as a clear violation of the Yalta Agreement, represented the first signal of such a threat. But in conjunction with Soviet actions in the Middle East (toward Iran, Turkey, and Greece), the level of threat seemed substantially greater. The U.S. reaction resulted in Truman's doctrine, followed by the Eisenhower doctrine, which was to "assist any nation or group of nations requesting assistance against armed aggression from any country controlled by international communism."[5] The main purpose of these doctrines and actions resulting from them (the chain of alliances in the area) was to contain the "communist threat." The intensity of the perceived Soviet threat seemed to fluctuate with the USSR's actions in the region and with the world view of the American administration in power. For example,

TABLE 5.   U.S. Military Assistance to Israel and Some
Arab Countries, 1968–1976 ($ millions)

	1968–1972	1973	1974	1975	1976
Israel	985.0	307.5	2,482.7	300.0	1,500.0
Jordan	126.2	54.8	45.7	104.6	138.3
Lebanon	15.6	10.7	0.2	0.1	0.1
Libya	1.6	—	—	—	—
Saudi Arabia	46.2	0.2	0.2	0.0	0.0

Source: Derived from Agency for International Development, U.S. Overseas Loans and Grants and Assistance for International Organization, July 1,
1945–September 30, 1976, *Congressional Quarterly,* September 1977.
   Note: Egypt, Iraq, and Syria received no U.S. assistance during this period.

Soviet cooperation with the United States to solve the Arab-Israeli conflict during the early 1970s has resulted in a perception of the Soviets as
committed to the status quo, while Soviet policy during the 1973 war
resulted in a U.S. nuclear alert on October 25, 1973.[6] The early years of
the Carter administration witnessed some relaxation prompted by SALT
II, whereas the later years were characterized by intensely strained relations, due to the Soviet invasion of Afghanistan, which resulted in the
grain embargo and the construction of the rapid deployment force (RDF).
   The Reagan administration has gone even further in its hostility toward
the Soviets, inspired by perceptions of the USSR that have evoked cold
war rhetoric and policies. As a result, the current administration developed its own doctrine for dealing with Soviets in the Middle East. In
the words of a State Department spokesman in 1981, this doctrine was
called the "the strategic consensus," according to which "the highest
priority in [the Middle East] at this time should be to arrest the deteriorating position of the West vis-à-vis the Soviet Union."[7] As William Quandt
put it:

   The anti-Soviet attitude is the starting point for a lot of people in the
   administration. For them issues don't have to do with Palestinians
   and Lebanese and Saudis. They have to do with Persian Gulf oil,
   and that is what we have to focus on, and bilateral relations out there
   are simply part of a larger strategic design containing Soviet expansion in the area. Period.[8]

Based on this American objective, one would assume that any conduct by the Libyan revolutionary regime that may be perceived as resulting in expanding Soviet influence in the region could result in viewing Libya as a source of threat to U.S. objectives.

U.S. PERCEPTIONS OF LIBYA'S REVOLUTIONARY ACTIVITIES ABROAD

It is often stated by U.S. officials that Libya's international misconduct is one of the factors that strains American relations with that country. Libya perceives its support of revolutionary movements, such as the radical factions within the PLO, the POLISARIO, in the Western Sahara, and some opposition groups within some of the Arab countries, as support for liberation movements. The United States sees this conduct as support for terrorists whose aim is to destabilize some of the Arab regimes friendly to the United States. Also, Libya's global revolutionary activities, either its alleged involvement in terrorist incidents or its financing and supplying weapons to revolutionary movements and radical regimes worldwide, has been one of the issues raised by U.S. officials against Libya. My discussion of this variable in the next part will be on two levels: regional and international.

THE STABILITY OF THE "FRIENDLY" ARAB REGIMES

Describing the first three objectives of U.S. foreign policy in the Middle East shows the obvious contradictions and uneasy tension that exists between these objectives. The first tension exists between satisfying the economic demands, specifically the demand for oil, of the American people and U.S. investment abroad, and the commitment to protect Israel and its well-being. The first objective necessitates a friendly approach toward the Arab oil-producing countries who are engaged in a confrontation with Israel, a de facto U.S. ally. In the United States, this contradiction led to domestic tensions between an economic group represented by the oil lobby and an ethnic group represented by the Zionist lobby. Each group tries to influence U.S. policy toward its own ends. The second tension is that the Arabs are dissuaded from turning to the Soviets for economic and military assistance in their conflict with Israel. This would constitute a threat to the United States in two respects: it would lead to an expansion of Soviet influence in the area, and it would threaten the security of Israel.

For the United States, the balancing formula that could solve these contradictions was to support friendly Arab regimes whose hostility toward Israel was confined to the rhetorical level, at the same time to oppose Soviet influence in the region, and (most important) to assure American access to oil. (Saudi Arabia and the Arab sheikhdoms of the Gulf represent the last type of regime). Thus, supporting those regimes became a vital derivative objective that the United States has been pursuing since 1957. Richard Cottam argues that this balancing formula was pleasing to both pressure groups since Israel is unthreatened and oil supplies and investments are not in jeopardy.[9]

Therefore, one expects that any act by Libya that aims at destabilizing those regimes would place the American formula in great jeopardy and consequently would be viewed as a threat. Such an act is usually described by the United States as "subversive and terrorist" and threatening to the status quo in the region.

LIBYA'S INTERNATIONAL ACTIVITIES

The United States has often charged Libya with involvement in terrorist activities such as assassinations, skyjacking, and financing terrorist operations against Western diplomats, in addition to supporting and training opposition groups in many countries worldwide (such as the Irish Republican Army, El Salvador, the Philippines), and supplying Nicaragua with arms. This study is not concerned with proving or disproving those claims. Rather, my concern is to explore how Libyan policy in this regard has affected the U.S. image of and policy toward Libya.

Because each of the U.S. objectives just discussed represents a vital interest to the United States, any antagonistic or friendly policies in relation to those objectives may change the U.S. image of the source of those policies—Libya, in this case. The essential task of this research is to find out which is the most important U.S. objective in the Libyan-American context. I will approach this task by exploring the Libyan policies and behavior vis-à-vis these objectives (independent variables) and studying the variations in the U.S. image of Libya (the dependent variable) as a consequence of Libya's actions.

PART II ≻ U.S. POLICY TOWARD LIBYA DURING THE NIXON AND FORD ADMINISTRATIONS

3 ➤ LIBYA'S FOREIGN POLICY, 1969–1976

Despite the controversy and the lack of agreement about the utility of focusing on the individual level in analyzing the foreign policy of a certain country, I believe this approach could be useful in studying the foreign policy of Third World countries because of the large decisional latitude enjoyed by most of those countries' leaders. The revolutionary regime in Libya is a case in point.

It is well known that Libyan foreign policy cannot be understood in isolation from the thinking and personality of Muammar el Qaddafi, not only because he is the leader of the revolution, but also because of the effect of his ideology and thought on other Libyan officials who participate in planning or executing the nation's foreign policy. To Qaddafi nationalism and religion constitute the basic drives of history. Without them history cannot be understood or explained. Economic factors, he contends, are secondary in comparison to nationalism and religion. Mohammed H. Heikal elaborates further:

> Two people and two backgrounds combined to make Qaddafi the man he was. The people were the Prophet Mohammed and Gamal Abdel Nasser. His thinking was an amalgam of the ideas of Islam at the time of Mohammed and the revolutionary doctrine of Nasser, particularly as expounded during the formation period of Qaddafi's life when, as a schoolboy and young soldier, he first became aware of what was going on in the world around him—in the period, that is, between the Suez War in 1956 and the June War in 1967. His two backgrounds were the army and the desert. It was in the army that he

43

first really found himself, but it was to the desert that he would return for solace.[1]

Unlike the Moslem brotherhood, Qaddafi sees no contradiction between nationalism and religion. For him "a reinvigorated Islam is the key to Arab rebirth."[2] Islam is perceived as the motivating, disciplining source of moral activism needed to mobilize the Arabs for national reconstruction.

Commenting on Mirella Bianco's depiction of Qaddafi as a prophetic "voice from the desert," Hinnebusch writes, "Qaddafi clearly does see himself as a man with a messianic vision and does seem to have that supreme inner conviction that he alone in a corrupt world is righteous and right, which is typical of the prophet."[3] Therefore, from Qaddafi's belief in Arab nationalism springs his conception of "the Arab world as a single homogeneous whole and of the Arab people as a single nation bound by the common ties of language, religion, and history."[4] Consequently he became chiefly preoccupied with the cause of Arab unity, the Arab-Israeli conflict, and inter-Arab politics as different dimensions of the same problem, "the revival of the Arab nation." On the other side, the Islamic factor in Qaddafi's thinking can help us understand not only his internal economic policy as translated in "socialism," but also Libyan conduct toward the superpowers, the Western world, the Third World, and liberation movements.

Qaddafi's concern with Arab unity and Islam furnished the philosophical frame for Libya's conduct internally and externally. They have been translated into the three goals of the Libyan revolution: freedom, socialism, and unity. (They are the same goals called for by Nasser's revolution of July 23, 1952.) Qaddafi saw these goals as essential to rid Libya of its misery. As he put it in a TV interview on October 14, 1969, "The true cause of the Revolution lay in the backward Arab life which reduced the Arab to an almost complete lack of affiliation to the 20th Century. It is by turning to the three slogans that the Arab world rediscovers [its] dignity and [its] place in history."[5]

Libya's foreign policy conduct from 1969 until 1976 illustrates the importance of ideological factors in Libyan foreign policy, which explain some of the policies that remain mysterious to many, particularly in the West. The following discussion will investigate Libyan conduct vis-à-vis the four U.S. objectives in the Middle East that were presented in the first chapter.

LIBYA AND THE ARAB-ISRAELI CONFLICT

The primary motivating factor that inspired the young military officers in Libya to take over the ailing monarchy on September 1, 1969, Qaddafi states, was the humiliating defeat of the Arabs in June 1967. Israel, to revolutionary Libya, is a strange entity that was artificially planted in the Arab land to serve imperialist and Zionist designs and to keep the Arab nation divided. The terms, "Arab-Israeli conflict," or "the Middle-East dispute," are unrecognizable terms in the dictionary of revolutionary Libya's foreign policy. The issue is the Palestinian cause, and what is called the Middle-East conflict is only a consequence of that basic cause. The right way of dealing with this strange entity, Qaddafi points out, is by eliminating it, and this can only be done by force. This goal cannot be achieved except through Arab unity. Thus, solving the Palestinian problem (by returning the Palestinians to their homeland, Palestine) and achieving Arab unity, are two sides of the same coin—you cannot have one without the other. That is why since the first day of the revolution Qaddafi's dream has been to achieve Arab unity, whatever the cost. John K. Cooley writes:

> One idea above all others obsesses Qaddafi: the unification of all Arabic speaking people. Only in total Arab union, he says, can there be Arab strength, and the Islamic faith is necessary to create that union. Nearly everything Qaddafi has said, written, or done since his classroom days in Sebha can be explained in terms of this dream. In order to achieve it the State of Israel, which Qaddafi regards as the last and most odious of the Western colonial implantations in the Arab body politic, must be eliminated, and the four million Palestinian Arabs must be returned to their original homes, or those of their families, in historic Palestine. Anything that contributes to those causes is right and just. Anything that works against them must be circumvented or eradicated.[6]

During the early 1970s Qaddafi's conviction was that both superpowers were imperial powers that could not be trusted or turned to for assistance in solving the Arab-Israeli conflict. The only effective solution was the Arab solution. Arabs through their unity and their own capabilities could solve the problem forever. Based on this conviction, Libya's foreign policy conduct moved in three consistent directions: first, toward Arab unity; second, to complete support of the Palestine Liberation Organization (PLO) as represented by al-Fatah—the other factions of the Fedayeen which are of Marxist origin were not considered genuine liberation movements but rather as divisive elements that handicapped the effectiveness of the Palestinian resistance movement; and third, to the enhancement of Libyan military capabilities and attempts to persuade the other Arab countries to participate effectively in the battle against Israel—"pan-Arabization."

Thus, it was only a matter of hours after the complete takeover on September 1, 1969, that Qaddafi instructed M. Heikal, the envoy sent by Nasser to find out the nature and orientation of Libya's new regime. "Tell Nasser that this is his revolution, we are his men, and all Libya's capabilities are under his disposal for the battle."[7] For Egypt, the changeover in Libya was of great importance; it removed a suspicious old pro-Western monarch from Nasser's flank, and provided him instead with a "neighbor committed to radical Arab nationalism."[8] Three months later, the presidents of Egypt, Libya, and Sudan held a conference in Tripoli which marked the first step toward an eventual political, economic, and military merger among the three countries. A communiqué issued after the meeting reaffirmed that "the responsibility of facing up to Israel's aggression is shared by all Arab revolutionary fronts" and envisioned a "new axis of armed struggle against Israel stretching from Tripoli to Khartoum by way of Cairo."[9] In mid-1970, Qaddafi, with the approval of Nasser, started moving toward mobilizing the Arab capabilities for the battle against Israel. He called his project the "pan-Arabization of the battle." In a tour that included almost all the eastern Arab states, Qaddafi tried to convince the heads of those states to mobilize their military capabilities under one command for the sake of establishing an eastern military front against Israel. The tour represented Qaddafi's first real encounter with the problems and complexities of Arab politics. For a puritan young leader with a simple vision, the results of the trip were disappointing. This led him to intensify his efforts in other directions: seeking unity with Egypt and Sudan, accelerating material support to the

Palestinian Fedayeen as represented by al-Fatah, and finally enhancing Libya's military capability using its oil revenues to purchase more weapons from the West. Thus, a deal was concluded with France to purchase 110 Mirage fighter planes—which aroused much controversy between the United States and France regarding the balance of power in the region, as will be explained later. On May 15, 1970, the Libyan leader, accompanied by Arafat, asked all Arab nations to allow their nationals who so desired to volunteer for the Palestinian Resistance Movement (PRM). Libya expressed readiness to train and arm them. All Libyan missions abroad were asked to open registers for volunteers from Arab countries and provide transportation to Libya for necessary training.[10] As early as September 1969, the "al-Jihad" fund was established to collect donations for the PRM.

Two incidents took place in 1970 that reflect the Libyan concern with the PRM. The first were the clashes between the Lebanese army and the PRM in Lebanon, which led to Qaddafi's visit to Lebanon in June 1970 in an effort to mediate the dispute. The other was the crisis of September 1970 between the PRM and Jordan. Libya sided with the PRM and officially stopped its economic aid to Jordan, which had been part of the financial support for confrontation states agreed upon in the Khartoum Arab summit of 1967. On September 26, 1970, Libya decided to break off diplomatic relations with that regime.[11] The UPI, citing State Department information, said that since 1970 Libya had provided over $100 million annually to the Fedayeen.[12] In addition to training, arming, and financing the PRM, Libya's involvement became more direct in 1972–1973 when a number of Libyans (estimates of the total go up to 600 during that time) joined the guerrillas in Lebanon, and some took part in a rocket attack on Safad in Israel on January 9, 1972.[13]

The death of Nasser on September 28, 1970, was a great setback to revolutionary Libya and to Qaddafi personally. As "a simple puritan caught up in a complicated world full of intrigue and manoeuvre,"[14] Qaddafi was completely relying on Nasser and his understanding of Arab and world politics. Heikal describes the effect of Nasser's death on him:

> Qaddafi was very upset by the death of Nasser. It was not just that he admired Nasser more than any other living man, but he had always believed in the central role of Egypt in the Arab world [and] when

Nasser died he felt that there was a vacuum in the Arab world which was too big for any one man to fill, and he thought that there should be a collective leadership by Egypt, Syria, and Libya.[15]

Thus, Libya intensified its efforts toward Arab unity, while at the same time enhancing its military capability by purchasing more weapons from the West and the Soviets. Yet Libya's attacks on the USSR became even stronger, as we will discuss later.

The efforts toward unity resulted in the establishment of the Union of Arab Republics composed of Egypt, Syria, and Libya. (Sudan had bowed out because of internal problems.) The confederation was small, measured by the aspirations of the revolutionary young officers in Libya. In addition, they suspected the Syrian Ba'athist's real motives. Thus, they started pushing for a complete merger between Egypt and Libya. After a long series of meetings and exchange of visits between Cairo and Tripoli, Qaddafi and Sadat agreed in August 1972 to "create a unified state and to establish a unified political command to bring about, in stages, the merger of the two countries by September 1, 1973." Heikal argues that Qaddafi was pushing hard for the merger because he "was prompted to this by his fear that the Soviets might exercise some sort of pressure on Egypt in retaliation for the withdrawal of the experts—pressure that might be military, political or economic—and that in consequence Egypt might find itself obliged to accept some partial and unsatisfactory settlement.[16] Nevertheless, signs of mutual suspicion between the two leaders were growing rapidly, mainly around how the battle toward Israel should be conducted and the form of the proposed state and its laws and institutions. Relations became more strained when Israel, in February 1973, shot down a Libyan civilian airplane which had lost its route to Cairo, and killed 107 passengers. The Libyans charged that the Egyptians could have protected the airplane. And Qaddafi became more upset when Sadat intervened at the last minute to reverse Qaddafi's orders to an Egyptian submarine in the port of Tripoli to sink the *Queen Elizabeth II*, which was carrying a group of wealthy Jews from the United States to the Israeli port of Ashdad. Then came the October War of 1973 which resulted in open differences and hostilities beween Sadat and Qaddafi about the purpose and conduct of the war. Qaddafi was very upset because Sadat did not inform him of the date of the war while informing other "reactionary" Arab rulers such as King Faisal of Saudi Arabia. He called the war a "comic opera" which was not intended for the liberation of Palestine.

Qaddafi makes it clear that his country will not take part in any war unless its objective is the liberation of Palestine and that the battle should be conducted on the enemy's territory. He advocates the return of European Jews to the countries from which they came. The Arab Jews, whom he calls "our cousins and brothers," should be allowed to "live in our midst in peace as they did in the past."[17] He does not see any way for the Arabs and Israelis to coexist because, as he puts it:

> In the Arab region are two nationalities, two entities, two religions, two civilizations, two nations and two heterogeneous histories, neither of which can absorb the other and the relationship between them is that of hostility. Therefore, it is inevitable for the conflict to continue until one of the two entities is finished off.[18]

Thus, all peaceful negotiations and the UN resolution 242-338-339 are refused by Libya—the only way is armed struggle.

Nevertheless, when war started in 1973, Libya financed and supplied with weapons both the Egyptian and Syrian armies, and used the weapon of its oil with other Arab oil-producing countries in the 1973 embargo. The size of the Libyan contribution is debatable. Sadat denied at the end of 1973 that Libya had supplied any arms or had participated financially in preparing for the battle. But Heikal, who took part in the preparations, states that "Libya contributed no less than $1,000 M towards preparations for the battle," and that Qaddafi "scoured Libya for arms and aid of every description, stripping shops of food and hospitals of medicines and piling them into lorries for dispatch to Egypt."[19] The Libyan newspaper *Al-Fatih* (May 18, 20 and 22, 1974) valued the aid provided to Egypt before the war at $542,164,000. On June 8 the paper said that Libya's support for the war amounted to $968,671,113. Reports said that seventy MIG-21 planes had been placed at Egypt's disposal, together with an extensive range of aircraft supplies, three hundred modern tanks, forty-seven armored troop carriers, and defense equipment, including missiles and antiaircraft guns.[20] John Cooley reports:

> At a meeting of Egypt's Supreme Defense council on October 25, 1972, General Al-Gamassi reported that Libya was readying "everything they have" for the coming war. "They have put at our disposal a squadron of Mirages, twenty-four self-propelled 155 mm.

guns, twelve 120 mm. mortars mounted on tracked vehicles and 100 armored personnel carriers." When the war did come, all of the promised Libyan equipment and more was already inside Egypt. There were not one but two Libyan Mirage squadrons, one with Egyptian pilots and another with Libyans.[21]

Libya did not approve of the ceasefire: "As long as the battle started it should continue." Friction became even deeper when Sadat started disengagement talks followed by the Sinai Accords I and II. There he finally became perceived by the Libyans as a traitor who sold out the Palestinian and Arab cause to the Zionists and the American imperialists. Sadat described Qaddafi as a "lunatic" and "terrorist" who enflamed the Lebanese civil war in 1975. There were charges of subversive activities between the two countries. Relations have never returned to normal since then, and in response to Sadat's visit to Israel (November 19–21, 1977) Libya broke relations with Egypt completely. Libya intensified its extremist position because of the peaceful negotiations, which it perceived as "surrender," and directed its support toward Syria and the PLO as a substitute for the "fall of Egypt to the imperial, Zionist, reactionary camp." Syria and the PLO were seen as the only hope to confront the "Zionist threat." At the same time, the Libyan arsenal began receiving huge amounts of the most sophisticated Soviet weapons, and Sadat talked about the increasing "Soviet threat and influence on his borders and on Africa." Colin Legum, an African affairs expert, explains the reason behind Libya's purchase of sophisticated Soviet weapons in 1974. He argues that Qaddafi

> was alarmed by the new rapport between the U.S. and Egypt, which he felt tipped the balance of international power in the Middle East towards the Americans. In retaliation—and in quest of arms—he turned for support to the Soviet Union in 1974. Previously his hostility towards Communism and his suspicion of Soviet intentions in international affairs had limited contacts between the two countries. Now Qaddafi—while maintaining his reservations about Soviet ideology, seems willing to go much further than before in the direction of official friendship.[22]

Kissinger believes that the "Soviet arms depots in Libya and Ethiopia fuel insurgencies all over Africa,"[23] and that they represent a strategic stockpile for use by the Soviets in an emergency in Africa, the Middle East or elsewhere. John Wright disputes the view on the grounds that the tanks had been bought by Libya for hard currency, and were not maintained to Soviet standards.[24] Dyer contends that the most plausible explanation is in Qaddafi's conviction that

> Libya proposes to be, in Qaddafi's words, "the arsenal of Islam," waiting for the day when other Arab countries agree on the necessity of fighting Israel and have need for arms. At this point, Libya would enjoy a far larger voice in Arab councils if she presented an immediate source of weapons in large quantities.[25]

This explanation is more congruent with Qaddafi's perception of the role that Libya should play, and how the Arabs should behave toward Israel. Talking in 1977 about "the historical conflict in Palestine," Qaddafi said: "The only thing that can save us is buying arms and preparing ourselves. This is because we believe this battle faces all the Arabs."[26] Ruth First wrote in 1975 that Qaddafi was the only Arab leader who had a stomach for conflict with Israel.[27] First's statement is not far from the truth, as this and the next chapters will testify.

OIL POLICY

No state developed and exploited newfound reserves of oil faster than the pro-Western conservative Kingdom of Libya in the 1960s. Only eight years after the start of its commercial production, Libya overtook Kuwait as the world's fifth largest producer.[28] Because Libyan oil was cheap (see table 6), available in great quantities, and of the best quality in the world because of its low sulphur content: because of the stability of Libya's pro-Western regime and its perfect location in relation to Europe, the West and the oil companies (mostly American) saw in Libya a golden opportunity.

Cooley points out that "the cheapness of Libyan oil, one of its greater virtues for the West, was its greatest vice in the eyes of other producing countries," and that "the majors were doing well in Libya: profits were soaring, and so was the value of their stocks."[29] But these golden days for the West were never to last, and "the proximate cause," Kissinger states, "was the overthrow in September 1969 of the pro-Western King Idris of Libya by the radical Colonel Muammar Qaddafi." Kissinger continues:

TABLE 6.   Libyan Oil Exports and Prices Before the Revolution

	Oil Exports (millions of barrels)	Revenues ($ millions)	Receipts p/b ($U.S.)
1961	6	3	.50
1962	67	40	.60
1963	167	108	.65
1964	314	211	.67
1965	443	351	.79
1966	547	523	.96
1967	621	625	1.01
1968	945	1,002	1.06
1969	1,120	1,175	1.05

Source: Petroleum Economist, OPEC Oil Report, 1979.

> Until then the dominant role among the oil-producing countries was played by essentially conservative governments whose interest in increasing their oil revenues was balanced by their dependence on the industrial democracies for protection against external (and perhaps even internal) threats. Qaddafi was free of such inhibitions. An avowed radical, he set out to extirpate Western influence. He did not care if in the process he weakened the global economy.[30]

Having expelled the British and American military bases, and the Italian community (which was perceived as a remnant of the colonization period), Qaddafi believed that Libya's freedom could not totally be achieved unless he liberated its economy from Western influence and domination. Thus he embarked on a fierce battle with the oil companies to control the oil industry.

The Libyan strategy vis-à-vis the oil corporations consisted of three successive stages: raising prices, demanding participation, and nationalizing the oil industry. It was less than five months after the revolution when Qaddafi told the representatives of twenty-one oil companies that Libyan oil was priced too low in relation to its production cost, its high quality, and its nearness to markets. He complained, also, that Libyan oil workers were not being treated fairly by their Western employers and warned that Libya could live without oil revenues while it trained its own oil technicians.[31] Qaddafi demanded a number of adjustments, the most important of which was a price increase of around 44 cents a barrel. The companies rejected the demand and made a counteroffer of 6 to 10 cents increase. At this, the Libyan government resorted to a successful strategy, comprised of the following elements (which represented the Libyan bargaining leverage): (1) Libya confronted the weakest part of the chain first, namely, the independent oil companies that develop and export most of the Libyan oil resources. Because the independents (Occidental, Continental, Marathon, Amerada, Bunker Hunt) have most of their Middle East oil investments and operations in Libya, if they lose Libya they lose everything. (2) It threatened to cut back production and to nationalize the companies' assets as a way to induce them to comply with the Libyan demands. (3) It coordinated its efforts with some "progressive" oil-producing Arab countries to show the companies that Libya does not stand alone in its oil battle. (4) It developed some contacts with European, Soviet, and Japanese firms to indicate that American oil companies could easily be replaced. (5) And, finally, the Libyan government showed signs of willingness to halt completely all sorts of oil production and exportation if the oil companies did not comply. John Wright comments, "The basic strength of the Libyan negotiating position was underlined by the fact that this producer had become Western Europe's largest single source of oil, supplying about one-third of total demand. No government was prepared for a confrontation with the Libyans."[32] Wright's statement applies also to the United States, although for different reasons, as we will see later.

Thus, on February 27, 1970, the Libyan negotiating team began separate talks with Occidental and Esso. And in March an official of the Oil Ministry stated that Libya would take unilateral action if the twenty-one companies did not agree to raise prices. In the meantime, in Moscow the Libyan oil minister declared that Libya was anxious to cooperate with the USSR in the exploration and development of Libyan oil and wanted to open East European markets for Libyan crude.[33] In April there were reports that a Soviet oil team would arrive in Libya for a geological mapping survey and that a French team would arrive to establish a petroleum institute. In May the Mitsui Group of Japan began conversations with Libyan officials on a proposal to form a joint oil exploration company.

The first move came on May 7, when Libya ordered Occidental to cut its production in the name of "conservation" and "good oilfield practice." By June, the company's output had fallen from its April peak of nearly 800,000 b/d to 485,000. Such cuts were crippling to a company with no other source of crude oil outside the United States.[34] Similar cuts were imposed on other companies that summer: reductions in the output of Amoseas, Oasis, Mobil, and Esso, together with the original and further cuts in permitted Occidental liftings (shipments), reduced total output by some 870,000 b/d between April and late August. (Note that this was the first time such an event had ever happened in the Middle East or North Africa.)[35] On September 4, it was announced that Libya had accepted Occidental's offer of a 30 cents' increase in the posted price, plus 2 cents a year increase for five years from 1971, and a rise in the tax rate from 50 to 58 percent. The company was allowed to increase production from 425,000 to 700,000 b/d on certain conditions. Although "the industry as a whole was shocked by these terms, it was unable to resist them, for it had failed to take any united and effective counter-action."[36] On September 21, the three independent partners in the Oasis group (Continental, Amerida, and Marathon) agreed to broadly similar terms. Before the end of the month all the other companies had fallen into line except Shell, which refused to sign the agreement. Consequently, the government stopped all Shell production, which amounted to 150,000 b/d, its share of the Oasis total of about 900,000 b/d.[37] On October 16 Shell complied with the demand.

The Libyan model inspired other oil-producing countries to go ahead with their own demands. In July 1970 Algeria imposed a raise of 72 cents a barrel on French companies. By the end of the year the shah of Iran was pressuring the oil companies working in Iran to pay him more. Most of the OPEC countries began demanding a 55 percent tax base and 30 percent increase in the posted price. The oil companies had to comply. However, as Hunt Oil's former representative in Libya, Henry Schuler, has pointed out, "If the companies had been able to hold the line there, they would oblige all the OPEC members—including Libya—to settle for these terms and expect no new rises in the near future."[38] Schuler was wrong. Only a week after the Gulf Agreement, Libya presented the companies with a new set of prices. Although the companies agreed among themselves, in the Tehran Agreement, to stand up to Qaddafi and to compensate any company that lost its oil share in Libya as a consequence of Qaddafi's reductions and nationalization, it did not work out that way. Libya refused to deal with G. T. Piercy, who arrived in Libya supposedly to represent all the companies working there and insisted on negotiating with each company separately. In John Cooley's words, the Libyan position "was strong and growing stronger. World oil supplies were getting tighter. Tankers to haul the oil to refineries and consumers were becoming more scarce. Western Europe was increasingly thirsty for Libya's high-quality nearby oil."[39] The companies had to give in again. The Libyan posted price rose 80 cents p/b and Libya's share of the additional take from 54 to 63 cents. So it was this combination of Libyan determination, successful tactics, the lack of unified counteraction, and the Western governments' support for the companies that made the Libyan oil price, which had started at $2.53 p/b, to reach $16.35 p/b in July 1976. And it did not stop there, as we will see later (see table 7).

TABLE 7. Libyan Oil Prices, September 1970–July 1976 (Marsa Brega, 40.0–40.9 degrees API) ($U.S. p/b)

		Posted Price	State Price
1970	1 September	2,530	—
1971	1 January	2,550	—
	20 March	3,447	—
	1 July	3,423	—
	1 October	3,399	—
1972	1 January	3,386	—
	1 April	3,642	—
	1 July	3,620	—
1973	1 January	3,777	—
	1 April	4,024	—
	1 July	4,391	—
	1 August	4,582	—
	1 October	4,065	—
	16 October	8,925	—
	1 November	9,061	—
1974	1 January	15,768	16,000
1975	1 April	15,000	11,560
	1 October	16,060	12,320
1976	1 July	16,350	12,620

Source: John Wright, *Libya: A Modern History* (Baltimore, Md.: Johns Hopkins University Press, 1982).

In the second and third stages of the Libyan oil policy, participation and nationalization, the use of oil as a political weapon was quite clear. It started at the end of 1971, when the companies agreed to resist a demand for increased revenues to compensate for the devaluation of the U.S. dollar. Libya retaliated by taking the disputed amount (about $1 million) from Esso's Tripoli bank account.[40] At that time the Arab oil-producing countries were calling for 25 percent participation in oil companies' capital and management. When, in November 1971, Britain withdrew from three little islands situated in the Strait of Hurmoz, leaving them to "Iranian occupation" (Iran was perceived then as a close ally of Israel), Libya announced a full nationalization of all British Petroleum's rights and assets in Concession 65, and primarily its share in the Sarir field, as a retaliation for this British "treachery" in the Arab Gulf.[41] The Petroleum Press Service commented on the BP takeover: "This demonstration of Colonel Qaddafi's revolutionary zeal on behalf of other Arab nations fits remarkably conveniently with Libya's current ambitions in the Arab world."[42] A general agreement of 25 percent participation, rising to 51 percent in 1982, had been reached in the Gulf in October 1972. This conservative soft approach by the "reactionary" oil Arab regimes was unsatisfactory to revolutionary Libya. Celebrating the third anniversary of the evacuation of the American forces on June 11, 1973, Qaddafi announced the nationalization of Hunt's assets as a "strong slap in the cool arrogant face" of the United States for its support of Israel. This action, he said, was a warning to the U.S. to "end its hostility to the Arab nation."[43] On August 13, 1973, the Revolutionary Command Council issued a decree nationalizing the U.S.-owned Occidental Company (a new model of seminationalization). Fifty-one percent of all the funds, rights, assets, shares, and interests of the company were nationalized. Occidental was allowed to continue to control 49 percent of its assets. On August 16, Oasis signed a similar agreement. This affected four other companies operated by Oasis, namely, Continental, Amerada, Marathon, and Shell. On September 1, 1973, Libya issued a sixteen-article law nationalizing 51 percent of the assets of all the remaining oil companies in Libya. This policy was not outright nationalization, it was part of a general program of Libyanizing the economy. A total nationalization could not be pursued until a Libyan staff of technicians and experts was ready to take over. But this was not to forbid the revolutionary government to use the oil as a political weapon. Libya took part in the oil embargo of 1973 and was opposed to lifting it. The embargo was lifted early in 1974. For instance, on February 11, 1974, following the Washington Oil Conference of the Consuming States, which was considered by the Arabs as an American attempt to intimidate them, Qaddafi decided to fully nationalize three American companies. That included the remaining 49 percent share of the California Asiatic Company, the American Overseas Petroleum Company, and the Libyan-American Oil Company. Once again, as John Cooley puts it, "Western resistance to Qaddafi collapsed" and Qaddafi "proved to Libya and the rest of the world that oil was indeed a political weapon, and that he could successfully use it, especially when it was to his advantage to do so."[44] Reflecting on this revolutionary policy, Charles F. Doran wrote in 1977:

> Ever since the Russian Revolution and the Mexican expropriation of foreign interests, nationalizations of oil have occurred. But Qaddafi rewrote the textbook on nationalization. It was the threat of nationalization of corporate assets in the producer countries that ultimately—to use a phrase current in the Middle East during the period—broke the back of the majors.[45]

Thus, by the end of the period under study, the price of Libyan oil was the highest in comparison with other producing states. (This resulted in huge revenues for the state.) The assets of almost all the companies working in Libya were either fully nationalized or an average of about 63 percent owned by the state. (See table 8.) In short, the oil industry came under Libyan control and the Western influence had been undermined.

POLICY TOWARD THE SUPERPOWERS

"Qaddafi was no one's agent but his own," writes John Cooley.[46] He is right. Only a few days after the revolution, a strict nonaligned policy was proclaimed by the new regime as the guide to Libya's conduct toward the superpowers. Qaddafi's conviction of nonalignment is based mainly on his rejection of both capitalism and communism, and this rejection, as Ruth First puts it, "stems not from any Maoist-type commitment that the U.S. and the USSR are equally imperialist super-states, but from nationalism and religion."[47] Those two factors are the sole basis of Qaddafi's Third Universal Theory as represented in the Green Book. The Libyan interpretation of nonalignment was spelled out in the fourth

TABLE 8. Private and State Ownership of Oil-Producing Companies in Libya, 1975 (in percent)

	Owned by Individual Companies	Group Total	Owned by the State
BP	—	—	100.00
Bunker Hunt	—	—	100.00
Amoseas			
Texaco	—	—	100.00
Social			
Elf-Aquitaine	11.25		
OMV	2.25	15.00	85.00
Wintershall	1.50		
Occidental		19.00	81.00
Atlantic Richfield	—		
Esso Sirte	24.50	36.50	63.50
W. R. Grace	12.00		
Oasis			
Amerada Hess	8.20		
Continental	16.30	40.80	59.20
Marathon	16.30		
Shell	—		
Esso Libya		49.00	51.00
Mobil	31.90	49.00	51.00
Gelsenberg	17.10		
Agip		50.00	50.00
Elf-Aquitaine	42.00		
Hispanoil	42.00	100.00	—
Murphy	16.00		

Source: John Wright, *Libya: A Modern History* (Baltimore, Md.: Johns Hopkins University Press, 1982), p. 249.

summit meeting of nonaligned states in Algiers in September 1973. At that meeting, Qaddafi deplored all types of military, political, economic, and cultural submission to both superpowers. He stated that the true meaning of neutrality is the liberation of a state from all those types of ties and the defense of liberty in the Third World from both Eastern and Western influence. To be nonaligned is to be aware of the attempts made by the United States and the USSR to dominate the Third World. Both seek the realization of their own self-interest economically and strategically; the big powers have no concern for the smaller powers. The Libyans pointed to the detente accord as evidence of their statements.[48] Mohammad Heikal recalls that "when Kosygin came to Egypt and some derogatory remarks were made there about Kissinger, Qaddafi's comment was: 'I don't make any difference between Kissinger and Kosygin. They are both enemies.' "[49] A look at the Libyan policy toward the superpowers is in order.

POLICY TOWARD THE SOVIET UNION

Until May 1974, Libya's attitude and policy toward the Soviets was intensely hostile. Because of his strong religious beliefs, Qaddafi saw the Soviet Union as the land of atheists. It is an imperial power that seeks the domination of smaller powers; thus its policies are no different from U.S. imperialism. This image of the Soviets was the motivating factor behind the Libyan anticommunist conduct in several situations. In January 1971, Qaddafi launched a severe attack on what he called the deviationist, Marxist-Leninist organizations within the Palestinian resistance movement, who caused trouble for al-Fatah. Left-wing Palestinians had been caught distributing booklets in Libya on the creation of a proletarian regime; over 100 of them were expelled.[50] In return, Georg Habash, the head of the Popular Front of the Liberation of Palestine, denounced Qaddafi as "a Fascist tyrant" and declared that "he is bound to be overthrown."[51] On May 15, 1971, when Sadat cracked down on the Nasserite elements in his regime, Libya stood by Sadat and offered its immediate assistance under the perception conveyed to them by Sadat that those elements were merely the Soviet agents in the Egyptian regime. Two months later, Libya played a decisive role in putting down the short-lived Marxist coup against Numerry in Sudan. Libyan jets ordered a BOAC plane en route from London to Khartoum to land in Benghazi (Libya), when the coup's two leaders were arrested and sent later to Sudan to be executed. In the Indian-Pakistani war, Libya supplied Pakistan (on Islamic grounds) with all the material assistance it could afford, including several American F-5 fighters. Qaddafi also supported the expulsion of Soviet military advisors from Egypt and suggested to Sadat the merger of their two countires for fear that the Russians might retaliate militarily or economically.[52] On October 10, 1971, the *New York Times* described the USSR as "pursuing a more aggressive Middle East policy including scoring the anti-Soviet regime in Libya." The paper said that "Soviet and Soviet-oriented Arab communist puppets have scored Qaddafi for his criticism of Soviet support of India in the India-Pakistan war." On March 29, 1972, Qaddafi told the Arab Socialist Union (the legislative branch in Libya at that time) that the communist system "permits the government to dispose people of their property. As everything is in its hands, the government enslaves people."[53]

Despite this ideological and political hostility, Libya started by February 1972 to establish some commercial contacts with the Soviets. (According to U.S. official reports, there was a Soviet shipment of arms to Libya as early as July 1970. But it was done through Egyptian contacts.) Major Jallud (then deputy prime minister and minister of economy and industry) visited Moscow briefly and signed an economic and technical agreement with the Soviets on March 4, 1972. The agreement covered cooperation in oil prospecting, extracting and refining, mineral prospecting, gas exploration, and the development of power production. However, the better atmosphere this agreement should have created was quickly dispelled the very next day. *Pravda* "bitterly criticized the Libyan newspaper *Al-Jundi* for having published a story claiming there was a Soviet-U.S. agreement for maintaining the "no-war, no-peace" stalemate in the Middle East."[54] A month later, the Libyan hostility toward the Soviets was highlighted when Iraq signed a friendship and cooperation treaty with the Soviets. Libya denounced the agreement and recalled its ambassador from Baghdad, protesting that such treaties represented imperialist pressures and would deprive the Arabs of the chance of leadership in the Third World. Libyan radio "warned the U.S.S.R that aid to the Arabs was welcome, but not at the expense of Arab freedom and sovereignty."[55] The exchange of verbal assaults between Libya and the Soviets continued throughout 1973 over the Soviet stand on the Middle East conflict and the October War in particular.

The signing of the first Israeli-Egyptian disengagement agreement on January 18, 1974, as a result of Kissinger's efforts, represented a turning point in Libyan-Soviet relations. Qaddafi saw Egypt falling under the American umbrella and he believed that the U.S. expansion of influence in the region would affect the international balance of power in the area. Thus, Libya accelerated its contacts with the Soviets, mainly in the field of arms, to achieve two interrelated strategic and tactical objectives. These were, first, to enhance the Libyan military capability, especially after being turned down by the United States and some Western countries for the supply of some sophisticated weapons. The enhancement of Libya's military capabilities stemmed from the Libyan leadership's perception that Libya became more threatened by the American-Israeli existence in Egypt and that Libya in reality became the new southern front against Israel as a result of Sadat's "treason." Also, Libya's accumulation of massive amounts of arms would serve as an arsenal for the Arabs when they realized that the Arab-Israeli conflict cannot be solved but by force. A second reason for strengthening ties with the Soviets was to balance the growing American influence in the region, which was seen as affecting the balance of power in the area. But it has to be kept in mind that the new Libyan approach to the Soviets was not based on ideological or political approval of the Soviet ideology or policy in the Middle East. As Qaddafi himself put it, "We deal with the Soviet Union on a commercial and not on an ideological basis."[56]

The Soviets, for their part, were eager to offset the loss of their foothold in Egypt and to demonstrate their determination to continue playing a major role in the region. This was in addition to their need for Libyan hard currency drained from oil revenues. The new Libyan approach was highlighted by Jallud's visit to the USSR. On this visit Jallud concluded the first of two arms deals that raised a great deal of controversy in 1975 about their amount or their content. The first, reported to be concluded in December 1974, included TU-22 supersonic bombers (with 1,400-mile range), various types of SAM missiles, tanks, and antitank missiles. The deal also was reported to include MIG-23 "Floggers." The second came after Kosygin's visit to Libya in May 1975. Western officials believe that it included an increase of 1,000 tanks and six F-class attack submarines. *Al-Alhram,* the Egyptian newspaper, valued the deal at $4 billion, while Sadat, in an interview with the *Los Angeles Times,* cited an even higher figure of $12 billion. A Libyan spokesman in Cairo, in early June, placed the value at $800 million.[57] Although Soviet-Libyan cooperation included some other economic and technical aspects (mainly regarding oil) the arms purchases represented the most important side of their relations (see table 9).

Soviet-Libyan relations were to grow even stronger after Qaddafi's first visit to the Soviet Union in 1976. Nevertheless, as Roger Pajak put it in

TABLE 9.   Libya's Trade with the Soviet Union, 1969–1976 ($U.S. thousands)

	Exports to the USSR	Imports from the USSR
1969	6,834	—
1970	9,867	—
1971	7,063	4
1972	9,351	49,287
1973	22,153	54,293
1974	36,371	—
1975	22,265	—
1976	20,371	—

Source: U.N. Yearbook of International Trade Statistics (1972, 1973, 1974, 1979).

1981, although "the current Soviet relationship with Libya is based on limited mutual interests, serious difficulties persist. Despite the close arms transfer and technical assistance ties between the two countries, the Soviets no doubt are concerned about Qaddafi's strong anti-communist feelings and his erratic behavior."[58]

POLICY TOWARD THE UNITED STATES

In contrast to Libya's perception of the Soviet Union, in which religion played a very strong role, the Libyan perception of the United States was mainly determined by nationalistic factors. The United States was perceived as an imperial power that seeks military, economic, and political domination over the Arab nation. Western imperialism in general, and the United States in particular, had transplanted Israel to the Arabs' land, to keep the Arab nation divided, backward, and dependent. This unholy alliance between Zionism and imperialism was to be perpetuated with the assistance of the reactionary Arab rulers who allied themselves with U.S. imperial power to protect their interests and survival. This perception is very crucial in explaining Libya's policies toward some of the Arab countries, as will be shown later.

Thus, it was only a few months after the revolution in September 1969 when the revolutionary regime called upon the United States and Britain to negotiate the withdrawal of their military bases from Libya. In the opening session of the negotiations, Qaddafi's tone was very strong and determined. He declared that if the United States did not comply with Libya's demand, Libya would be turned into another Vietnam. Within six months both the U.S. and U.K. military bases were out of the country. The American bases (Wheelus and Alwitia) were very important to the United States. In his statement before the Subcommittee on U.S. Security Agreements and Commitments Abroad of the Committee on Foreign Relations (July 1970), the former assistant secretary for African affairs, David Newsom, specified the value of the U.S. military bases in Libya as very important to U.S. operations in Europe:

> Wheelus Air Force Base was originally used as a USAF Air Transport Command field. In the early 1950s its primary mission became that of a USAF gunnery and training base. . . . It served an important training function for U.S. Air Force NATO committed tactical aircraft. . . . Alwitia range, south of Tripoli, provided an opportunity for every form of gunnery and bombing except nuclear, something that we could not duplicate anywhere else in that hemisphere, and for that reason it was a convenience and valuable as long as we could keep it on satisfactory grounds.[59]

To Qaddafi, the expulsion of the foreign military bases represented not only a necessary step toward the achievement of a true Libyan independence, but also an Arab victory—there had been some reports from Radio Cairo indicating those bases' involvement against Egypt in the 1967 war. It was also Qaddafi's conviction that he could not negotiate with the United States regarding the establishment of a new type of relations based on equal mutual respect while part of his country was still "occupied."

Having expelled the military bases, Qaddafi believed that the main obstacle to the establishment of healthy U.S.-Libyan relations was American support of the "Zionist enemy." His contention was that the U.S. policy toward the Arab-Israeli conflict did not serve even the American interests in the region because the Zionist lobby in Washington dictated U.S. policy in the Middle East. In his statement after the reelection of President Nixon in 1972, Qaddafi repeated:

> Whenever any U.S. president, whether Richard Nixon or anyone else, is able to get rid of the Zionist influence on U.S. policy, that day will not only be the beginning of the establishment of sound and

healthy relations between this nation and the U.S., but will also be a national day for the United States, to celebrate the restoration of the right to determine the policy of a major state like the United States.[60]

Ruth First writes, "One has the distinct impression that once the U.S. changed its policy on the Palestine issue, Qaddafi would have little to quarrel with."[61] Other than this problem, Qaddafi saw no hindrances to good relations with the United States, especially as the latter had no past colonial experience in the Arab countries. He clarified this notion more adequately in a meeting with some Egyptian intellectuals in 1972 in Cairo, by arguing that "unlike other great powers, the U.S. had not shared in the accumulation from colonialism. . . . All American capital is American." He told his audience, "It is the U.S. steel, copper, U.S. rivers that did it—not the exploitation of the world."[62] The only exploitation the United States was guilty of in Libya was the domination of the American oil companies over the Libyan economy. And thus, by eliminating this element, together with the elimination of the military bases, Qaddafi thought that the door would be open for better relations with the United States.

Based on this notion, Libyan policy from 1969 to 1976 followed a dual track. The first emphasized strengthening economic and cultural relations, taking into account that most of the oil sector in Libya was staffed and operated by American companies and that Libya also needed the

TABLE 10. Libya's Trade with the United States, 1969–1976 ($U.S. thousands)

	Exports to the U.S.	Imports from the U.S.
1969	111,087	126,425
1970	63,233	76,459
1971	161,871	48,508
1972	227,048	65,770
1973	310,727	95,556
1974	7,055	107,226
1975	1,498,813	141,542
1976	2,466,253	131,720

Source: U.N. Yearbook of International Trade Statistics (1972, 1973, 1974, 1979).

advanced American technology for its development programs. Thus, this period witnessed stronger economic relations—in 1973 Libya ranked as the second Arab oil exporter to the United States—and thousands of Libyan students were sent to the United States for study in different fields of education (see tables 10 and 11).

The other track emphasized the necessity that the United States change or moderate its stand regarding the Arab-Israeli conflict as a prerequisite for better political relations. In this regard, Libya used all means at its disposal to pressure the United States to change its policy in the Middle East. This included using oil as a political weapon (as explained above) and attempting to create a unified Arab stand against U.S. policy. Aside from its unilateral action against the American oil companies, Libya rejected the lifting of the 1973 oil embargo (this is despite some unconfirmed reports that half of the oil shipments leaked to the United States during the embargo came from Libya).[63] The U.S. decision not to sell Libya any arms and halting delivery of eight C-130 transport planes to Libya in 1973 fueled the intensity of Libya's perception of the United States as an enemy to the Arab world and helped intensify Libya's hostile policies vis-à-vis the United States. In June 1972, Libya declared a special restricted airspace within a 100-mile radius of Tripoli, far beyond the conventional twelve-mile limit. On March 21, 1973, the U.S. State· Department announced that two Libyan Mirage fighters had fired on an unarmed U.S. Air Force plane. (The *Washington Star* suggested on March 23 that the plane was on an espionage mission.) Libya denied the

TABLE 11.   Oil Exports to the United States from Arab Producers, 1973 (thousands of b/d)

Saudi Arabia	600
Abu Dhabi	150
Kuwait	150
Iraq	50
Libya	350
Algeria	150
Other Arab countries	150
Total	11,600

Source: U.S. Department of State Bulletin, no. 1801, December 31, 1983.

attack. Another incident took place on March 30 when Libyan fighters intercepted fourteen U.S. Phantoms because they were seen in the territorial waters Libya claimed. The nationalization of 51 percent of three American oil companies in September 1973 was seen by many observers as a sign of further deterioration in U.S.-Libyan relations.[64]

The October 1973 War and its results represented a crucial turning point in Qaddafi's perception of the United States and some Arab countries. He bitterly attacked the Geneva peace talks in December 1973 and with the beginning of the Egyptian-American rapprochement in 1974 he saw the major Arab countries, especially Egypt, as falling into the imperialist-Zionist camp. The Arab cause, to him, had been sold out by Egypt and other "reactionary" Arab regimes to the "imperial masters," and hence he engaged himself in an attempt to establish the "rejection front" composed of the "progressive" Arab regimes to confront this "imperial-Zionist, reactionary" threat. As I have explained, this new situation made Qaddafi temper his approach toward the Soviets in an attempt to balance the increasing "imperial" influence in the region.

By 1976, the Libyan approach toward the United States was back on the double track, calling for better relations while showing complete dissatisfaction with U.S. policy toward Israel. On September 27, 1976, Libya's press minister, Mohammed Zwai, stated, "Libya would like to establish normal relations with the U.S. but the U.S. is deliberately opposed to any improvement in relations."[65] He urged the establishment of a new dialogue.

On the same line, Qaddafi told *Jeune Afrique* on October 8, 1976, that he wished his relations with the United States were as good as those he enjoyed with the USSR. He blamed the Americans for the coldness of relations, noting that they refused to exchange ambassadors and that Libya was willing to buy arms and nuclear technology (for its agricultural projects) from the United States but had been turned down.[66] But on October 14, 1976, the Libyan permanent representative at the UN attacked the conduct of both President Ford and Jimmy Carter in their presidential election campaigns, accusing both of behaving "as if they were running for Mayor of Tel Aviv."[67] Again, it was obvious that the American backing of Israel constituted the stumbling block, in the Libyan view, to better relations between the two countries. This factor will continue to play the major role in Libya's perception of, and policy toward the United States and other Arab regimes that are seen as "puppets" of U.S. imperialism in the region.

REVOLUTIONARY ACTIVITIES ABROAD

The support by the Libyan revolutionary regime of the revolutionary movements in the Arab world and elsewhere stems mainly from the two ideological factors I have referred to above. A careful scrutiny of the Libyan revolutionary activities abroad suggests that both nationalistic and religious factors were motivating forces behind these activities. As a fervent nationalist, Ruth First writes, Qaddafi "conceives of the Arab world as a single homogeneous whole and of the Arab people as a single nation."[68] Three stumbling blocks are seen by Qaddafi as standing in the way of the reunification of this nation. First, Israel, as a political entity, keeps the Arab nation separated; consequently, the Arabs remain divided into small fragile entities as long as Israel continues to appear on the map of the Arab world. Second, U.S. "imperial" policies in the region help not only to perpetuate the existence of Israel, but also to spread its influence (militarily, economically, and politically) over other Arab regimes in the area. A third stumbling block are the "reactionary" Arab regimes who allied themselves with U.S. imperialism for the sake of survival. The rulers of those regimes, to Qaddafi, have no base of legitimacy within their countries and the only reason for their continuous existence is U.S. protection.

Thus, since the early years of the revolution, Libya has expressed its overt support and encouragement to any revolutionary movement within those "reactionary" Arab regimes. For revolution is the only way to Arab rebirth. Thus, on July 10, 1971, after an attempt to overthrow King Hassan of Morocco, Libya immediately expressed its full support by placing its army on full alert and releasing statements that troops were prepared to fly to Morocco if there was any danger from reactionary forces. The coup attempt failed, and on July 22 the two countries withdrew their ambassadors.[69] The next month, Qaddafi suggested to the Palestinians that they should assassinate King Hussein of Jordan.[70] In March 1973, Libya was alleged to have supported a guerrilla attack in Morocco for the purpose of assassinating King Hassan.[71]

In his speech to the Nasserite volunteers on July 23, 1972, Qaddafi outlined three methods for achieving Arab unity. The first was the Nasserite method, namely, the unity of the revolutionary Arab regimes. The second was reunion by bringing the Arabs together within existing regimes. Third was conquest. He declared that "if the rulers of the Arab nation do not want to enter Arab unity through the method of reunion, they should then expect the two other methods because the Arab nation is determined to achieve Arab unity."[72] Apparently Libya chose to support the revolution within the "reactionary" Arab regimes, after the unification attempts with Egypt, Syria, Sudan, and Tunisia had failed. This method was intensified by the perceived American-Egyptian detente and Sudan's backing of the Egyptian policies after 1974. In an interview with Beirut's *Al-Usbu-Alarabi* (October 21, 1974), Qaddafi attacked Sadat saying that Sadat did not want to see the people rule. He called on an "alliance of Egyptian peasants, workers, students and officials to seize power, to throw out the present 'usurping administration,' and to set up a 'people's government' to carry out the plan for union with Libya."[73] Egypt accused Libya of financing acts of subversion on April 18, 1974, and of directing Libyan agents to blow up the presidential rest house at Mersa Matruh and to kill some Egyptian journalists. A bomb explosion in an Alexandria night club on July 27 was also blamed on Libya. Libya, on its part, accused Cairo of financing subversive activities in Libya. On May 12, Numeiry claimed to have discovered a plot to overthrow his regime and that Libya was involved in the act. Such acts of subversion and countersubversion became more acute between Egypt and Libya, when the former granted asylum to two ex-Libyan officials who were involved in a plot against Qaddafi in 1975. Another coup attempt in Sudan on July 2, 1976, "provided much more alarming proof," in the eyes of Numeiry and Sadat, "of Qaddafi's intention to spread revolution in neighboring states."[74] They claimed that Libya spent $140 million in financing the plot.

On March 21, 1976, President Bourguiba of Tunisia stated that Libya had sent a "terrorist unit" to Tunisia with orders to kill him or his prime minister. He described the alleged plot as an act of revenge for the failed attempt at unity between Tunisia and Libya in January 1974.[75] On July 8, 1976, the Tunisian News Agency claimed that Libya was also training about 2,400 Tunisians at twenty camps in Libya operated in conjunction with Tunisian opposition leaders. On August 14, Sadat claimed that Libya was training men "in four camps for subversive activities in Egypt,

Chad, Sudan, and Tunisia."[76] But in an interview with the *London Daily Telegraph* (September 5, 1976), Major Jallud said that "apart from the Palestinians, the only guerrillas who had received training in Libya were those from Guinea-Bissau and Mozambique."[77]

Libya was very instrumental in its support (financing, training, and arming) of two revolutionary movements in particular: the Palestinian Resistance Movement and the Polisario Front in the Western Sahara. (The latter was created by Libya and Algeria for the purpose of liberating the Western Sahara from Spain. But the support of the two countries continued when Morocco and Mauritania took over the Sahara.)

Libya's revolutionary activities worldwide could be attributed, in most cases, to the Islamic factor in Qaddafi's thinking. In other cases, Islam was interwoven with nationalism to furnish the ideological base of Libyan conduct. Qaddafi sees the world divided into northern "oppressors" and southern "oppressed" and thinks that the only path that can restore the "oppressed" south is the path of revolution. In his statement to the first Arab Socialist Union (ASU) National Congress, March 29, 1972, Qaddafi maintained: "One-third of the world is still suffering from injustice, racial discrimination, oppression and deprivation and is still denied human rights and the right to live free under the sun. To these people who are still fighting for freedom we must extend a helping hand and initiate a discussion with them."[78] Thus, on April 7, 1972, the First National Congress of the ASU proclaimed its support for all liberation movements and revolutions throughout the world. Nathan Alexander's interpretation of this Libyan stand is that

> support of liberation movements was intended to symbolize that the Arab revolution was passing from the defensive to the offensive. Ideologically, support of selected liberation movements, such as the Filipino Muslims, was also an expression of Islamic solidarity. Finally, Libya's support to liberation movements was a tactic employed to enhance its international status as a leader in the Third World's struggle against colonialism and neocolonialism.[79]

As early as August 1971, Chad accused Libya of financing a coup attempt against the Tombalbay regime. In retaliation, Libya openly announced its full support to the Chad National Liberation Front in September 1971. Two reasons lay behind this Libyan action: the perceived need of the Moslems in northern Chad who were seen as oppressed by the "Christian" Tombalbay regime, and the desire to undermine the strong Israeli influence in Chad.

Libya's concern for persecuted Muslims went further when on October 7, 1971, Qaddafi expressed his readiness to send arms to Guinea and warned the Filipino regime that Libya would take the necessary action if persecution against Muslims in the south did not cease. In the same year, Libya stood by Pakistan, militarily, in its war with India.

Qaddafi's religious sympathies also were the motive behind supporting Black Muslims in the United States. The Beirut daily *Al-Bayraq* (August 11, 1972) stated, without naming the sources of the information, that in 1972 Libya provided $13 million for the Tunisian opposition, and $10 million over two years for the Irish Republican Army. At the same time, Libya's efforts in Africa to help Moslems in different countries, and to undermine the Israeli influence, were making some progress. On April 12, 1972, the Chadian regime resumed diplomatic relations with Libya and announced its support for the Palestinian fight against Israel. In April also, Idi Amin expelled the Israeli mission from Uganda, and established diplomatic relations with Libya. This was the result of his visit to Tripoli and after he had received a Libyan promise of economic and military help. The Libyan campaign against Israel in Africa accelerated its speed in 1972–1973. During these two years, Mali, Dahomey, Burundi, Congo People's Republic, Zaire, Gabon (President Bongo of Gabon was converted to Islam on his visit to Libya), and Togo broke diplomatic relations with Israel and declared their firm support for the Palestinian cause.

Libyan support to liberation movements in Africa was also a cardinal sign of Libya's opposition to the existence of all forms of racial discrimination and colonization. In 1973 the following liberation movements were reported to have received Libyan arms and financial aid: ZAPU and ZANU (against Rhodesia), SWAPO (in Namibia), PAIGC (in Guinea-Bissau), FRELMO (in Mozambique), and MPLA (in Angola).

Aside from the Libyan support to liberation movements and the alleged Libyan intervention in some Arab and non-Arab countries, Libya also was accused of financing and/or helping some terrorist activities such as airplane hijacking and acts of assassination and sabotage. For instance, Libya was accused of cooperating with members of the Black September Movement (who in September 1972 killed eleven Israeli athletes at the Olympic Games in Munich). Libya received the bodies of five Palestinians killed in the operation "and gave them a ceremonial funeral."[80]

Also the three Palestinians released after the hijacking of a West German airplane were received in Tripoli on October 30 and were given shelter in Libya. The Munich incident led to deterioration in relations between Libya and the West German government. On July 24, 1973, a Japanese Boeing 747 hijacked from Amsterdam landed in Benghazi (Libya) and was blown up by the hijackers after the passengers were released. Libya announced that the hijackers would be tried for their crime.

During 1974–1975 the most notable involvement of Libya in revolutionary activities was its alleged involvement in subversive activities in some Arab countries (Egypt, Sudan, Tunisia), in addition to its support to the radical Palestinian movement and its involvement in the Lebanese civil war in 1975. But in 1976 the list in the Western press of alleged Libyan "terrorist" acts was unusually long. In addition to charges of subversion in neighboring countries, Libya was held responsible for an attack on an El-Al Israeli plane in Istanbul in August 1976. Also, in August Sadat claimed that Libya and George Habash were behind the Entebbe hijacking affair (although Israeli sources said that the affair was the work of Wadei Haddad who defected from the Habash organization in 1972). The London *Times* reported on April 19, 1976, that Libya trained its own commando units for "terrorist" operations abroad. And on May 20, 1976, Iran claimed that the three guerrillas killed in Tehran "had been receiving arms and money from Libya. The men were said to have received $100,000 every three months."[81] Libya was also accused of having connections with some terrorists such as Ilyich Ramirez Sanchez (Carlos) and some terrorist organizations such as the West German Baader-Meinhof, the Japanese Red Army, and the Italian Red Brigade. But Qaddafi, in an interview with the West German *Der Spiegel* (July 26, 1976) rejected all these charges, denying any connection with these organizations. In the London *Daily Telegraph* (September 5, 1976), Major Jallud said that "apart from the Palestinians, the only guerrillas who had received training in Libya were those from Guinea-Bissau and Mozambique." Jallud suggested that "Palestinian hijackers should be tried before 'revolutionary' courts, perhaps even facing the death penalty." He believed that "past hijackings were 'mistakes' carried out by Palestinians acting as individuals, and not as part of any movement."[82] In April 1976, Libya refused to give asylum to three Muslim Filipinos who hijacked a Philippine Airlines plane to Tripoli.

Qaddafi's version of what constitutes terrorism is much broader than the common usage of the term, and his solution to the problem is quite different from what some countries had suggested. In his statement before the first Arab-American People-to-People Dialogue Conference (held in Tripoli October 9–12, 1978), Qaddafi said this about the problem and its solution:

> Foreign bases, nuclear weapons, starvation, economic warfare, naval fleets, hijacking of planes, the holding of hostages for ransom, and the killing of innocent people are all acts of terrorism. If we are serious in combatting terrorism, we have to put all these deeds on one list and find the necessary solution for them. We are ready to put all our sources in the service of this objective.
>
> Why do Americans forget that the Palestinians have been expelled from their homeland and that the U.S. is helping the occupier keep hold of the land of the Palestinians? But when a Palestinian hijacks a plane to express his despair, the U.S. shakes the world by saying that this is terrorism and an end should be put to it. We are in agreement with the U.S., an end must be put to terrorism, but we should seek solutions to the underlying problems which have led to this kind of terrorism.[83]

4 ➤ THE U.S. IMAGE OF LIBYA, 1969–1976

HISTORICAL BACKGROUND

Aside from the period 1792–1832, when the United States was forced by the Karamanli rulers in Tripoli to pay annual tribute to ensure immunity for U.S. ships from the attacks of "Tripoli pirates," U.S.-Libyan relations (until September 1969) were those of "close friendship." Libya's strategic position was the crucial factor in the policies toward Libya of Ottoman Turkey, Italy, Germany, Britain, and France.

Until the late 1950s, Libya was considered by the United States as "less a country or a state than a strategic position for a series of military bases."[1] Libya's strategic position became more important after Stalin's failed attempt for trusteeship over Libya after World War II. In 1949 a committee of the U.S. Joint Chiefs of Staff, headed by President Truman, designed a contingency plan for World War III (expected in 1957). The plan was called Operation Dropshot. Dropshot was declassified in 1977 and became public through the Freedom of Information Act. Anthony Cave Brown, who obtained Dropshot and published it in 1978, states that one of the major assumptions of the plan was that "there would be no permanent Soviet military presence in the Middle East or North Africa that could seriously interfere with Allied war operations."[2] The plan also called for the United States to provide air and naval protection for its military bases in the region. As for Libya, Dropshot recommended defending the Libyan ports through the deployment of marine and air forces in the ports of Tripoli and Cyrenaican. The plan, in essence, reflects the strategic context of U.S. official thinking during the late 1940s and the 1950s, when the containment of the communist threat was the major concern for U.S. decision makers. Twice, U.S. operations at Wheelus Air Force base (near Tripoli), in 1944 at the time of the Korean War, were integrated into the U.S. Strategic Air Command.[3] The base's existence in Libya was formalized through a treaty signed in 1954. The United States agreed to pay the pro-Western Libyan monarchy $1 million a year for twenty years in exchange for use of the base. (The treaty did not survive the 1969 revolution.) In his welcome speech to John Foster Dulles, who came to inspect the base, the American ambassador proclaimed, "Libya has acquired a powerful new protector in addition to its British ally. As a stakeholder in Libya's future, the U.S., it stands to reason, will have a natural interest in the defense of that none too strongly unified country."[4]

U.S. protection of this pro-Western regime also took the form of economic assistance. During the 1950s the United States provided about $3 million in grain commodities. It was this assistance in conjunction with British economic assistance that helped sustain the weak economy, considered by the UN in 1959 as one of the poorest in the world. As for the United States, it was important to have a pro-Western regime that promoted not only Western influence in Libya but also tried to spread it throughout in the entire region. (Ruth First maintains that when American foreign policy failed to enfold the whole of the Middle East in its embrace, Libya's King Idris in 1958 went personally as the emissary of the Baghdad Pact to Turkey and Lebanon.)[5] The U.S. policy of protecting the monarchy was pleasing to Congress, which advised in 1956: "It is to the American interest that the people in the areas where [military] bases are located have a peaceful government friendly to the U.S. and its interests."[6]

Apart from Libya's strategic position and its role in countering radical Arab nationalism in the region (seen as a destabilizing force in the Middle East), came the discovery of oil in the late 1950s to lend even more importance to Libya in American eyes. By 1969 the United States had virtual total domination over the oil industry in Libya, with twenty American companies exploring and producing Libyan oil. By 1968, Libya was second only to Saudi Arabia as the most profitable source 'for U.S. oil companies. In that year their total investment reached $1,500 million. An American official report estimated in July 1970, "These U.S. companies' investments in Libya have a market value of several billion dollars and their oil operations in Libya account for 88% of Libyan oil production and returned about $60 million to the U.S. balance of payments in 1969."[7] As of August 31, 1969, Libya was a paradise for Western interests in the region. A pro-Western regime furnished its land for Western military installations, supplied the West with low-priced oil under comfortable conditions, and promoted Western influence in the region through its opposition to Arab radicalism.

On September 1, 1969, there was a revolutionary upheaval in Libya that brought to power a nationalistic young officer who vowed to undermine Western influence not only in his country, but also in the whole region. How did the United States see the new revolutionary regime's policies? And through what lenses did it view the new Libyan leadership in its early years?

THE U.S. IMAGE OF LIBYA, 1969–1976

The 1969 Libyan revolution took the entire world by surprise, and the Nixon administration was no exception. There was no information at all about the identity of the new rulers or their orientation. The few statements issued by the Libyan radio were not enough to paint a picture of the newly born regime. In his first dispatch after the takeover, the Ameican ambassador in Tripoli, Joseph Palmer, told the president and Secretary of State Rogers that "the still-anonymous young men of the Revolutionary Command Council (RCC) promise to protect all Western interests, including the pumping of oil" and that they have "proclaimed a kind of Muslim welfare state, drastically raising wages and banning alcohol as a step toward implementing Koranic law in the new republic."[8] The statements issued by the RCC gave the impression that the new rulers were anticommunist, and that they were nationalists who considered Nasser their ideal.

Two men and two elements played the major role in the U.S. recognition of the new regime. The two who knew most about Libya were Assistant Secretary of State for African Affairs David Newsom, former ambassador to Libya, and Ambassador Palmer. The two elements were the obvious anticommunist line of the new regime and its promise to keep Libya's international commitments. Commentators on Libyan-American relations such as John Wright, Ruth First, John Cooley, and Ellen B. Laipson agree that Newsom and Palmer were convinced that the new regime "would prove to be an important asset in the struggle to keep Soviet influence and Communism out of the Arab world."[9] In a personal discussion, Newsom confirmed to me his role in the U.S. recognition of the new revolutionary regime and described the rationale behind the recognition. He also confirmed that he was the one who convinced Britain, through its ambassador in Washington, to follow the U.S. policy toward Libya. Nevertheless, the official U.S. statement of recognition was worded very cautiously:

> The U.S. government has noted the statement of the RCC that all nations maintaining diplomatic relations with Libya are considered as recognizing the new Libyan government. The U.S. is maintaining diplomatic relations with the government of Libya and looks forward to a continuation of traditionally close ties between our two countries.[10]

U.S. officials viewed Libyan policies from the time of the revolution until 1972 with some objectivity. The revolutionary regime's orientation and conduct were seen as motivated by Muammar el Qaddafi's nationalistic conviction and Islamic zeal. His policies were seen as radical and extreme but not the result of the influence of a foreign power such as the USSR. During this period, three areas of Libyan foreign policy dominated the U.S. administration's concern: (1) Libya's stand against the Soviet Union, (2) Libya's position vis-à-vis Israel, and (3) Libya's oil policy.

As I have noted, Libya's antagonism toward communism in general and the USSR in particular was used by some U.S. officials to convince President Nixon and his top officials to recognize the newborn regime. All official statements about U.S.-Libyan relations delivered before congressional committees and subcommittees from 1969 to 1972 emphasized Libya's antagonism toward the Soviets. For example, in July 1970, while delivering a statement before the Subcommittee on U.S. Security Agreements and Commitments Abroad about U.S.-Libyan relations, David Newsom relayed what he called "some rather *dramatic* news from Libya." He announced, "It just came in at noon, and we have not had a chance fully to evaluate its significance, but large quantities of Soviet arms, including T-54 tanks, were unloaded at Tripoli Harbor July 18 and 19."[11] However, Newsom and the deputy assistant secretary of defense for international security affairs assured the subcommittee that the arms were for "parade purposes" and that they did not reflect any Soviet-Libyan rapprochement, because the deal was concluded through the Egyptians and not through a direct Libyan contact with the Soviets. His interpretation later turned out to be correct. Despite the insignificance of the incident, though described as "dramatic," it shows the intensity of U.S. concern about Soviet influence in that part of the Arab world which used to be within the U.S. sphere of influence. Later I asked Newsom why he had described the Soviet arms shipment to Libya as "dramatic news." He replied, "because it was the first contact between Libya and the Soviet Union, even if indirect, and it might lead to change in the Libyan policy toward the Soviet Union."[12]

Thus, U.S. officials continued to view Libya as an anti-Soviet country whose policy was to combat communism not only internally but also in other Arab and non-Arab countries. The Libyan stand toward the communist coup attempt in Sudan, Libya's support to Sadat's expulsion of Soviet advisers and his crackdown on what was described as "Soviet agents in the Egyptian regime" in May 1971, and Libya's support of Pakistan in its war with India, all were policies that made the American view of Libya as anti-Soviet grow even stronger. The economic and technical agreements that were concluded between Libya and the Soviet Union did not change this view. If other issues had not become involved, such as differences over the Arab-Israeli conflict and the Palestinian question, Libya's anti-Soviet approach could have served as a solid basis for establishing better relations between the United States and Libya. The U.S. officials themselves were aware of this. As Newsom stated, "Although strongly anti-Communist, [Libya] is at the same time cool to the United States and Britain because of the stand of these governments on Arab issues."[13]

By May 1974, when Libya concluded its first major arms deal with the Soviet Union, concern about the Libyan-Soviet rapprochement started to surface among U.S. leaders. This concern was fueled in 1975 and 1976 by Egyptian and Sudanese allegations of growing Soviet influence in Libya. Some rumors even suggested that the Soviets had established military bases there. However, Western sources, including those of the CIA, disconfirmed Egypt's allegations. Nevertheless, the Soviet-Libyan rapprochement caused worry in the United States that it might develop into a stronger Soviet influence in the Middle East. This concern intensified because of two factors. First, the Soviet-Libyan rapprochement

Turn to pg. 21

took place at a time when Soviet influence was declining in the Middle East, as witnessed by the expulsion of the Soviets from Egypt, and the growing American influence in Egypt after the 1973 war. Thus, it was feared that the Soviets might come back to the Middle East through a different door. Second, by 1973 Henry Kissinger had assumed responsibility for the State Department. Given his analysis of world events, he might have viewed the Soviet-Libyan rapprochement as more threatening than it actually was. The Libyan and American officials I interviewed agreed with this line of argument.[14] In an interview, Harold Sandres (former National Security Council member and former deputy assistant secretary of state for the Near East) added another factor: Kissinger's personal friendship with both Sadat and the Saudis might have accelerated the intensity of U.S. worry about the Soviet role in Libya, through the allegations they used to feed Kissinger with. "Qaddafi was perceived as anti-Communist," Sandres maintains; "we regretted the change in his relations with the Soviets."[15] However, because there were no military bases or facilities given to the Soviets in Libya, in line with Qaddafi's assertions that his relations with the Soviets were purely commercial, the U.S. perception was that Libya still kept a distance from the Soviet sphere of influence.

The Libyan revolutionary stand regarding the Arab-Israeli conflict was based, essentially, on the rejection of Israel as an entity. Qaddafi has reiterated his belief that the only solution to the problem is through armed struggle in which either Israel or the Arabs must annihilate the other. Obviously, the United States could do little to change this belief, given Qaddafi's conviction that the United States is the main supporter of the Arab's enemy. Despite this stand, described by U.S. officials as "militant," "radical," and "extreme," the United States was less concerned with the Libyan policies in the Arab-Israeli conflict than with Libyan policies toward the Soviets and oil. This was in part because of Libya's geographic position, relatively far from Israel, and also because Libya was perceived as weak and unlikely to affect the Arab-Israeli balance of power.

From September 1969 to 1973, Libya's military capabilities were evaluated as poor in quantity and quality.[16] Even purchase of 110 Mirage fighters from France did not change the official American view, despite the arguments of Israel and the Zionist lobby in Washington that the deal was ultimately intended to supply Egypt with aircraft. There was mounting pressure from Israel's friends in Congress that the Nixon administration should do something about this deal. In a press conference on January 31, 1971, Nixon promised that he would discuss the matter with French President Pompidou, who was scheduled to visit the United States the following month. The pressure turned into disturbance during Pompidou's visit in February 1971, because "Israel's friends organized demonstrations everywhere he went, with blows falling upon both Mr. and Mrs. Pompidou in a Chicago crowd."[17] The official U.S. position was clarified by Secretary of State Rogers when he was asked in January 1970 whether the deal would upset the balance of power in the region:

> Well, the sale by France to Libya does not become operative until 1971. And it is true that there are, I think, very few trained Libyan pilots, so they would have difficulty for some time until they train pilots. France's position is that they are going to train some of the Libyan pilots and that they have made provisions to prevent the planes being transferred by Libya to other countries.[18]

Despite Rogers's assurances, two squadrons of the planes were transferred to Egypt and took part in the 1973 war. The Congress and the Zionist lobby achieved some results when the administration decided, "The arms deal injects a new sense of urgency into the administration's consideration of Israeli requests for U.S. aid."[19]

The U.S. view of Libya's inability to affect the course of events in the Arab-Israeli conflict started to change gradually by 1974 as a result of Libya's efforts to build the "rejectionist" front, composed of Syria, Iraq, Algeria, the PLO, and South Yemen. Moreover, its military capabilities improved because of the increased amounts of sophisticated Soviet equipment imported from Moscow. In addition, Libya's rapprochement with the Soviets, if utilized, might give it leverage in the Arab-Israeli conflict. By 1975–1976 some concern started to surface in the American press that what was called "Libya's subversive activities within some Arab regimes friendly to the U.S." might lead to destabilizing those regimes who were involved in the "peace process" under the American umbrella.

A third issue about which the United States was concerned at the time of the Libyan revolution was American oil interests in Libya. Early statements of the RCC gave the impression that U.S. interests were not in jeopardy. This was apparent in the interagency paper prepared for the

Washington Special Action Group on what attitude to take toward the new revolutionary regime: "We see no immediate threat to these [oil] interests, although such could result if the regime is threatened or becomes increasingly unstable."[20] When in 1970–1972 Libya started its battle against the oil companies for higher prices and higher participatory ownership status, the official American view did not change. As a matter of fact, the administration's position was to support Libya's demand for higher prices. In the view of James E. Atkins, head of the Office of Fuels and Energy of the Department of State, the demands were justified: "You take the Persian Gulf price, take the transportation costs to Europe, and then subtract transportation costs to country X, Libya in this case, and you get a value of oil in that particular spot, Libya. Libyan oil by most calculations seemed to be underpriced."[21]

David Newsom presented to Congress in July 1970 the administration's point of view that both Libya's cutback in production and its demand for higher prices were justifiable. His contention was that both issues had been raised by the previous royal government and before Qaddafi's takeover.[22] It is clear that the U.S. administration had expected the Libyan actions against the oil companies. Only expropriation was not expected. Thus, Libya's steps toward nationalization in 1973, using oil as a political weapon against the American oil companies, began to cloud the official U.S. perception of Libya's oil politics. The official view became public on July 8, 1973, in the U.S. government's reaction to Libya's nationalization of Bunker Hunt Oil Co.: "Under established principles of international law, measures taken against the rights and property of foreign nationals which are arbitrary, discriminatory, or based on considerations of political reprisal and economic coercion are invalid and not entitled to recognition by other states."[23]

Libya's nationalization of other American oil companies in 1974 was viewed through the same lenses. But the official U.S. perception of those actions was never intense enough to describe them as hostile. As Newsom explains, "Despite all the differences with the Libyan government oil policies, their oil was still available for us."[24] Former Libyan Foreign Minister Mansur Kikhia agrees with Newsom's point of view: "The real American interest lies in the continuing supply of oil. That was not affected. Besides, we have utilized the law of the market very carefully."[25] Two other former American officials condone the same argument. In Harold Sandres's words, "Every country has the right to nationalize, but we wanted fair compensation."[26] Harold Josif, former

chargé d'affaires of the U.S. embassy in Tripoli (1969–1973), went even
further: he personally met with the Libyan oil minister to tell him, "We do
not object to the nationalization with fair compensation." He believes that
"the companies themselves were interested more in getting access to oil
than in owning it."[27]

By 1975 Libya's lead in the oil market started to decline. Its oil was
overpriced and it was clearly not competitive with relatively cheaper
crudes from the Gulf. By February 1975, Libyan output fell to only
912,000 b/d.[28] Hence, there was not much ground left for contention
between the United States and Libya over the issue of oil—the battle was
over by 1974.

Libya's revolutionary activities within other Arab countries and
worldwide did not receive any U.S. official attention at all in the 1969–
1975 period. Despite the multiplicity and the intensity of these activities,
only one official statement during that period, worded in very neutral
language, referred to them. Words such as "terrorist," "subversive,"
"destabilizing," were not used in describing Libya's revolutionary actions. Instead, in 1971 the official U.S. statements read as follows:
"Libya has increasingly interested itself in sub-Saharan Africa through
expressions in the past of support for Moslem populations in other states
and opposition to what it regards as Israeli influence detrimental to the
Arab cause in Africa."[29] Former Foreign Minister Kikhia recalls that
during that period "Libya's worldwide revolutionary activities were
never rejected by the U.S. The only exception is our support to the
Filipino Muslims where the U.S. expressed to us its fears that our action
may turn [the Philippines] into a tension spot that could be exploited by
the Soviets."[30] I asked David Newsom about this deliberate neglect of
Libya's revolutionary activities. He responded:

> Actually, there has been a contest between the Congress and the
> executive about designating some countries as "terrorists." One
> administration after another fought legislation by the Congress in
> this regard. The Nixon and Ford administrations did this in the
> Libyan case. Congress wanted us to prepare a list, but we never did.
> This does not mean that [the executive branch] did not know about
> Libya's "terrorist" activities at that time.[31]

By late 1976, when Libyan-Soviet relations had improved substantially, the official American view of Libya began changing. Libya's
revolutionary activities were not neglected any more. Nevertheless, the

language used in official public statements still was not strong or assertive in its condemnation of Libya's acts. This was clear in President Ford's July 19, 1976, press conference, when he responded to a question about whether the administration had any evidence or information about Qaddafi's connection with terrorism. The president's reply was: "We do know that the Libyan government has in many ways done certain things that might have simulated terrorist activity, but I don't think we ought to discuss any evidence that we have that might prove or disprove that."[32]

Having reviewed all the publicly available official American statements regarding Libya during this era, and having interviewed U.S. and Libyan officials who played a major role in formulating and executing the relations between the two countries, I can safely infer that the official U.S. view of Libya at this time saw Libya as a "militant Arab nationalist regime," and Qaddafi as an "erratic and extreme leader but still representing a strong stream in Libyan life which is based on Islam and nationalism." These are the words of David Newsom, who maintains that "there was no conflicting image of Qaddafi and Libya during those early years. But there were differences of opinion about how to deal with him."[33]

The prevailing U.S. image of Libya between 1969 and 1976 was as follows.

1. *Motivation*. Libya's foreign policy after 1969 was seen as motivated solely by Qaddafi's thinking and personality. Because he was a nationalist and Muslim zealot, the regime's orientations were characterized as nationalistic and radically Islamic. Libya was also seen as independent from the influence of any foreign power. With its hostility toward the Soviets and its coolness toward the West, the United States held a particularly "complex" view of Libya during the early months of the revolution. Libya was not seen as under the Soviet influence, although some caution started to surface in official statements after the Libyan-Soviet rapprochement. With Libya's expulsion of the U.S. military bases in 1970 and its radical oil policies, the orientations of the regime were not seen as serving American interests in the region. Thus some threat started to be perceived, though it was not regarded as significant because Libya was not associated with a foreign power equal to the United States in capability or culture. The threat was also felt to be moderate because oil was still flowing to the West; moreover, Libya's rhetoric in the Arab-Israeli conflict could not be taken seriously because of its poor military capabil-

ity. Thus from mid-1970 to 1973, the prevailing U.S. image of Libya was complex, but approaching the "agitator" category.

2. *Capability*. Because Libya apparently posed no threat to the United States during the early months of the revolution, Libya's modest economic and military capability was seen in a detached manner. With the increase of Libyan rhetoric and involvement in the Arab-Israeli conflict, the U.S. perception of Libya's capabilities tended to underestimate Libya's ability to affect the regional balance of power. But with the Libyan-Soviet rapprochement after May 1974, the United States began to regard Libya as an "affiliate with the enemy," because of the perceived potential of using the influence of a third power (the USSR) as leverage.

3. *Decisional Style and Locus*. The decisional style of the revolutionary regime was seen through the whole 1969–1976 period as highly

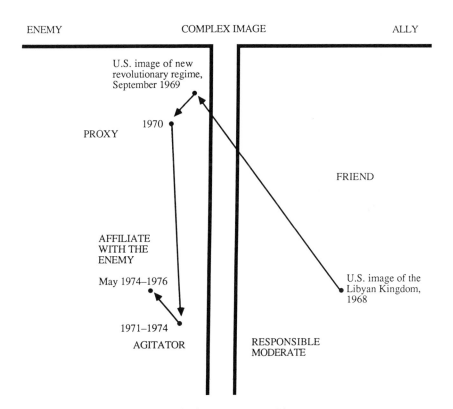

FIGURE 4.   U.S. Images of Libya, 1969–1976

individualistic. All decisions were seen as Qaddafi-made or Qaddafi-inspired. The unsuccessful attempts to overthrow Qaddafi were not viewed as affecting his power position or his decisional latitude.

The prevailing U.S. image of Libya during this era underwent three successive stages: the first lasted from September 1, 1969, until the end of 1970 when the U.S. officials saw the newly born revolutionary regime through "complex" lenses. The second stage lasted from 1971 until May 1974 when some threat started to be perceived as a result of the Libyan conduct. During this period the revolutionary regime was viewed as an "agitator" due to its inferior capability and its inability to use as leverage the influence of a third power comparable in capability and culture to the United States. The third stage lasted from May 1974 until the end of 1976. In this period the prevailing U.S. image of Libya started moving toward the "affiliate of the enemy" category because of Libya's improved relations with the Soviets; it was feared that such a rapprochement would enhance Libya's economic and military capabilities. Thus, the threat perceived from Libya's conduct was more intense than in the previous two patterns. (See figure 4.)

5 ➤ U.S. POLICY TOWARD LIBYA,

SEPTEMBER 1969–1976

Despite the fact that U.S. officials shared a perception of Libya during the early years of the revolution as a "militant nationalistic revolutionary Arab regime," they disagreed on what policy the United States should pursue vis-à-vis the new regime. This issue was under serious discussion by the Washington Special Actions Group (WSAG) in November 1969. Two points of view characterized these discussions. The first, represented by Henry Kissinger (then national security advisor), was hostile toward the new regime. In his *Years of Upheaval,* Kissinger recalls:

> In a meeting of November 24, 1969, I raised the question whether to have the 40 committee canvass the possibility of covert action. A study was prepared of economic and political pressure points on Libya, but the agencies did not have their heart in it. All options involving action were rejected, causing me to exclaim that I was averse to submitting to the President a paper that left us with the proposition that we could do nothing.[1]

This antagonistic policy line was rejected by the majority of U.S. officials represented in the WSAG. Newsom explains the basis of this rejection: "We had about 5,000 citizens in Libya, we had economic interests (oil) to protect. Besides, the hostile action would attract hostile reaction from other Arab countries."[2] According to the dominant view, Kissinger narrates:

> The real danger of radicalization resided in our opposition to Qaddafi. The huge Wheelus Air Base—which Qaddafi asked us to

evacuate—was alleged to be of marginal significance. We would protect our oil interests best, it was said, by separating them from military matters.[3]

This bureaucratic consensus was reflected in a paper prepared for the WSAG meeting which emphasized that the best choice was to try to get along with Libya:

> Our present strategy is to seek to establish satisfactory relations with the new regime. The return to our balance of payments and the security of U.S. investments in oil are considered our primary interests. We seek to retain our military facilities, but not at the expense of threatening our economic return. We also wish to protect European dependence on Libyan oil. It is literally the only "irreplaceable" oil in the world, from the point of view both of quality and geographic location.[4]

Mansur Kikhia, former Libyan foreign minister, argues convincingly that the real issue behind the U.S. intention to initiate some rapprochement with revolutionary Libya was Qaddafi's apparent strong anti-Soviet attitude. Hence, the Americans had no fear that their interests, including oil, were in danger. The U.S. ambassador's first dispatches to the president and secretary of state assured them of the anticommunist nature of the regime. This complacency is also apparent in statements delivered by U.S. officials before congressional committees and subcommittees. Even when Libya started its battle against the oil companies, the official U.S. reaction was passive, if not supportive of Libya's actions.

Rapprochement is a policy to be undertaken when one state sees the possibility of thereby changing the character of another state. However, when the target state cannot be completely trusted because of the changing character of its policies, or because more time is needed to judge its foreign policy line, the policy pattern to be followed involves what could be described as "cautious cooperation." According to this policy, some of the target state's needs (usually economic and technical) are to be responded to favorably, while other demands (usually military) are to be delayed or turned down politely.

U.S. policy toward Libya from September 1969 until 1973 corresponds to this pattern to a large degree. It started with the fast withdrawal of the American military bases from Libya in compliance with the Libyan demand. This fast compliance was intended, as one U.S. official put it in July 1970, "to remove an irritant from the U.S.-Libyan relations"[5] and to prove the good intentions of the United States to establish a satisfactory relationship with the new revolutionary regime. Eight of the sixteen C-130 military transport planes purchased by the royal regime before 1969 were delivered under the justification that they were representing "a commercial deal" between the royal regime and Lockheed Company. The delivery of some F-5 military aircraft was under serious consideration. Some officials were against the delivery, in light of Libya's acutely antagonistic policy toward Israel, while others, especially in the State Department, favored the delivery as a way to more rapprochement with the new regime. However, the former point of view grew stronger when Libya concluded its Mirage deal with France and it became even harder to get congressional approval of the delivery. (Libya later canceled the F-5 deal under the pretext that the aircraft were not advanced enough to match other types of aircraft acquired by Israel.)

Libya's efforts to improve relations with the United States (through Tunisia's mediation) and its appointment of a new ambassador to Washington in 1971, gave the impression, as David Newsom puts it, that "the U.S. started to have effective and satisfactory relations with Libya."[6] During this period, some rumors circulated in Beirut and in Washington that the CIA discovered and informed Qaddafi of at least three plots to overthrow the regime. In the first of these, reported by the Lebanese newspaper *Al-Nahar* on October 1, 1971, and by the *New York Times* on October 3, Ambassador Palmer betrayed a group of army officers who were plotting to overthrow Qaddafi. *Al-Nahar* said: "Palmer got names of the plotters by feigning sympathy with them and then turned names over to Qaddafi." The second incident in 1971 was what became known as the "Hilton assignment," when a group of Libyan exiles, headed by Omar Al-Shalhi (the former monarch's special adviser), hired a band of expert European mercenaries to overthrow the revolutionary regime. The operation called for seizing Tripoli's main prison, freeing the prisoners, arming them, then moving to Qaddafi's residence to assassinate him. (Morocco was also involved in the plot.)[7] This incident was said to have been discovered by the CIA and some other European intelligence agencies and reported to Qaddafi.

The third plot, allegedly discovered and revealed to Libya by the CIA, was the attempt made by Abdullah Abid Al-Sanussi, a close relative of the monarch, to overthrow the revolutionary regime in 1970. John Cooley states that "the Israeli intelligence closely followed and may have actually supported or contemplated actively supporting" the attempt.[8] The plot depended on using Chad as the base for smuggling weapons and mercenaries into Fezzan in southern Libya where tribal elements could be used to control the city. From there they could move to the northern cities of Tripoli and Benghazi. Cooley claims, "The CIA Special Operation Directorate, in its infinite wisdom, seems to have examined the plan and found it somewhat less than practical. This opinion was passed on to Mossad with a clear indication of American disapproval."[9]

The former Libyan minister and some of the former U.S. officials with whom I had discussions (David Newsom, Harold Josif, and Harold Sandres—though Sandres did not seem to remember the incident well) all confirmed the U.S. assistance in discovering the "Hilton plot." However, Mansur Kikhia asserts, "We had been informed of the plot by Italian intelligence first, then the Americans told us." He explains:

> The American act was not because they liked Qaddafi or his revolutionary regime, but because they realized that the attempt would fail because of Qaddafi's overwhelming popularity at that time. And most important, Qaddafi's hostile line toward the Soviets made them realize that he is better than a pro-communist element ruling Libya.[10]

David Newsom explains the rationale of the U.S. action in slightly different words: "We had about 5,000 Americans in Libya to protect, and what we had learned about the plot suggested that its chances of success were slim. Landing in Tripoli would be exploited by Qaddafi against us." He adds, "It was a deliberate decision to let the Italians inform the Libyan regime first because Qaddafi would believe them more than he would believe us should we have acted first."[11]

To me, the incident (if it really took place) reflects part of the rapprochement the United States was trying to establish with Libya; it occurred because American interests were perceived as better served by making this gesture. Despite Qaddafi's antagonistic policies toward Israel and the U.S. oil companies, and despite his revolutionary activities, he was still seen as a very strong anticommunist figure, and that outweighed his hostile policies in American eyes. For instance, Colin Legum states: "In midsummer 1972, according to two U.S. officials, the U.S. formally considered and rejected a proposal to furnish clandestine assistance to Chad to enable it to counter Libya's Qaddafi and dissident Chadian groups." Legum also claims that the United States "had exerted pressure on Israel not to make a retaliatory strike"[12] when in November 1972 some speculated that Israel was preparing a direct reprisal against Libya. Israel was angry because of Qaddafi's open support for the guerrillas in Lebanon and his providing sanctuary for the survivors of the Black September group (who killed the Israeli athletes in Munich during the Olympic games). Sandres told me, "We did not have any interest to be served, if Israel attacked Libya. Thus we told Israel not to take any reprisal action against Libya."[13]

U.S. trade relations with Libya during the period 1970–1973 corresponded to a large degree to the cautious U.S. rapprochement with the new revolutionary regime. By 1970 the United States was Libya's second-largest supplier of primary capital goods. The value of U.S. exports to Libya was estimated at $104.4 million. In 1971, the amount dropped to only $77.7 million, but it grew steadily to reach $103.7 million in 1973. This fluctuation could be attributed mainly to the nature of the private sector which tries to find the most stable places for its trade deals and investment. In contrast, imports from Libya grew steadily after 1970 from $39.1 million to $215.8 million in 1973. This was despite the fact that early in 1972 the United States, through a mutual agreement with Libya, terminated about ten economic and military agreements signed in 1955–1957. The U.S. response to Libya's radical oil policies during this period was generally passive, if not supportive of the Libyan side, as explained above.

By mid-1973 until 1976, U.S. policy toward Libya started to witness some signs of pressure because of new developments in Libyan foreign policy. These changes were: first, the growing intensity of Libya's involvement in the Arab-Israeli conflict, reflected in Libya's military involvement in the preparations for the 1973 October War and its opposition to the American-sponsored peace plans that followed the war. Second was the increased aggressiveness of Libya's oil policies and its use of oil as a political weapon, namely, the nationalization of four U.S. companies in 1973–1974. Third was the growing Libyan-Soviet rapprochement which began in May 1974 with the purchase of substantial quantities of sophisticated Soviet arms.

In early 1973, the United States sent its first signal of dissatisfaction with Libya's policies by not appointing a successor to the American ambassador in Tripoli, who resigned late in 1972. From that time until May 1980, U.S.-Libyan relations were conducted through a chargé d'affaires. Also in 1973, the United States blocked the delivery of another eight C-130 planes to Libya, despite the fact that Libya had paid for them, and decided not to sell Libya military weapons and certain other equipment "which could add significantly to Libya's military capabilities."[14] Former Libyan Foreign Minister Kikhia attributes the above actions to the intensity of Libya's stand in the Arab-Israeli conflict and to the pressure exerted by the Zionist lobby in Washington. He recalls the U.S. secretary of state, in a meeting with him at that time, calling the Libyans "troublemakers, because they refuse the peaceful solutions to the Arab-Israeli conflict."[15] David Newsom explains the U.S. decision not to deliver the eight C-130s:

> In 1973–74, the feeling in Washington was that our cooperation with Libya was not reciprocated. [Ambassador] Palmer was not getting access to Qaddafi. It became apparent that the regime was going to have different objectives in the area from ours. Thus the initial willingness to deliver the rest of the C-130s changed.[16]

The U.S. reaction to the Libyan nationalization of the American oil companies is in contrast to its earlier passivity in 1970–1972. For instance, when Libya nationalized the shares of Bunker Hunt Oil Company in June 1973, the United States protested officially by calling the measure "arbitrary and discriminatory." Libya retaliated by nationalizing another three companies in September. The United States moved to support the companies' legal claims against Libya, informed other companies not to export oil from the fields under the legal dispute, and requested other governments not to receive oil from those fields. But the New England Petroleum Company violated the State Department's advice and started shipping oil from the disputed fields to the New York area, which was totally dependent on Libyan oil. In a letter to Henry Kissinger in September 1973, New England Petroleum's President Manning argued that unless the company could purchase oil from Libya, some 20 million U.S. citizens would be threatened with electrical blackout. No reply to the letter was ever received.[17] The U.S. position also came under severe attack from the press, especially the *Wall Street Journal* and the *New York Times*, which argued that the U.S. position led to Libya's switching to the communist market instead of the West. The State Department circulated a note to the companies stating, ''The State Department leaves to the companies concerned the decision whether they wish to proceed with such purchases.''[18]

To put the U.S. reaction to the Libyan nationalization of the American oil companies in its proper perspective, one may argue that it was intended more to symbolize official sympathy with the companies than to exert pressure against Libya. For the United States realized, accurately, that it did not have much leverage to use against Libya. President Nixon expressed this fact on September 24, 1973, when he was asked what could be done against the Arabs who use oil as a political weapon against the United States. Nixon replied:

> Obviously, we are having discussions with some of the companies involved. Obviously, as far as some of the nations involved—for example, Libya—our relations are not that close that we could have too much influence. The other problems, of course, are the radical elements that presently seem to be on the ascendancy in various countries in the Middle East, like Libya. Those elements, of course, we are not in a position to control.[19]

Thus, I would argue that the U.S. position was merely a symbolic action of solidarity with the companies that could not change Libyan oil policy. After all, the flow of oil to the American market was not threatened, and that was all that really mattered. In a hearing before the Senate Foreign Relations Subcommittee on Multinational Corporations in August 1974, it was stated that Libyan oil was exported to the United States even during the Arab oil embargo.

After the Libyan-Soviet rapprochement in May 1974, the United States began to exert more pressure on Libya. On January 21, 1975, the Libyan purchase of a $200 million air-defense system (a Westinghouse computer and radar equipment from Northrop) had been delayed. In August 1975, the State Department confirmed the action and refused to permit Libyan air force trainees to enter the United States for training in aircraft maintenance.[20] By the end of 1976, Soviet-Libyan relations grew even stronger when Qaddafi visited the Soviet Union for the first time. The United States started using a different kind of political pressure. In President Ford's press conference of July 1976, he stated that Libyan activities might have stimulated terrorism. This charge became a policy line in the thirty-first session of the UN General Assembly when the United States led a group of European countries in attempting to accuse Libya of financing and supporting terrorism.

Despite this marginal political and military pressure, U.S.-Libyan economic relations between 1973 and 1976 were growing even stronger. U.S. imports from Libya rose from $215.8 million in 1973 to $2,188 million in 1976; in the same period, U.S. exports to Libya grew from $103.7 million to $277 million. The two countries' healthy economic relations indicates not only that political frictions did not spill over into their mutual economic interests, but also that U.S. criticism of Libya in 1973–1976 was meant only to register dissatisfaction with Libya's growing hostility vis-à-vis U.S. objectives in the region, not to force a change in those policies. Should that have been the purpose, pressures would have been stronger and would have involved economic relations, as occurred during the Reagan administration. For instance, when in March

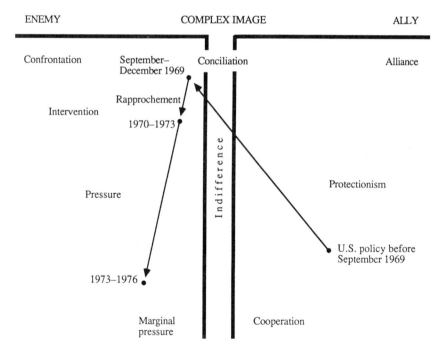

FIGURE 5.   U.S. Policy Toward Libya, 1969–1976

and April 1973 Libyan jets intercepted and fired upon U.S. military planes in the Mediterranean, the United States did not respond or raise the issue publicly. Not only this, the U.S. chargé d'affaires in Tripoli sent a cable to Washington asking for the cancellation of the military maneuvers that were scheduled to take place in the area. The maneuvers were postponed.

Thus, it is quite obvious that the changes in U.S. policy toward Libya from 1969 to 1976 conform, to a large extent, to the changes that took place in the image held by the U.S. official of the revolutionary regime at that time. (See figure 5.)

PART III ➤ U.S. POLICY TOWARD LIBYA DURING THE CARTER ADMINISTRATION

LIBYA AND THE ARAB-ISRAELI CONFLICT

The Arab-Israeli conflict, perceived entirely in terms of the Palestinian cause, continues to be the central concern for Libyan revolutionary leaders. Libya's policies toward other Arab countries are still basically determined by those countries' conduct toward this issue, which was of crucial importance during 1977–1980.

As I have stated, Sadat's new course of conduct after the 1973 war resulted in acute tensions between Egypt and Libya. For Qaddafi, Sadat was not the man to be trusted with the Arab cause; his new approach toward the United States was in essence a selling out of the Arab cause; the region, as a result, would fall under the "imperial-Zionist" umbrella. The Libyan-Soviet rapprochement was seen as a necessary strategic step to encounter this perceived imbalance of superpower influence in the region. According to Libya's outlook, the Arab regimes were judged on their stand from the new developments in the Arab-Israeli conflict. They were either "progressive" regimes rejecting Sadat's "defeatist" approach, or "reactionary puppets" supporting Sadat and the "imperial Zionist" designs in the region. To Sadat, the Libyan-Soviet rapprochement was an annoying factor. Libya was accused of being a base for Soviet influence in the area. The increasing quantities of sophisticated Soviet arms in Libya were perceived to be for the sole purpose of destabilizing other regimes in the Middle East and Africa, and Sadat saw Egypt as the first target. Each government accused the other of subversive activities.

By 1977, Egypt and Libya were on a confrontation course, and in July verbal hostilities gave way to four days of border clashes. Two factors explain this military confrontation. First was each leader's perception of the other. Sadat saw Qaddafi as conspiring with the Soviets to overthrow his regime. On the second day of hostilities, he blamed "that very strange person" Qaddafi for the deteriorating relations and accused him of being "an agent of a foreign power." Sadat and other Egyptian officials claimed that their attacks against Libya were primarily aimed at "Soviet-built installations in the country."[1] To Qaddafi, Sadat's diplomacy in the Middle East was seen as part of an "American-Zionist" conspiracy aimed at dominating the region and destroying Arab and Palestinian interests.

Both sides claimed the superpowers' involvement in the hostilities. Libya's Major Jalloud, for instance, stated at the beginning of August that Egypt had hit the radar station in Tobruk because it was monitoring the U.S. Sixth Fleet. He also claimed that the United States concluded an arms deal with Egypt immediately after the incident as a way of rewarding Egypt for aggression against Libya. Egypt, on the other hand, claimed that helicopters from the Soviet warship *Noscova* had interfered with its radio communications during the military operation.[2]

The second factor that led to the military clashes was the Egyptian-Sudanese attempt to encircle Libya and isolate it externally. It started when Sadat and Numeiry signed a defense treaty in July 1976 to counter what they called "Soviet-Libyan influence in the Red Sea and the horn of Africa." The attempt continued in February 1977, when Egypt, Sudan, and Syria, backed by Saudi Arabia, called for a coordinated policy against "Soviet and Libyan activities in the Horn of Africa."[3] It was only two weeks before the military clashes when Sadat tried to expand his circle to southern Libya. On July 6 Libyan Radio announced that Egypt was flying arms to Chad. Then on July 12, Hosni Mubarak (then vice-president of Egypt) visited Sudan and traveled on to Chad as head of a joint Egyptian-Sudanese delegation to discuss support for the Chadian government against what they called "foreign aggression." Libya called the visit "a declaration of war on Libya."[4] Taking into account Libya's deteriorating relations with Tunisia during that time, the Egyptian, Sudanese, and Chadian encirclement, should it succeed, would have left Libya with hostile powers along its borders. Since that time, Chad has become a security area of special significance in Libya's foreign policy.

The relaxation in relations between Libya and Egypt that came about as a result of Arab and African mediation attempts was short-lived. Sadat's visit to Israel (November 19–21, 1977) widened the political gulf between the two countries; Libya denounced the visit as soon as it was announced, in mid-November. An emergency meeting of the General People's Congress, the highest authority in the country, issued a statement expressing concern for the "regrettable and dramatic collapse of Arab confrontation against the Zionist enemy,"[5] and a special envoy was sent to Damascus and Cairo voicing the country's objection.

Reacting to Sadat's visit to Israel, Libya's Middle Eastern policy became intensely aggressive. Libya unilaterally broke diplomatic relations with Egypt, called for its expulsion from the Arab League, and decided that the rules of Arab boycott of Israel would also apply to Egypt. Libya further called for a summit meeting of the "progressive" Arab countries in Tripoli on December 2–5 to organize opposition to Sadat. The meeting, attended by Syria, Libya, Iraq, South Yemen, Algeria, and the PLO, issued the Tripoli Declaration, which set up the Front of Steadfastness and Confrontation to counter what it called the "high treason of Egypt."[6] However, Iraq withdrew from the summit, while the other members decided only to freeze relations with Egypt—which was short of Libya's demand for a complete break of diplomatic relations. On the popular level, Libya convened a permanent congress comprised of parties and organizations from all Arab states that opposed Sadat's approach. Sadat's new policy not only pushed Libya into a more extreme stand in the Arab-Israeli conflict, but also provided Libya with more freedom of action at the Arab level. That is because all Libya's predictions about Sadat's "defeatist" policy since 1974 have been borne out. Thus, Libya's "extremism" could not be objected to, even by the most conservative Arab regimes. Marius and Mary Deeb wrote in 1982, "Libya's activism in the Arab world increased and since November 1977, its aspirations to play a major role in Arab politics were to some extent realized."[7] In a sense, Libya tried after November 1977 to assume the role of the leading power of Arab nationalism and Arab struggle against Israel, since Egypt—which historically has held this position—had, according to Qaddafi, retreated from this responsibility. In addition, this brought Libya into acute competition and conflict with Iraq, which tried to claim the same role for itself.

By 1978, revolutionary Libya seemed unsatisifed with the effectiveness of the Steadfastness Front in opposing Sadat's policy and effectively combating Israel. In particular, Libya was disappointed with Syria's failure to respond militarily to Israel's "Litani Operation" in south Lebanon. Qaddafi maintained:

> Syria has become an onlooker as regards the driving out of the Palestinians by the Israelis in south Lebanon. The Steadfastness and Confrontation Front stipulates that any attack on any party is an attack on the other parties and now that the Palestinian side has been attacked, why is it that Syria has not entered the fighting on the side of the Palestinians?[8]

Nevertheless, the signing of the Camp David Accords by Egypt and Israel brought the members of the Front together again when they decided in Damascus to break all political and economic relations with Egypt.

Libya took part in the Arab Summit held in Baghdad in November 1978, although Qaddafi did not attend the summit personally. It was reported that Libya's share of the $3.5 billion annual fund allocated by the summit to finance opposition to Sadat's approach would be about $500 million.

The Egyptian-Israeli peace treaty posed a security problem for Libya. For the Libyan leadership saw that not only would Egypt be free to turn its attention to Libya, but also Israel itself might operate militarily against Libya across the Egyptian-Libyan border. Thus, in June and July 1979 Qaddafi made an extensive tour of the Arab countries, visiting Algeria, Syria, Jordan, Iraq, Kuwait, Bahrain, Saudi Arabia, and the UAE. In Damascus he discussed the possibility of opening a new front against Israel in southern Lebanon. It was reported that "he offered Syria 12 MIG-25s, with ground to ground and ground to air missiles, and promised to replace all planes lost by the Syrian Air Force."[9] In the Gulf states, he was said to have suggested the coordinated use of oil as a political weapon against Israel. In spite of the Arabs' apparent lack of enthusiasm for Libya's suggestions, Qaddafi's tour resulted in rallying Arab support behind Libya against any Egyptian future attack. This signal was quite clear in the tenth anniversary celebration of the Libyan revolution, which was attended by many Arab heads of state.

Libya's noticeable support of the PLO became more intense after Sadat's new policy in the Middle East. This took the form of not only financing, arming, and training military personnel, but also direct participation in the Palestinian operations against Israel from south Lebanon. However, early in 1980 a rift took place between Qaddafi and Arafat. To Qaddafi, Arafat was losing his revolutionary zeal, while Arafat, for his part, did not approve of Qaddafi's financing of the radical factions within the PLO and his attempt to organize the Palestinians in Libya into revolutionary committees that might remove them from the PLO's spheres of influence. It was a difference of style, not of content.

Thus, Libya's policy toward the Arab-Israeli conflict during 1977–1980 became more extreme and more aggressive. Most important, it became more effective at the Arab level. Sadat's visit to Israel and the Camp David agreements were the two stimuli that pushed Libya toward radicalism and gave it the opportunity (in Egypt's absence) to play a leading role. Qaddafi's was convinced that the only solution to the Arab-Israeli conflict was through armed struggle and using Western economic interests as a pressure tool against any country that backs Israel, especially the United States.

OIL POLICY

As I have stated, Libyan oil production in 1975 fell significantly, mainly because of world recession which in turn affected world demand for oil. But between January and June 1977, the average rate of Libyan oil production was over 9 percent higher than during the same period of 1976.[10]

Despite those fluctuations in oil production and demand, Libya was still a hawk among OPEC countries. Its aggressive oil policy could still be felt in 1977–1980, but it was much less intense than it had been in the early 1970s. Libyan leaders were no less determined to control oil policy and to get the maximum revenue possible for exports; however, because of the world recession that hit the industrial societies so badly, and also because the battle against the oil companies' monopoly was almost over by 1975, with Libya controlling about 80 percent of its oil industry, Libya maintained a less aggressive stance.

Moderate in comparison with the early 1970s, Libya's oil prices were still among the highest in the OPEC organization during the late 1970s (see table 12). Its stand in the OPEC meetings during this period was no different from that of the early 1970s—radical, aggressive, calling for higher prices and more control by OPEC countries of their oil wealth, and

Turn to
pg. 69

TABLE 12.   OPEC Oil Prices, 1977–1980 ($U.S. p/b)

	1977	1978	1979	1980
OPEC[a]	12.88	12.93	18.67	30.87
Algeria	14.37	14.14	19.65	37.59
Ecuador	12.90	12.33	22.41	34.42
Gabon	12.80	12.80	18.20	31.09
Indonesia	13.55	13.55	18.35	30.56
Iran	12.81	12.81	19.45	34.54
Iraq	12.61	12.62	18.56	30.30
Kuwait	12.37	12.26	18.48	29.84
Libya	**14.06**	**13.89**	**21.26**	**36.07**
Nigeria	14.45	14.07	20.86	35.50
Qatar	13.19	13.19	19.72	31.76
Saudi Arabia	12.40	12.70	17.26	28.67
United Arab Emirates	12.88	13.26	19.81	31.57
Venezuela	12.75	12.75	17.22	28.44

Source: National Foreign Assessment Center, U.S. Central Intelligence Agency, *Handbook of Economic Statistics, 1981: A Research Aid* (Washington, D.C.: GPO, 1981).

a. Average prices as weighted by volume of production.

resisting any attempt by the oil-producing regimes (such as Saudi Arabia) to lower prices.

Using oil as a political weapon was less apparent in this period, though during his tour of the Gulf states in 1979 Qaddafi had raised this possibility as a weapon in the Arab-Israeli conflict. The nationalization of foreign-owned industry was also less feasible during this period, although in September 1977 Standard Asiatic Oil and Texaco Overseas Petroleum were nationalized as a way of ending their differences with Libya. Full compensation to both companies was promised by the petroleum secretary.[11] Clearly, Libya's oil policy was detrimental to Western interests during most of the 1970s. Through price wars and the Libyanization of the oil sector, Libya not only inflicted heavy damage on the economic interests of the West, but also created a pattern for other oil-exporting countries to follow.

But from Libya's perspective, its oil policy was the best course to follow for a country that was almost entirely dependent on oil as a source of revenue. Taking into account its ambitious development plans, its active foreign policy, and its program of building a strong army, Libya needed to increase its revenues from oil. Libya's oil policies during the 1970s achieved these objectives. Thus, while per capita income was $4,567 in 1975, it reached $10,309 by the end of 1980, making Libya, by this measure, one of the richest countries in the world.[12] The Libyan army became one of the strongest in the Middle East, with increasing amounts of sophisticated weapons from the Soviet arsenal bought with the hard currency from oil revenues. In John Wright's words:

> It was as true in 1980 as it had been in 1970 that Libya's international standing stemmed from its oil. The continued production and export of crude earned the revenues to finance an extraordinarily ambitious, forward, and sometimes alarming, foreign policy. It was the importance of maintaining this apparently vital flow that inhibited many exasperated governments from taking a firmer attitude towards a state whose policies were widely regarded as disruptive, if not downright dangerous.[13]

POLICY TOWARD THE SUPERPOWERS

POLICY TOWARD THE USSR

The Libyan-Soviet rapprochement that started in 1974 seemed to grow stronger during the 1977–1980 period. To Libyan leaders, Sadat's visit to Israel and the Camp David Agreement upset the strategic balance in the region in favor of the "imperialist-Zionist" camp. Also, they feared that as a result of Sadat's new "defeatist" line, if Egypt were to fall, Libya's eastern border could be invaded by Egypt, Israel, and the United States. Thus, their option was to enhance Libya's military capability to the largest extent possible, not only to defend itself (Egypt's attack on Libya in July 1977 made Libyan fears more credible), but also to build a strong arsenal for the Arabs, should they decide to give up their "defeatist" policies and resort to military force. The USSR was the natural choice to fulfill Libya's needs, not only because it was the only power that could counter the perceived growing "imperialist" influence in the region, but also because of the Western nations' reluctance or refusal to supply Libya with its military requirements. Thus, resorting to the Soviets for arms became for the Libyans a matter of necessity.

As for the Soviets, closer relations with Libya, despite its criticism of communism and disapproval of some of their policies, represented an opportunity to reestablish a foothold in the Middle East. Being expelled from Egypt and Somalia, and being excluded from the Egyptian-Israeli negotiations under the American umbrella after 1977, the Soviets had been left with the only option of backing the members of the Steadfastness and Confrontation Front, of which Libya was the leading member. Thus, despite their ideological differences, Libya and the Soviet Union found themselves with congruent strategic objectives in the area. This was, of course, in addition to the Soviets' need for hard currency and Libya's willingness to pay cash for its military purchases.

Some scholars believe that the Soviet strategy toward Libya was based on a formula suggested by Khrushchev to expand Soviet influence in the Middle East.[14] The formula, they suggest, calls for breaking the Arab states' dependence on the West by supplying them with Soviet arms and thus creating new dependence on the Soviets, creating political and economic relationships with those states based on mutual self-interest, and developing a "vague ideological solidarity based on anti-colonialism, anti-imperialism, anti-Zionism, revolutionary change and 'socialism.' "[15]

These arguments do not hold up, however. A careful scrutiny of the Libyan rhetoric and policy toward the Soviets during this period suggests that Libya's relations with the USSR could barely result in any significant Soviet influence on the Libyan leadership, not only because of Qaddafi's well-known opposition to communism, but also because of Libya's efforts to diversify its source of arms by purchasing from other Western countries such as France and Italy, and its policy of importing the spare parts for the Soviet weapons from other countries such as India, Yugoslavia, Romania, and China, who sell them under more comfortable terms and cheaper prices. Moreover, Qaddafi's criticism of some of the USSR's policies, such as the invasion of Afghanistan in 1979 and support for the Steadfastness and Confrontation Front, is a clear indicator of the Soviet's failure to use their massive supplies of arms to Libya to gain a significant influence in that country.[16] Moreover, Libya has refused to grant the Soviets any military bases on its soil or naval facilities in its ports, facts confirmed by Western intelligence reports, in spite of some Egyptian claims to the contrary.[17]

Thus, despite the increased massive supplies of Soviet arms to Libya during 1970–1980, which included the most sophisticated weapons in the Soviet arsenal such as MIG-23, MIG-25, MIG-27 aircraft and the most advanced Soviet T-72 tanks (some of the Warsaw Pact members have not yet received some of these types of weapons),[18] Libya was still dealing with the Soviets on a commercial basis. This is not to neglect the fact that Soviet-Libyan relations were stronger than they had been in the early 1970s. But this cautious friendship was based on pragmatic mutual interest and was strengthened by a congruence of objectives between the two countries. Nevertheless, it was an accidental congruence resulting from the new circumstances that came about after Sadat's visit to Israel. In this context, Qaddafi's threat to join the Warsaw Pact can be understood as only a bargaining device against the United States, which tightened its squeeze on Qaddafi during that time.[19] Thus, as one scholar put it, "While many Libyan policies may coincide with Soviet interests, there is little evidence to suggest that the former are dictated or even strongly influenced by the Soviet Union."[20] He went on to state that the main principle in Soviet-Libyan relations remains as follows: "We need each other for the time being, let us play down our differences for a while."

From 1977 to 1980, economic relations between Libya and the USSR also grew stronger than they had been during the early 1970s, though not to the same level as military relations. This is due mainly to the inability of the Soviets to satisfy Libya's needs for technological goods; Libya imports these from Western Europe and Japan. A Soviet radio survey of economic aid to Libya on May 18, 1979, referred to Soviet assistance for over twenty major industrial projects.[21] (These included two nuclear reactors, one, of 10 megawatts, for research purposes, and the other, agreed upon in 1978, with a capacity of 400 megawatts.) But again, with the exception of military supplies, the level of Soviet trade with Libya has been relatively low, compared with Libya's trade with the West or several other Western European countries,[22] simply because stronger ties would require a political or ideological base that does not exist in the Soviet-Libyan case. (See tables 13 and 14.) As one scholar succinctly puts it:

"While Qaddafi wants Soviet arms and is anti-Western, he is not a Marxist, and his relationship with the Soviet Union has always been characterized more by cautious cooperation than by friendship. In this sense, he seems determined to retain a degrée of neutrality in the world power struggle."[23]

TABLE 13. Libya's Trade with Some Western European Countries, 1977–1980 ($U.S. millions)

	Italy	West Germany	France	United Kingdom
Exports				
1977	1,916,603	1,942,192	445,876	271,143
1978	2,156,293	1,063,103	538,661	175,148
1979	2,896,479	2,375,013	945,879	172,474
1980	4,061,083	2,674,206	603,676	35,398
Imports				
1977	1,037,842	488,535	284,903	216,311
1978	1,108,902	586,870	383,193	326,302
1979	1,401,806	761,408	436,769	365,060
1980	2,001,743	902,508	458,055	471,820

Source: U.N. Yearbook of International Trade Statistics, 1982, vol. 1, p. 614.

POLICY TOWARD THE UNITED STATES

The election of Jimmy Carter was a welcome event to the Libyan leadership. Qaddafi saw Carter as a religious man who would be morally motivated in his outlook toward issues and foreign policy. Implied in Qaddafi's perception was the notion that Carter might look at the Arab cause, the "Palestinian issue," in a more just way than other U.S. presidents and that he might realize "the biased stand" of U.S. policy toward Israel. Such a change in attitude would remove the most serious problem that had been preventing a healthy relationship between Libya and the United States. This hope was articulated by Qaddafi during his visit to the USSR in June 1977: "We hope that the current American administration will, perhaps, avoid the mistakes that were made by the previous American administration. We are ready to meet halfway any new American steps, if they are in keeping with the aspirations of the peoples."[24] Thus, on June 11, 1977, Qaddafi urged Carter to improve relations by consenting to appoint an ambassador (instead of a chargé d'affaires) to head relations between the two countries.[25] But these hopes faded not only because U.S. policy toward the Arab-Israeli conflict did

TABLE 14. Libya's Trade with the USSR, 1976–1980 ($U.S. thousands)

	Exports to the USSR	Import from the USSR
1976	—	20,371
1977	104,292	20,042
1978	156,228	29,791
1979	427,318	130,399
1980	443,072	251,676

Source: U.N. Yearbook of International Trade Statistics, 1981, vol. 1, p. 614.

not change, but also because the new administration started as early as May 1977 to be more antagonistic toward Libya. The United States publicly accused Libya of terrorism and blocked the sale of Italian transport aircraft to Libya, because the planes' engines were assembled under license from an American company. Libya's perception of U.S. hostility grew even stronger when the United States sided with Egypt in its assaults against Libya in July 1977. (Libya stated that the United States not only supported Egypt but also was directly involved in the military operations against its territory).[26] America's continuing refusal to sell military equipment to Libya was also interpreted as a sign of hostility. The announcement of the sale of military equipment worth $200 million to Egypt just after the Libyan-Egyptian war was seen as a clear indication of U.S. antagonism.

The two interrelated issues which the Carter administration declared of crucial importance to the United States—namely, human rights and combating terrorism—were seen by Libyan leaders as not worth talking about. According to the Libyan view, the United States is guilty of terrorism by establishing military bases in other countries, by sending its fleets to the territorial waters of other states, and by pursuing a nuclear policy that jeopardizes world peace and stability. The revolutionary leaders also believed that the Americans' claimed support for human rights lacked credibility, since the United States stands against the human rights of the Third World people, such as the Palestinians, and protects the regimes of fascists and dictators regimes such as the shah of Iran, Sadat in Egypt, and Somoza in Nicaragua. At the first Arab-American People-to-People Dialogue Conference held in Libya in 1978, Qaddafi clarified the Libyan point of view:

> History has recorded the insult to the Americans by their mobilization of all their resources in the service of evil, reaction, backwardness, dictatorship, fascism and oppression. Therefore, United States' talk about human rights is worthless to us. I personally do not attribute any significance to such talk.[27]

The Libyan leadership maintained that the Carter administration's accusation of Libya as "supporter of terrorism," was in fact a reaction to policies of the early 1970s. However, to deny the American administration any pretext for using such accusations as the reason for blocking sales and deliveries of aircraft and equipment to Libya, Libya signed the three UN conventions regarding terrorism in 1978. However, this did not result in any major change in U.S. policy toward Libya. Certainly it did not change the status of the eight C-130 planes that the United States had refused to deliver to Libya since 1973. Libya attached a great significance to this issue in particular.

Based on the above events, and in congruence with Qaddafi's theory that people-to-people diplomacy is the correct way to handle affairs among nations, Libya initiated a kind of dialogue directly with the American people. This approach was also designed to overcome the perceived hostility of the U.S. Congress and to change the American image of Libya which was believed to be distorted due to the Zionist influence in Congress and in the media. In an interview with *Newsweek*, June 18, 1979, Qaddafi stated:

> Your so-called Congress does not know anything about what is happening around the world. And we reached that conclusion after we saw the influence Congress had on the American stand toward Libya. It looks as if Congress is in the dark. Certain elements are distorting facts. The State Department itself does not agree with Congress on Libya. . . . The Libyan delegation which visited America came back with quite different ideas of the American people. Their ideas are completely different from Congress. So if the American government's attitude is different from that of Congress toward Libya, and the American people's attitude is different from Congress, then who is Congress representing?

Thus, during 1978–1979, Libyan policy vis-à-vis the United States was moving in two directions. The first was the diplomatic official line that focused on intensive contacts with U.S. officials for the purpose of explaining the facts of Libya's foreign policy and eliminating some of the misunderstanding of Libya's policies, especially regarding terrorism. It was hoped that improved Libyan-American relations could start by securing the release of the purchased C-130 planes. The second direction focused on establishing some circles of friendship with some American celebrities (such as Billy Carter, Lillian Carter, Senator Fulbright, Mohammed Ali) who were perceived as having some potential for influencing U.S. policy toward Libya. Libya's people-to-people approach was centered mainly in Georgia, the president's home state, and Idaho, the home state of Frank Church, chairman of the Senate Foreign Relations Committee, who was opposed to the delivery of the C-130 planes to Libya. Delegations of farmers and businessmen from both states visited Libya in 1978, and also Libyan delegations were received in both states in 1978–1979. The prospect of strengthening the economic relations between the two states and Libya was discussed. Billy Carter, the president's brother, was a member of the Georgia delegation in 1978 and in September 1979 he attended the tenth anniversary of the Libyan revolution with his mother and sister, where it was reported that he was photographed with Yasir Arafat and other liberation movement members. Also it was claimed that he promised to try to do something about the release of the C-130 planes to Libya.[28]

Libya's contacts in both states attracted media attention, especially from those journalists with connections in the Zionist lobby in Washington. William Safire claimed that Libya was trying to win the support of Idaho's Senator James McClure, and Representative Steven Symms, in an effort to get the delivery of the planes. He also suggested that the same objective was behind "the Libyan flirtation with Billy Carter."[29] Other press reports suggested that the Libyan "infiltration" of Idaho was mainly for the purpose of backing some candidates who sympathized with Libya, such as Steven Symms, against Frank Church in the coming elections of 1980.[30]

Another major effort at the people's level, which did not get much attention in the press, was Libya's hosting of the Arab-American People-to-People Dialogue Conference in Tripoli, October 1978. The conference was attended by former Senator William Fulbright, Najeeb Halabi, and G. Shadyac representing the United States. It was a good opportunity for the Libyans to clarify and explain their point of view regarding many issues in general, and terrorism and the Camp David Accords in particular. Again it was reported in the press that Fulbright pledged "to be going home to have the planes released that Libya had paid for and never received."[31]

Despite its active diplomacy both at the official and unofficial levels, Libya continued during the whole 1977–1980 period to attack American "imperialist" policy in the Middle East, and to resist Sadat's "defeatist" line as reflected in the Camp David Accords under the U.S. umbrella.

From late 1978 until the end of 1979, some improvement in Libyan-American relations took place. However, there is no empirical evidence that could attribute this improvement to Libya's unofficial connections. Instead, the improvement may have been brought about as a result of the official contacts that took place between officials from both countries during 1978–1979, where some kind of "agreement to disagree" was reached to lay the basis for a "workable relationship."[32]

But the improvement of relations was superficial and did not touch some sensitive issues, such as the C-130 planes. (Libyan officials threatened to use the oil weapon to secure their release, but the threat was never translated into action.) Because this "workable formula" was not based on some kind of political mutual understanding, the improvement in relations was short-lived.

By December 1979, relations between the two countries were at their lowest ebb. It started on December 2 when more than 2,000 Libyan demonstrators, responding to the siege at the Grand Mosque at Mecca and the burning of the U.S. embassy in Pakistan, sacked and burned the U.S. embassy in Tripoli. Relations went from bad to worse when the United States accused Libya of sponsoring the attack on the Tunisian town of Gafsa. Both the United States and France provided prompt military assistance to the Tunisian regime. On February 4, 1980, the French embassy was sacked and as a reaction the United States withdrew its chargé d'affaires from Tripoli. Soon after a press report revealed that a Libyan assassination campaign against Qaddafi's opponents abroad was under way in Europe, the United States reacted by ordering its two remaining diplomats in Tripoli home and closing the embassy.

The spread of U.S. alliances and its access to military facilities or bases in Egypt, Sudan, Somalia, and Oman, was interpreted by the revolutionary regime of Libya as a real "occupation" of Arab land. The joint American-Egyptian maneuvers and the American navy exercises in the Mediterranean were seen in particular as hostile military actions against Libya. By summer and autumn 1980, Libyan fighters were intercepting American planes over the Mediterranean Sea, reflecting the highest degree of tension between Libya and the United States. These tensions were clearly reflected in Qadaffi's message to President Carter and to Ronald Reagan, published in the *Washington Post* on October 22, 1980, that "relations had reached a grave stage. There was no longer room for friendly initiatives and a distinct possibility of armed conflict existed, for which America was to blame." He complained bitterly of "America's support of Israel, and urged the U.S. to take steps to avoid confrontation with the Arabs by withdrawing from its bases in Muscat and Oman, and from Somalia, removing reconnaissance planes from Saudi Arabia, ending the 'occupation' of Egypt, and keeping its naval and air forces away from Libyan borders."[33]

REVOLUTIONARY ACTIVITIES ABROAD

Sadat's new approach toward the United States and Israel, which became more obvious in 1977, had resulted in an intense perception of threat in Libyan eyes. As the Libyan leadership saw it, Sadat's policy could lead not only to irreparable damage to the Arab cause (the Palestinian cause), but also to the fall of the whole Arab region under "imperialist" domination. Libya's first consideration was that the Egyptian masses might do something to prevent a further deterioration in this grave situation. Libya declared its firm support to the Egyptian people, urging them to revolt against Sadat's regime. Sadat, in return, saw Libya as a security risk to his regime not only because of its Soviet military buildup, but also because of its alleged interference in Egypt's internal problems. Thus, during the whole of 1977, accusations of subversion, destabilization, and assassination were exchanged between the two countries. Sadat's visit to Israel at the end of 1977 not only aggravated Libyan fears, but also left them with the question of what to do about it.

The Libyan option, as the policy conduct suggests, had one objective, namely, of isolating Sadat and preventing other regimes from supporting him. This option resulted in some policy changes toward some Arab regimes which Libya considered "reactionary" and enemies of the revolution in the long run. But it is important to mention that the change that took place in Libya's policy was tactical for the sole purpose of rallying Arab opposition to Sadat's policy, and did not extend to the strategic thinking of the Libyan leaders that revolution within the "reactionary" Arab regimes is the only way to bring about Arab unity and progress.

Thus, by late 1977 and until 1980 Libya's relations with the Maghreb States were surprisingly good, including those states that for a long time accused Libya of subversion and terrorist activities, such as Morocco and Tunisia. Libya also showed some flexibility toward some issues, such as reducing the level of its support to the Polisario movement in Western Sahara. Diplomatic relations with Sudan were restored and it was reported that "Libya and Saudi Arabia both exerted pressure on Sudan's President Numeiry to detach him from his Egyptian alliance."[34] Jordan's refusal of Sadat's approach was also satisfactory enough for the Libyan leadership to resume diplomatic relations with Jordan, which had been severed since 1970. To complete its effort at Egypt's encirclement, Libya in 1977 reversed its policy in Ethiopia, withdrawing its support from the Eritrean rebels and trying to mediate between them and the new Ethiopian regime. Based on the same consideration, Libya kept its active policy toward Chad, switching sides in the internal conflict of that country. Libya's policy culminated in 1980 in direct military intervention, first, to secure its southern borders, and next, to protect a Chadian regime that could resist any Egyptian pressure on Libya's southern frontier. The attendance by delegations from most Arab countries at the tenth celebration of the Libyan revolution was a good indicator of Libya's improved relations with those countries. It also indicated the change in Libya's tactical policy from supporting revolution within those countries to a temporary peaceful coexistence. That is because Sadat constituted more of a threat in Libyan eyes than temporarily promoting "reactionary" Arab regimes.

Also, in 1977–1980, Libya actively attempted to live down its reputation as a supporter of terrorism. (Libya excluded the Palestinian and South African liberation movements, which were considered struggles for freedom.) Thus, on September 26, 1977, Qaddafi was quoted in *Le Monde* as disavowing his country's association with international terrorism. On January 5, 1978, Mansur Kikhia, Libya's UN representative, wrote to the secretary-general that "Libya condemned the serious and worsening phenomenon of international terrorism, and that Libyan laws provided severe penalties for crimes of terrorism."[35] Libyan officials maintained that the U.S. accusations of terrorism against Libya were merely a reaction to policies pursued in the early 1970s.[36] Libya's policies seemed to conform very strongly to its antiterrorist rhetoric. In early 1978, Libya signed three UN conventions dealing with airplane hijacking. It also provided the U.S. State Department with documents confirming its accession to these conventions. On February 14, 1978, Libya refused to permit a Cypriot plane hijacked by Palestinians to land in Tripoli, despite requests by the Cypriot president to grant the plane landing permission for humane reasons. In January 1979, Libyan authorities "negotiated the freedom of 83 hostages on an Air Tunis plane hijacked by Tunisians trying to secure the release of some political prisoners in Tunis."[37] And by late 1979, Libya condemned the seizure of the American hostages in Iran, and even tried to negotiate their release.

However intense Libya's efforts to dissociate itself from terrorist activities during 1977–1979, Libya was again accused of supporting and sponsoring terrorism beginning in 1980. It started when Tunis, France, and the United States charged Libya with sponsoring a raid on the Tunisian town of Gafsa in January 1980—a charge that Qaddafi refuted, openly challenging Tunis and France to provide evidence of Libya's involvement. Then came the European assassination of opponents of the Libyan regime; these linked Libya even more closely with terrorism in Western and American eyes.

SUMMARY

Libya's foreign policy from 1977 to 1980 can be characterized as follows:

1. Libya strengthened its opposition to any negotiated settlement with Israel and refused all American-sponsored "peace projects" toward the Arab-Israeli conflict. Sadat's visit to Israel and his signing of the Camp David Accords resulted in a more militant Libyan position, coupled with a more intensive effort to bring about the destruction of this "defeatist" approach.

2. It pursued a more moderate oil policy, compared to its policy of the early 1970s. But this was a moderation created more by the world recession than by a change in the Libyan leadership's revolutionary approach toward the oil companies; in addition, most of the oil battle had been fought and won by the early 1970s.

3. It increased its friendly relations with the Soviets, especially regarding military aid. But continuing ideological and political differences separated the two countries.

4. Despite the severe criticism of U.S. policy in the Middle East, Libya showed some signs of flexibility toward the United States for the sake of improving relations between the two countries. It also undertook efforts at the popular level to change Libya's image in the States and to overcome some of the difficulties that were blocking good relations.

5. Libya tempered its revolutionary activities vis-à-vis other Arab regimes, to rally solid Arab opposition to Sadat and to dissociate itself from terrorism. Consequently, although Libya was linked with subversion, destabilization, and terrorism in 1970–1976, such activities were discontinued between 1977 and 1979. However, they started to surface again by early 1980.

When the Carter administration assumed power in 1977, some officials and observers talked optimistically of new "visions" and orientations in U.S. foreign policy.[1] Those new visions, which soon constituted the basis of a new policy approach toward the world, were based on the following assumptions:[2]

1. U.S.-Soviet relations could no longer be regarded as the central organizing factor of U.S. policy toward other regimes. This would lead to an increased willingness to deal with radical and anti-American regimes.

2. The Third World as a force in world politics could not be ignored any more. Zbigniew Brzezinski was obsessed with what he called the "new fundamentals" such as India, Brazil, Nigeria, and Saudi Arabia.[3] Also, more emphasis was put on world organizations such as the UN as a forum for U.S. diplomacy. Consequently, less reliance on force as a means of achieving foreign policy objectives was a cardinal feature of the new approach.

3. As a result also, a greater focus was put on economic and human issues (called the north-south dialogue) and Carter's human rights campaign. These assumptions constituted the broad strategic frame for what was called by some "liberal internationalism."[4]

The implications of this new global approach were quite obvious in the U.S. perception of the Soviet Union as a potential partner in settling the Arab-Israeli conflict (the 1977 October Declaration). The new approach was also behind the Carter administration's efforts to find a comprehensive solution to the Arab-Israeli conflict using the "fundamentals" such as Saudi Arabia, Iraq, and Syria as pillars for negotiations. More attention to the Palestinian issues was expressed in the administration's call for a homeland for the Palestinians. Implied in this Middle Eastern policy was the perception that regional stability and continuous stable access to oil could not be achieved without a comprehensive Arab-Israeli settlement.

During 1977, the Carter administration's image of Libya was solely centered on the issue of terrorism. All official U.S. statements in 1977 explicitly described Libya as pursuing subversive, destabilizing policies in neighboring countries and as one of the main supporters of international terrorism. Only a few months into the Carter administration, the State Department officially accused Libya of supporting international terrorism. In a letter to Senator Jacob Javits (R, N.Y.) dated April 17, 1977, the State Department named Libya, Iraq, South Yemen, and Somalia as abettors of international terrorists. The letter asserted that Libya had, at least since 1972, "actively assisted a number of terrorist groups and individuals, including the Palestinian 'rejectionist' factions."[5] Another official report in 1977 stated that "Libya remained at the forefront of such activity."[6] It was predictable that the Carter administration, with its moral and ideal emphasis in foreign policy, would respond thus to terrorist activities by any country; however, there was no such activity on Libya's part during the 1977–1979 period.

Three explanations may be suggested for this paradox. First, the Carter administration could have been reacting to a specific Libyan action vis-à-vis a government deemed an important U.S. ally in the Middle East or elsewhere. But this possibility must be excluded, because Libya was on friendly terms with almost all the countries of the region, including neighbors with whom it had experienced sporadic tensions and disputes in the past. The only exception was Egypt; Libya opposed Sadat's policies and declared its support for efforts to overthrow Sadat. This stand resulted in hostility between the two countries and mutual accusations of subversion and destabilization. This could explain U.S. policy toward Libya, given Sadat's friendship with Carter and the importance of Egypt in any U.S. plans for the area. But Egyptian-Libyan tensions went back as far as October 1973; they were not new in 1977. As a matter of fact, both governments ceased their hostile operations following the short-lived military clashes of July 1977 and Arab mediations to bridge their differences. Besides, accusations of subversive activities were made on both sides. Thus the first possibility is not plausible enough to explain the U.S. image of Libya as a terrorist-supporting country in 1977.

Second, the Carter administration could have singled out Libya as a "terrorism sponsor" to demonstrate a new line of policy. The Libyan case could be used by the administration to demonstrate its determination to emphasize human rights and combat terrorism. Nevertheless, there is no concrete evidence to support this explanation.

The third and most plausible possibility is that the Carter administration came to office with a preestablished image of Libya as a supporter of international terrorism. This image was not a reaction to current Libyan policies so much as policies pursued by Libya in the 1970–1976 period. There is verbal evidence to support this idea. All official U.S. statements that connected Libya to terrorist activities during 1977, without exception, refer to alleged Libyan actions during the 1970–1976 period as a basis for that perception. For instance, all the evidence provided by State Department officials in a hearing before the Senate Subcommittee on International Terrorism (September 14, 1977) was related to terrorist incidents that took place from 1972 to 1975 in which Libya allegedly took an active part.[7] Also, the letter sent to Senator Javits by the State Department contained the same kind of evidence.[8]

Thus the second and third explanations complement each other. Given the moral orientation of Carter's foreign policy, Libya's conduct in the early 1970s was used as a basis for the administration's description of Libya as a continuing supporter of terrorism; its disapproval of Libya served as proof of its support for human rights.

Thus I disagree with John Cooley, who argues that the "turning point for the Carter administration and for U.S. policy toward terrorism, whether of the Libyan or other varieties" was an alleged Libyan conspiracy in late 1977 to assassinate Herman F. Elits, the U.S. ambassador in Cairo. Without giving the source of his information, Cooley states that the CIA learned of the Libyan plan through "an American 'mole' " inside Libya, and that Carter prevented the incident by sending a personal message to Qaddafi.[9] Even if we consider this story hypothetically true, we could not consider the event the "turning point" in the U.S. perception of Libya as a terrorism sponsor; Libya had been officially accused of terrorism as early as the first four months of the Carter administration, whereas the Elits incident allegedly took place late in 1977. Hence, the administration's conception of Libya existed prior to the alleged incident.

The second feature of the U.S. image of Libya in 1977, as verbal evidence reveals, was a reaction to Libya's intense opposition to the "peaceful projects" to settle the Arab-Israeli conflict. Libya was seen as an "extreme, radical element that opposes the American efforts to solve the conflict." As David Newsom, the undersecretary for political affairs, put it: "We can and we have differences with Arab states on the peace process. But with Libya, the differences are more profound and involve active and often violent opposition to the process of peace."[10] Behind this view was not a conception of Libya's ability to block any agreement about the process of peace, but of its potential capability to destabilize some of the Arab countries directly involved in the peace process, and hence to destroy any agreement to solve the conflict. Alfred L. Atherton, Jr., clarified this perception on June 8, 1977:

> By itself Libya does not have the influence to block a Middle East peace settlement. However, Colonel Qaddafi's willingness to use Libya's resources to support Palestinian extremists and undermine moderate Arab leaders gives him a significant potential for disruptive activity, especially if the peace process appears to be reaching a deadlock.[11]

Libya's military capabilities, though they had grown rapidly due to the increase in imports of Soviet arms, were underestimated not only because of Libya's distance from Israel, but also because of the poor quality of the Libyan forces, as seen by U.S. officials. Atherton continued:

> The net result of Libya's arms purchases, however, has been little more than a massive accumulation of weapons. The Libyan armed forces remain undermanned and lack the capability to absorb and maintain their new arms, many of which are not operational. The situation is not likely to change significantly in the near future, even with expanded foreign technical assistance.[12]

Thus, a direct Libyan military threat to Israel was not feared; the only threat came from Libya's "disruptive revolutionary activities."

This analysis indicates that the United States was primarily concerned with Libya's revolutionary activities and its support of "terrorism"; its threat to any Middle Eastern peace settlement was derived from the Carter administration's perception of Libya as a destabilizing factor in the region.

In 1978–1979, as a result of Libya's efforts to dissociate itself from terrorism, the intensity of the U.S. image of Libya as a sponsor of terrorism dropped dramatically. This was quite obvious in Cyrus Vance's response to a question in January 1978 about whether the United States had changed its view of Libya as a supporter of terrorism: "With respect to Libya and terrorism, Libya has now signed the three conventions with respect to hijacking in the air—which is different from the past. We are continuing to watch and observe the situation there."[13] At the same time, Libya's growing hostility toward efforts to solve the Middle Eastern conflict, especially after Sadat's visit to Israel and the signing of the Camp David Accords, were not of much concern to U.S. officials. This again proves that the U.S. perception of Libya's Middle Eastern policies was derived from its image of Libya's revolutionary activities abroad. Because they were thought to have decreased, Libya's actual behavior was less threatening to the West.

It is interesting to compare how the U.S. officials viewed Libya's conduct abroad in 1970–1976 and 1977–1980. In the first period, Libyan revolutionary activities were very intense and covered many different spots in the world. Nevertheless, they were not a significant issue to either the Nixon or Ford administrations and did not affect the U.S. image of Libya. In contrast, Libya's revolutionary activities were minimal in 1977–1980, because of Libya's efforts to dissociate itself from terrorism. Yet Libya's activities abroad were the main factor shaping the U.S. image of Libya during the Carter administration.

There is a logical explanation for this phenomenon. The first-priority concern of decision makers usually serves, intentionally or unintentionally, as a yardstick by which the conduct of other actors is measured. So when the overriding concern of the Nixon and Ford administrations was to contain Soviet influence in the Middle East, Libya's hostility toward the Soviets in the early 1970s made both administrations intentionally neglect what were called Libya's "terrorist" activities. In contrast, the Carter administration saw the Soviet Union as less threatening, and thus its overriding concern was not East-West tensions, but an international liberal policy that emphasized defending human rights and combating terrorism. Thus, the administration came in with a stereotyped image of Libya based on past experience; it took it about a year and a half to come to grips with the new realities. Nevertheless, the view of Libya as a destabilizing force surfaced again when the United States accused Libya of intervening in Uganda in 1979, of sponsoring the Gafsa attack in Tunisia, and finally of sponsoring the liquidation campaign against Libyan dissidents abroad.

Libya's attitude and conduct toward the USSR between 1977 and 1980 had little impact on the Carter administration's image of Libya because Carter was less paranoid about the Soviets and the threat of communism than either Nixon or Ford. The Carter administration's attitude was apparent in its conduct toward events such as South Yemen's attempted penetration of North Yemen and the conclusion of the SALT II Agreement. And it was also behind the U.S. failure to respond to the August 1979 intelligence report that the Soviets for some time had been stationing a complete combat brigade of 2,000–3,000 soldiers in Cuba. Thus, in the U.S.-Libyan context, Libya's policy toward the Soviets was not perceived as constituting much of a threat. This was despite the efforts made by Sadat and Begin to exaggerate the Soviet influence in Libya and the threat it represented to Egypt. As Carter states in his memoirs, Begin suggested even the use of "the power of Israeli's land forces and their readiness to join Egypt in an attack on Libya."[14] During his visit to Washington in April 1977, Sadat used "the threat to his country by Soviet influence in neighboring Libya" as a pretext to request more American arms for Egypt.[15]

Despite the USSR's growing involvement with Libya, Libya's distance from the Soviets remained intact in American eyes. As a State Department official put it: "The Soviets do not have any base facilities in Libya. So far Qaddafi has resisted Soviet efforts to parlay its arms sales and economic cooperation into a strategic foothold. The Libyans do not even permit Soviet military ships to make port visits."[16] The same kind of image still prevailed in 1978, as reflected in congressional hearings on the Middle East:

> The central feature of the relationship is the Soviet sale to Libya of arms which the Libyans, for the most part, are unable to obtain elsewhere. . . . The Libyans are somewhat wary of the Soviets, and have not acceded to Soviet requests for bases or other facilities in Libya. Qaddafi, a devout Moslem, much prefers the West for assistance in educating Libyans and for assistance in the economic development of Libya.[17]

Interestingly enough, Libya's relations with the Soviets were seen as indirectly serving U.S. efforts to mediate the Arab-Israeli conflict. U.S.

officials assumed that all moderate Arab countries abhorred and resisted
Soviet influence in the area, as reflected in the following statement:

> Libya's isolation from mainstream Arab thinking is intensified by its
> close relations with the Soviets. Although this relationship provides
> the arms and a certain degree of political support for Qaddafi's
> disruptive posture, it also serves to alienate Libya from Egypt and
> other moderate Arab states, further limiting its influence in the
> area.[18]

By the end of 1979, the Carter administration's ongoing image of the
Soviets was abruptly shattered as a consequence of the Soviets' invasion
of Afghanistan. The USSR began to seem more aggressive and more
threatening to U.S. vital interests. Consequently, a rapid deployment
force was established to indicate a return to gunboat diplomacy. By late
1979, also, the U.S. image of and policy toward Libya had become more
hostile. It was somewhat coincidental that the United States began to see
an intensified threat in both the Soviet Union at this time, for the shift of
image and policy toward Libya preceded the Soviet invasion of Afghanistan, though it grew more hostile after the invasion. The change in U.S.
policy toward Libya, as U.S. officials contended, was a result of Libya's
"interventionist" policy in Uganda in February 1979.[19] The fact that
their image of Libya as a "disruptive, destabilizing force supporting
terrorism" grew stronger in 1980 was clearly a reaction to Libya's alleged
sponsorship of the attack on the Tunisian town of Gafsa in January 1980,
and the series of assassinations carried out by the Libyan Revolutionary
Committees against some of the regime's opponents in Europe. To
conclude, Libya's policy toward the Soviet Union from 1977 to 1980 was
not a crucial factor, as was the case during the Nixon and Ford administrations, in shaping the U.S. image of Libya at that time.

Libya's oil policies from 1977 to 1980 were even less important in
shaping the U.S. image of Libya during this period. This was, in part,
because these policies were not as extreme as they were in the early 1970s
(due to the world recession on the one hand, and because Libya by 1975
had nationalized almost all oil production). Also, by the late 1970s, most
of the oil companies (mostly American) had worked out some agreement
with the Libyan government. Undersecretary for Political Affairs
Newsom put it as follows: "By late 1970s, however, most claims had
been settled, and the American companies there had largely come to an

acceptable working relationship with the Libyans."[20] Evidently, U.S. policy was obeying the principle that what is good for General Motors is good for the American government.

The prevailing U.S. image of Libya during 1977–1980 were as follows:

1. *Motivation*. Libya's foreign policy continued to be seen as motivated primarily by Qaddafi's views. As "a devout Moslem and a radical nationalist," he was perceived as pursuing an extreme revolutionary policy the aim of which was to overthrow moderate Arab regimes in the region and to establish revolutionary radical regimes. This policy was seen as disruptive to the status quo (in Morgenthau's terms) and hence potentially dangerous not only to American efforts to achieve a solution to the Arab-Israeli conflict, but also to U.S. interests in the region in general. This image (which lasted throughout 1977) was preestablished in the minds of Carter's officials before the administration assumed office in 1977. For Libyan policies in 1977, as I have discussed above, were generally friendly toward most Arab regimes, including the moderate ones.

By 1978 this image was less intense as a consequence of Libya's efforts to dissociate itself from international terrorism. Libya's policies continued to be seen as motivated by the independent will of its leaders. Its distance from outside influence (the Soviet Union) remained intact in the prevailing U.S. image of Libya through the whole 1977–1980 period. Protecting U.S. economic interests in Libya—oil—was viewed as indispensable. Hence, the administration was caught between two forces: one, the perceived threat from Libya's "disruptive" policies; the other, its perceived vital economic relations with Libya that had to be preserved. On August 5, 1980, President Carter articulated this mixed perception more clearly:

> There are few governments in the world with which we have more sharp and frequent policy differences than Libya. Libya has steadfastly opposed our efforts to reach and carry out the Camp David Accords. We have strongly differing attitudes toward the PLO and the support of terrorism. Within OPEC, Libya has promoted sharply higher prices and the interruption of oil shipments to the U.S. and other Western nations.
>
> On the other hand, Libya illustrates the principle that our relation-

ships with other nations can never be cast in absolute terms. Libya is a major oil supplier, and its *high quality crude oil is important to the mix of our East Coast refineries. Libya had publicly and privately opposed Iran's seizure of our hostages and for a time joined other Moslem states in opposing the Soviet invasion of Afghanistan.*[21]

The administration's image of Libya's policies as motivated solely by the independent will of its leadership, which was "radical," "extreme," and "fanatic," stood in sharp contrast with the image held by Congress. Most members of Congress saw Libya as a "surrogate state" promoting Soviet influence and designs in the Middle East and Africa. Some congressmen, such as Larry McDonald, a noted anti-Soviet figure, went even further to suggest a termination of diplomatic ties with "the Soviet surrogate Libya."[22]

2. *Capability.* Libyan capabilities were generally underestimated. Despite the increasing amounts of sophisticated arms purchased from the Soviet Union, and the rapidly growing size of its armed forces, the United States did not see Libya's military capability as significant enough to affect the course of events in the Middle East, especially in relation to the Arab-Israeli conflict. This is because of the American perception that Libya's military capability was no more than a "massive accumulation of arms" that were not properly manned or maintained. Its potential capability of mobilizing the power of a third powerful actor, the Soviet Union, to strengthen its bargaining leverage vis-à-vis other actors in the region, was also underestimated because of the administration's perception that "the Soviet Union does not approve of many of Libya's extreme policies in the Middle East,"[23] and because of U.S. officials' perception of Qaddafi as a devout Moslem whose approach opposed any foreign influence on Libya's foreign policy orientation. Thus, Qaddafi's threat in 1978 to join the Warsaw Pact if the United States did not modify its hostile policy toward Libya, did not acquire much credibility in American eyes. Libya's only potential power perceived by U.S. officials was its ability to block a Middle Eastern settlement through its "disruptive and destabilizing" activities within moderate Arab countries that were directly involved in the peace process. And even this started to lose much of its significance in 1978–1979 due to Libya's efforts to dissociate itself from terrorism and its apparent friendly relations with most moderate Arab countries. This was despite growing friendly relations with the Soviets, and Libya's

124

opposition to the United States' Middle East efforts in the same period. By late 1979 and throughout 1980, Libya again began to seem threatening, because of its alleged intervention in Uganda and Tunisia. Moreover, President Carter's brother's connection with Libya was thought to have damaged the president's reelection campaign in 1980.

3. *Decisional Style and Locus.* Despite the basic changes that took place in Libya's political structure after 1977, according to which the highest authority in Libya became the General People's Congress (at least theoretically), the Carter administration continued through the 1977–1980 period to view Qaddafi as the central figure in Libyan decision making. He was perceived "to be popular among broad segments of the Libyan population"; no organized opposition was perceived within the country that could constitute any threat to his power.[24]

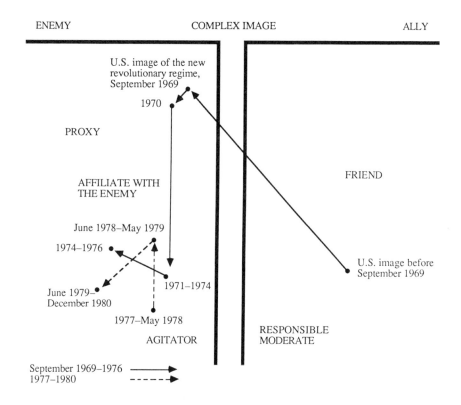

FIGURE 6.   U.S. Images of Libya, 1977–1980

On the basis of the above indicators, I would argue that the prevailing U.S. image of Libya during 1977–1980 approached the agitator type, because the United States underestimated Libya's capability to block the peace efforts in the Middle East. In addition, it believed that Libya had kept its distance from the Soviet Union, and thus it could not mobilize the influence of a third actor (comparable in culture and capability to the United States) for bargaining leverage. Therefore, the threat perceived from Libya's conduct was not intense enough in American eyes to characterize Libya as an affiliate with the enemy or as a surrogate. Libya's only threat was associated with its ability to destabilize regimes friendly to the United States in the region, and this perceived threat did not become intense until 1980 when Libya was accused of sponsoring the attack on the Tunisian town of Gafsa. International and internal political circumstances in the United States were the main reasons behind the administration's exaggerated fear of Libya and the U.S. response to it. The U.S. image of Libya, 1977–1980, is plotted in figure 6.

The U.S. image of Libya during the Carter administration was characterized by a fear of Libya's "subversive and terrorist" activities in neighboring countries on the one hand, and consideration for American economic needs on the other. This resulted in a dual-track policy: to maintain marginal political and military pressure on Libya, while protecting economic and trade relations.

Thus, in 1977 the United States publicly condemned what it called "Libya's support of international terrorism" and its subversive activities in neighboring countries. Therefore it granted Sadat's request for arms in April 1977, under the pretext of countering the Libyan threat. More weapons were also sent after the Libyan-Egyptian military clashes of July 1977. In the meantime, the United States continued its ban on the delivery of the eight C-130 planes to Libya, and rejected Qaddafi's proposal (June 1977) of appointing an ambassador (instead of a chargé d'affaires) to manage relations between the two countries. In contrast, U.S. trade relations with Libya seemed to flourish in 1977–1978: principal U.S. exports to Libya increased by 59.9 percent in the 1976–1978 period (see table 15).

By mid-1978, U.S. policy toward Libya seemed less restrictive. The State Department in May 1977 lifted its ban on the sale of two Boeing 727s (worth $30 million) ordered by Libyan Air Lines after Boeing warned that Libya might buy the European airbus instead. The opinion of U.S. officials that "the ban was a mistake" was reflected in President Carter's directive of September 26, 1978, to "take export consequences

TABLE 15. Principal U.S. Exports to Libya, 1976–1978
($U.S. millions)

	1976	1977	1978
Agricultural equipment	7.5	5.8	16.4
Construction and mining equipment	49.9	20.3	28.9
Building supplies and fixtures equipment	9.5	13.3	43.3
Drilling equipment (mainly oil)	17.1	34.2	89.7
Electrical equipment (mainly oil)	8.2	12.0	16.6
Purification equipment	0.9	5.0	21.3
Pumps, valves, and compressors	12.0	20.5	17.9
Engines and mechanical power equipment	5.7	9.5	12.9
Aviation and avionics	3.3	1.2	15.7
Prefabricated buildings	2.2	2.6	24.6
Total	116.3	124.7	287.3

Source: U.S. Department and U.S. Embassy, Tripoli, quoted in *Middle East Economic Digest* 23, no. 49 (December 7, 1979, p. 46).

fully into account when considering the use of export controls for foreign policy purposes."[1]

The delivery of the two Boeings in November was followed by the sale of 400 heavy trucks worth about $70 million from the Oshkosh Truck Corporation. The deal had first been approved by the Commerce Department, but in March 1978 the State Department had banned delivery under the pretext that Libya intended to use the trucks to haul tanks across the desert to intervene in neighboring countries.[2] The lifting of the two bans could be seen as a consequence of Libya's attitude toward "international terrorism" which lasted until mid-1979. Early in that year, the U.S. Department of State also recommended the sale of three Boeing 747s to Libya on condition that they would not be used for military purposes. David Newsom comments, "We entertained hopes that these decisions would not only be commercially advantageous but would also open opportunities for a more constructive dialogue with Libya on issues which have divided us."[3]

Consistently with this new policy, the State Department in December refuted the Federation of American Scientists' charges that Libya was developing a nuclear bomb. The FAS chairman, George Rathjens, claimed that Libya's nuclear reactor, purchased from the USSR in 1978, was capable of producing enough spent fuel to manufacture a half-dozen nuclear weapons a year. The State Department refuted these allegations, pointing to Libya's ratification of the Nuclear Nonproliferation Treaty since 1975, and noting that the treaty had been adhered to in the sale of the Soviet reactor to Libya.[4]

In line with these initiatives, several rounds of talks between American and Libyan officials took place from late 1978 until November 1979. The talks were conducted at a level higher than at any time since the early days of the revolution. U.S. Secretary of State Cyrus Vance, Undersecretary for Political Affairs David Newsom, and Ambassador Quainton participated in those talks, as did the Libyan foreign secretary, Dr. Turayki, Major Jallud (perceived by U.S. officials to be the second man in Libya), and Mansur Kikhia, Libya's representative to the UN. Though the talks confirmed the wide differences that divided the two governments, they also suggested, as Newsom put it, that "Libya wanted to find a way to contain those differences and to agree to disagree."[5] Also, in summer 1979, it was reported that the United States had convinced Sadat to give up a planned attack on Libya.[6] This development—the report turned out to be true—indicated the improved relations between the two countries.

Thus, from mid-1978 until mid-1979, U.S.-Libyan relations moved toward a cautious rapprochement. This U.S. policy line, mainly sponsored by the State Department, was opposed by Congress members who saw Libya as a Soviet surrogate whose policy was to expand Soviet influence in the area. The Pentagon, which in 1978 ranked Libya only after the Soviet Union, China, and North Korea as a possible source of hostilities, also disagreed with the State Department's policy toward Libya.[7]

This cautiously moderate policy toward Libya was short-lived. The return to marginal pressure started to emerge when the United States expressed its dissatisfaction with Libya's alleged intervention in Uganda in February 1979. In May, as we have noted, the State Department recommended that the Department of Commerce not allow the export of the three Boeing 747s ordered by Libya early in 1979 because of reports that Libya had used a Boeing 727 in evacuating Libyan troops from Uganda. As one official put it, "The State Department was left with no alternative but to regard the 747s for Libya as having a potential significant military application."[8]

The attack on the U.S. embassy in Tripoli by some 2,000 demonstrators on December 2, 1979, in support of the seizure of the U.S. embassy in Tehran, further complicated relations. The United States accused the Libyan government of sponsoring the attack because the demonstrators were wearing militia uniforms. However, the accusation was unconvincing. "Since . . . Qaddafi announced in September 1979 that all schools were to be militarized, uniformed students from the age of 14 [were] a regular feature both in Tripoli and Benghazi."[9] Whether the charge could be substantiated or not is less important than the fact that the incident accelerated U.S. distrust of Libya. The embassy episode, along with Libya's alleged role in Uganda, convinced the United States that "Qaddafi was a major obstacle to American interests in the Middle East."[10] Libya's official apology and offer of compensation for damages were "considered unsatisfactory in the absence of Col. Qaddafi's willingness to receive the U.S. charge and to establish clear responsibility in the Libyan government for contacts in the case of new threats."[11]

Libya's official denuniciation of Iran's seizure of the American hostages and its readiness to mediate their release helped in reducing U.S. dissatisfaction with Libya's conduct. Hence President Carter, through his brother Billy, asked Libya to help in releasing the hostages. Qaddafi's statement, during those contacts, that Carter had promised to follow a "more moderate policy toward the Arab-Israeli conflict if reelected in November, 1980,"[12] was an irritant to the Carter administration. The State Department issued a statement emphasizing the United States' established policy toward the region.

When, in January 1980, Libya was accused by some Tunisian dissidents of sponsoring the attack on Gafsa, the United States rushed to send arms to the Bourguiba regime under the justification of helping a friendly government to defend itself against the "Libyan threat." Though many observers doubted Libya's responsibility in the incident,[13] the event marked the beginning of a series of U.S. policy steps to put more pressure on Libya. In February, the United States withdrew its chargé d'affaires from Tripoli, and in May expelled six members of the Libyan's People's Bureau in Washington and ordered home the two American diplomats remaining in Tripoli. Thus, the U.S. embassy in Tripoli was closed, though the State Department still insisted that those measures did not constitute a formal break in relations with Libya.

On May 9, 1980, it was reported that Libyan citizens in the United States were under constant surveillance by the FBI, "as a precautionary measure against any assassination attempts against Libyan dissidents living in the U.S."[14] In summer 1980, U.S. reconnaisance flights over Libya were increased, and Libya intensified its efforts to intercept them. By October, Qaddafi warned Carter and Reagan that if the United States did not keep its naval and air forces away from Libya's borders, an armed conflict could take place at any moment. Jeff McConnell reported that "Carter did overrule the Pentagon and refrained from conducting naval maneuvers close to Libyan coastlines," because the Carter administration was convinced that military action against Libya could create unforeseen problems. One such problem would be that of a general war."[15]

Because the United States had followed a hard policy line in response to Libya's perceived conduct in Uganda and Tunisia and the burning of the U.S. embassy in Tripoli, one might ask (if those events were studied in isolation) why did the United States not respond to Libya's intervention in Chad in 1978, and why did it not react to Pakistan, when the U.S. embassy was sacked and burned in Islamabad, as it had responded to Libya? The answer is that U.S. relations with Libya cannot be comprehended without an understanding of the overall environment. First, a sequence of events took place that badly affected the U.S. image as a leader in world politics, starting with the seizure of American hostages in Iran in November 1979. Next came the Soviet invasion of Afghanistan by the end of the year, in addition to the burning of the U.S. embassy in Islamabad and the siege of the Grand Mosque in Mecca. The overall picture that emerged was of a weak United States that could be pushed around even by a Third World country. Thus, from an international perspective, the U.S. response to Libya's alleged conduct could be seen as only one step among others—such as the establishment of the RDF, the grain embargo against the USSR, the boycott of the Olympic games, the military attempt to rescue the hostages from Iran—to restore its lost image. Libya was not seen as a friendly country, and a tough stance would not make any difference in already strained relations. Pakistan was a friendly nation; this could answer why the United States did not respond to Pakistan as it had to Libya.

Second, the president's brother's connection with Libya was causing too much trouble to the administration and to the president personally. By late 1979 and throughout 1980, Billy Carter's connection with Libya, along with other alleged Libyan connections with ex-CIA employees (Frank Terpil and Edwin Wilson) were widely reported in the media. Billy Carter was said to have accepted money and gifts in return for using his relations with the president to influence U.S. policy toward Libya, especially regarding the issue of the banned C-130 aircraft. The matter gained more publicity when the press reported that the president "had interfered in the Justice Department investigation of Billy and given him confidential information about the case, and that Libyan money had been given to the president or transferred to Carter's warehouse in Plains."[16] When Billy Carter was asked whether his relations with the Libyans would be criticized by American Jews, he replied, "There are a hell of a lot more Arabs than Jews."[17] Billy Carter was accused of being anti-Semitic, and the president was urged by the American Jewish Congress to repudiate his brother's statement and actions.[18]

The whole affair of Billy Carter and the ex-CIA officials resulted not only in accusations of the administration's "softness" toward Libya, but also in irreparable damage to Carter's reelection campaign. In Carter's words:

> As the Convention approached, I needed to work to heal the wounds in the Democratic Party and to hold Congress together on our legislative program. Instead, I was bogged down answering a multitude of charges about myself and my administration that were absolutely baseless. The Libyan mess, which was dominating the news, was wreaking havoc with our efforts to deal with anything else on the political scene or in Congress.[19]

Taking into account internal American politics, the U.S. response toward Libya could have served the purpose not only of retaliating against Libya's perceived misconduct and strengthening America's international image, but also of proving the president's dissociation from Libya. Thus, the hard U.S. policy line throughout 1980 was not only a reflection of the prevailing U.S. image of that country, but also a reaction to internal and international factors.

The only dimension of U.S. policy toward Libya that was unaffected by the ups and downs of politics were trade relations. While U.S. exports to Libya were valued at $197,601 million in 1977, they jumped to

$426,169 million in 1980. And while its imports from Libya were at $4,542,014 million in 1977, they became $7,778,571 million in 1980 (see table 16).

Politics did not affect economics in this case; Libya did not extend its hostility toward U.S. policy into actions against U.S. economic interests—U.S. businesses were encouraged to develop economic ties with Libya. This was the subject of a December 1979 article entitled "Politics Do Not Intrude in Day to Day Business," which argued that U.S. businessmen in Libya "have not found that politics spills over into working relationships. Even crude oil contracts—where politics impinge most directly on economics—are unaffected once work starts."[20] The International Monetary Fund emphasized the same point: "While the U.S. is not among countries to which, for political purposes, the Libyan government channels import orders, U.S. goods have done well on their own merit. U.S. exporters should therefore not be deterred by the political factor from seeking export markets in Libya."[21]

U.S. trade relations with Libya continued to flourish. It is true that the revolutionary regime's moderate approach toward U.S. economic interests had created a comfortable environment for U.S. business during the Carter period. Nevertheless, the main factor, as verbal evidence suggests, lay in the U.S. officials' pragmatic view of Libya. This view was based on the assumption that despite its perceived role as a hostile agitator, Libya still represented an economic interest to the United States that should be maintained and promoted. This idea was apparent in the 1980 statement of the undersecretary for political affairs, who argued that despite the United States' differences with Libya, "we also have impor-

TABLE 16.   U.S. Trade with Libya, 1977–1980
($U.S. thousands)

	Exports to Libya	Imports from Libya
1977	197,601	4,542,914
1978	187,709	4,024,993
1979	283,670	5,797,833
1980	426,169	7,778,571

Source: U.N. Yearbook of International Trade Statistics, 1981, vol. 1, p. 596.

tant general trade interests in Libya. Given the high volume of U.S. oil purchases from Libya which may surpass $9 billion in 1980, we may be running a bilateral balance of payment deficit of around $8.5 billion this year. . . . With its high oil revenues and its major development programs, Libya represents a valuable potential market for American products and services."[22]

These market opportunities, especially in light of acute European competition, were emphasized heavily in a 1979 report prepared by the U.S. embassy in Tripoli calling for more American investment in and exports to the Libyan market. The report stated:

> Future opportunities for American construction and consulting companies should be good. . . . Outstanding opportunities for further sales of commercial aircraft, large and small. . . . The disappointing record in food and feedstuff sales should be improvable. . . . U.S. exporters should therefore not be deterred by the political factor from seeking export markets in Libya.[23]

The same conviction was held by Carter himself who wrote, in reaction to his brother's affair in Libya: "It was not an earthshaking event. We had full diplomatic relations. Libya supplied us with more than 10% of our imported oil, and there were many American investments in the country."[24]

Thus, using the policy-mapping framework introduced in the first chapter, we can see that U.S. policy toward Libya from 1977 to May 1978 was obviously approaching marginal pressure, involving politically strained relations and bans on all types of exports of "potential military significance." From June 1978 until May 1979, U.S. policy toward Libya was moving toward some kind of rapprochement in which there was some political relaxation—as represented by intensive American-Libyan rounds of dialogue to solve the differences between the two governments. Also some bans on some types of U.S. exports to Libya were lifted. By late 1979 and throughout 1980, however, the United States returned to a policy of marginal pressure. The pressure during this third period was greater than before, as represented by the withdrawing of U.S. diplomats from Libya, the expulsion of some members of the Libyan People's Bureau in Washington, the military support to Tunisia to defend itself against "the Libyan threat," and reenforcing the ban on some U.S. exports to Libya perceived to be of some military potential. Nevertheless, the pressure was still marginal because it did not cover the economic aspects of the relations—which flourished, as shown above—and did not involve escalating the military pressure against Libya, as was the case when Carter decided to stop the naval maneuvers along the Libyan coastline. This type of pressure applied by the Carter administration will look even more marginal when we compare it with the type of pressure applied by the Reagan administration in the next section. (See figure 7.)

The above discussion of the U.S. image of and policy toward Libya, 1977–1980, makes it quite clear that a substantial congruence between the prevailing official image and policy had taken place, though a minor divergence between the two variables started to emerge during the last year of the Carter administration. At that time the policy started to look

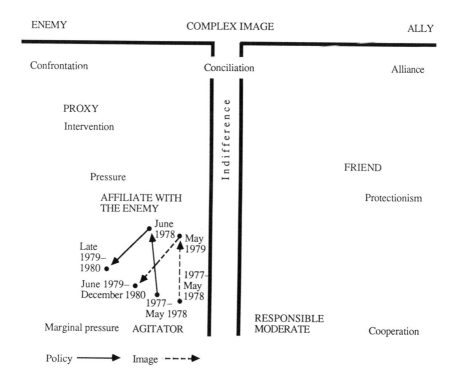

FIGURE 7.   U.S. Policy Toward Libya, 1977–1980

tougher (yet still defined as marginal pressure) than the then prevailing U.S. image of Libya would have indicated. This minor divergence was attributed to certain internal and international factors that accelerated the quality and speed of U.S. policy toward Libya in 1980. Therefore, Carter's policy during that period was not only a reflection of the prevailing image of Libya, but also a reaction to events in the international and U.S. internal environments. This incongruence between policy and image should serve as a reminder that such congruence should not be regarded as axiomatic, but rather as a logical hypothesis that has to be confirmed empirically.

PART IV ➤ U.S. POLICY TOWARD LIBYA DURING THE REAGAN ADMINISTRATION

9 ⊱ LIBYA'S FOREIGN POLICY, 1981–1982

No major change took place during the early 1980s in the general trend of Libya's policy toward the four dimensions set forth for study: Libya's policy vis-à-vis the Soviet Union; its policy toward the Arab-Israeli conflict; its oil policy; and its revolutionary activities abroad. As a matter of fact, Libya's foreign policy became more radical and extreme toward the Arab-Israeli conflict and its friendly relations with the Soviets grew even stronger than before. Its radical stand toward oil, though not changed in tone, lost much of its effectiveness due to world economic conditions in the 1980s. It still supported revolutionary activities and movements abroad in principle, though its behavioral aspect in this regard was less noticeable if compared with its conduct in the early 1970s. A more detailed description of Libya's foreign policy along the four dimensions under study is now in order.

LIBYA AND THE ARAB-ISRAELI CONFLICT

The struggle against Israel still represented the basic concern for the Libyan decision makers in 1981–1982. No compromise or coexistence was considered possible with the "Zionist enemy." Only military force, if the Arabs mobilized their capabilities, could solve the problem and for good. Arab unity was still seen as the ideal road to Arab victory. And Arab "reactionary" regimes who sold out to the "Zionist enemy" and continued to promote "American imperial" designs, should be isolated and fought. Based on this conviction, in April 1981 Qaddafi called for an alliance between Algeria, Libya, Mauritania, and the Sahara, and urged the Arab countries to expel Sudan from the Arab League because of its continued recognition of and dealings with Sadat's regime.[1] It was reported also that in April Libya moved some of its Soviet-built SAM-9 missiles into Lebanon to defined Palestinian bases south of Beirut, and that Libyan volunteers had joined the Palestinians during the period of high tensions on Lebanon's border with Israel. Israel claimed on May 28 that it had raided the missiles and destroyed them.[2] Qaddafi also repeated his offer to the Lebanese government that Libya deploy its missiles across all of Lebanese soil to defend itself against Israeli jets. A Libyan envoy arrived at Beirut in May 1981 to promote the Libyan proposal, but no official reply was received.[3] In conjunction with this effort, Qaddafi sent a letter to the Arab heads of state asserting, "The situation in Lebanon is one of external armed aggression. Depending on the charter of the Arab League, all Arab countries should immediately intervene militarily to assist an Arab country."[4]

The Israeli bombing of the Iraqi nuclear reactor on June 7, 1981, led to a tactical change in Libya's policy toward the perceived "reactionary" Arab regimes. Qaddafi believed that Israel threatened the whole Arab homeland without distinction between "revolutionary" or "reactionary" regimes; thus Arab differences could be overlooked for the sake of creating a unified Arab action against a common enemy. This new conciliatory approach toward "conservative" Arab regimes was quite apparent in Major Jallud's visit to Jordan and Iraq to negotiate the establishment of a unified Arab front against Israel. And it became more clear when Libya restored diplomatic relations with Iraq, Morocco, and Saudi Arabia by the end of the year. (The Libyan-American air clash of August 19, 1981, helped to accelerate Libya's reconciliation with those regimes.) Qaddafi described Sadat's assassination on October 6, 1981, as a victory and "a death sentence on a traitor carried out by the Arab nation."[5] Sadat's death was seen as an opportunity for the new Egyptian president to break out of the "Zionist, imperial camp." But Egypt's permission to 4,000 American troops to join Egyptian, Sudanese, Somali, and Omani troops in military exercises (called Bright Star) in its western desert, was seen as a continuation of Sadat's "treason." Sadat, Qaddafi said, "was not the last of the traitors."[6]

The Libyan conciliatory approach toward "conservative" Arab regimes was short-lived. That is because the Arabs had no intention of confronting Israel militarily and using their oil weapon against the United

States and "its foster spoiled child, Israel." Instead, they made one concession after another to the Zionist enemy, as was the case with the "Fahd plan" which Libya condemned and rejected. Thus, as early as January 1982, Qaddafi threatened that Arab revolutionaries would take the necessary steps against "the reactionary Arab governments" who were perceived to be hostile to the Arab nation, and urged Syria to establish a "strategic cooperation with the U.S.S.R."[7]

Another factor that deepened Libya's distrust of "reactionary" Arab regimes was their overproduction of oil. Libya accused Saudi Arabia of taking an important part in the United States' plan to impose an economic blockade on Libya, and in March 1982 Libya severed relations with Saudi Arabia.

Libya's militant stand toward the Arab-Israeli conflict grew even stronger when, in April 1982, it proposed officially to convene the Arab Joint Defense Council in an urgent session to discuss a comprehensive Arab strategy to repulse "Zionist" aggression. The strategy called for sending urgent military and financial backing to consolidate the Palestinian People's Steadfastness, and placing part of the Arab countries' military forces at the disposal of the Palestinians and the national Lebanese movement.[8]

Libya's dismay and anger toward Arab regimes reached a climax when Israel invaded Lebanon in June 1982. Libya called for an urgent Arab summit because "the current situation is among the gravest faced by the Arab cause" and also because "the fall of Beirut would mean the fall of Arab dignity. Forcing the resistance out of Beirut would be equal to being forced out of our wives' quarters."[9] The solution, as suggested by Qaddafi to the Arab heads of state,

> lies in sending Arab forces from every country to immediately take part in the Beirut battle, to bolster the Syrian front and to allow volunteers to fight in any front. All this must be agreed upon with Syria. America must immediately be placed on the Arab blacklist and its envoy thrown off the Arab land. The humiliating U.S. mediation must be rejected and the U.S. must be refused audience.[10]

Libya refused to take part in the Arab foreign ministers' summit under the pretext that the situation needed to be confronted by the Arab heads of state themselves, not by their ministers who did not have enough power to act. Qaddafi sent another cable to the Arab governments suggesting the creation of a military force supported by air squadrons from different Arab countries and offering himself as leader of this force in the battle against Israel. The Arabs' failure to respond favorably to his repeated calls infuriated Qaddafi, who charged that the Arab governments had "lost every justification for their existence for even one more day."[11] Libya sent military units to the Syrian front, and Qaddafi cabled Arafat asking him to commit suicide rather than comply with Israeli, American, and "reactionary" Arab plans to force him to leave Beirut. He felt that the Palestinians' departure from Beirut to various Arab countries was the worst of the Arab defeats at the hands of "Zionist imperialism." He condemned all the Arab governments for their failure to confront Israel and for their promotion of the Israeli-American plan of evacuating the Palestinians from Lebanon, which he saw as a longtime Israeli strategic objective. Qaddafi attacked not only "reactionary Arab regimes," but also "the regimes of the Arab nation, the parties of the Arab nation and the opposition of the Arab nation, rightist and leftist, which displayed their incapacity at the battle of Beirut."[12]

Thus, as in September 1969, Libya remained opposed to Israel's existence because it conflicted with the Arabs' future unity and progress. Military force continued to be seen as the only effective approach to deal with the "Zionist entity" which represented "all the evil on earth."[13] Qaddafi rejected all peace initiatives and proposals, including those of the Fez summit of September 1982, because, as Qaddafi put it: "The Zionists are determined to slaughter the Arabs even if they raise white flags. They very much fear the Arab race because it will destroy them. Therefore, the Zionists are trying every possible means to exterminate the Arabs."[14] Consequently, he believed, no Arab survival was possible without a unified Arab front using its military and economic capabilities to confront the "Zionist enemy" and its prime supporter, the United States.

OIL POLICY

Libya's radical oil policy was most strongly felt during the early 1970s through pricing, nationalization, and boycotting. However, these forms of pressure were virtually ineffective during 1981–1982. World economic recession, conservation efforts by the leading industrial countries, and the resulting decline in international oil prices, all created an economic environment that reduced the effectiveness of Libya's radical oil policy. For instance, during the first half of 1981, Libya opposed Saudi Arabia's selling at lower prices than other members of OPEC and called, instead, for production cuts to keep the price level as it was. But after the May OPEC meeting, Libya started lowering its own oil prices; another price reduction followed in October. The price of Libyan oil fell from $41 p/b at the end of 1980 to $38 p/b in October 1981. Nevertheless, Libyan oil was still uncompetitive because some other OPEC members, Nigeria for instance, were selling their oil at $34.50. This led Libya to further price reductions in November and December 1981.

The effect of this international economic environment was obvious. Libya's revenues dropped from $24 billion in 1980 to less than $14 billion in 1981, and its average level of oil production in March 1981 dropped to 1.6 million b/d, a decline of 35 percent from 1980. It dropped again to about 600,000 b/d as a result of the developing oil glut and the uncompetitiveness of Libya's oil prices.[15] By 1986 revenues had fallen to only $4.5 billion.

Things turned from bad to worse when in October 1981 the Reagan administration asked the American companies operating in Libya to terminate their operations and leave Libya. Then came the American embargo (Libya had been the third largest supplier of oil to the United States after Saudi Arabia and Nigeria) to inflict even harder economic conditions on Libya. Though some American companies (Esso Standard and Esso Sidra), under this political and economic pressure, relinquished all their rights and assets in Libya as early as January 1982, Libya had little difficulty replacing the American technicians with Canadians and Iranians, in addition to the assistance offered by the United Arab Emirates and Kuwait.

The U.S. economic pressure, which came during an oil glut in the world market, inevitably caused considerable damage to the marketing of Libyan oil and Libyan plans for development. In March 1982, Qaddafi described the situation as follows:

> What is happening is that the oil market has been flooded. There is a glut. Oil tankers are loaded with oil but no one wants to buy. This is due to the increase in Saudi oil production which has reached 8.5 million b/d. As a result of the surplus of Saudi oil, we cannot sell the quantity which we decided to sell because those who would buy from us will say that they are buying from Saudi Arabia.[16]

The Libyan petroleum secretary stated, "Our own revenues, our plans and our assistance to friendly and sisterly countries have been harmed as a result of this hostile imperialist stance imposed on our people."[17]

The U.S. economic pressure on Libya was perceived as an imperial plot against Libya and its revolutionary stands. This plot could never have had much effect on Libya's economy if it were not for the "reactionary" Saudi regime which assisted in the U.S. blockade of Libya through its overproduction of oil. Qaddafi's reaction to this perceived "imperial" conspiracy was a determination to continue the revolutionary course despite the economic pressure on his country:

> There is a challenge to us . . . a challenge to which our dignity, our revolution, our sovereignty and all our values are linked to our stomachs and not to any other values. With or without oil, we are against the U.S., against reaction and for Arab unity and Palestine.[18]

> The U.S. wants the Libyan people to submit to Arab reaction or to the will of the U.S. But to hell with the U.S., to hell with Arab reaction. We will not submit.[19]

Libya severed relations with Saudi Arabia because, as Qaddafi put it, "it has become a bigger threat to the Arabs than Israel and the U.S."[20]

Libya's repeated calls and proposals to Arab governments in 1981–1982 to use oil as a tool of pressure against the United States and any Western country that supported Israel, was ignored by other Arab regimes. Consequently, the possibility of using Arab oil as a political weapon, as was the case in October 1973, never materialized.

Thus, it is safe to conclude that in 1981–1982 Libya's radical stand toward oil was more of a verbal threat than a policy that could affect the structure of the world oil market or exert political pressure on the United States or Western Europe, as had occurred during the 1973 oil embargo.

REVOLUTIONARY ACTIVITIES ABROAD

Libya continued to insist upon a distinction between "liberation movements," which Libya strongly supported, and "terrorist organizations," which Libya opposed and condemned.[21] Libya officially asserted its backing of the PLO and other liberation movements in Africa and worldwide. This stand was clearly reflected in Qaddafi's speech of September 1, 1981: "In addition to participating with the Palestinian Revolution and the realization of Arab unity through Arab Revolution, I am also committed to participate in the revolutions in Nicaragua, Guatemala, El Salvador, Namibia and to fight U.S. colonialism everywhere."[22]

Apart from its financial and military support to the Palestinians, Libya also stood by Nicaragua financially when a cooperation agreement was signed in April 1981 according to which Libya provided $100 million for investment to the Central Bank of Nicaragua.[23] The empirical evidence suggests as well that Libya provided assistance to Namibia, Angola, the Somali Salvation Front, El Salvador, and Grenada.

As a reaction to the Reagan administration's accusations that Libya supported terrorism and acts of subversion in neighboring countries, Libyan officials demanded evidence for these accusations. They described the United States as the main sponsor of terrorism through its intervention in the affairs of Third World countries and through its military bases and naval fleets that "terrorize" the small countries of the world.

By 1981, also, the campaign of assassinating Libyan dissidents in Western Europe was called off, and Qaddafi was reported to be ready for a dialogue with opposition groups during his visit to Austria in March 1982. Libya's relations with most Arab countries (except Egypt and Sudan) were generally good during 1981–1982. Despite Qaddafi's repeated warning that Arab revolutionaries might take action against the "reactionary" Arab regimes that failed to confront Israel in Lebanon, there was no evidence that his threats ever materialized.

Libya's intervention in Chad in 1980 was condemned by various foreign governments, particularly the United States, who called Libya a subversive and destabilizing force in the African continent. This military involvement, though in response to the request of the legitimate Chadian government, aroused other African governments' fear that Qaddafi's "expansionist designs were only the first step in his ambitions to establish an 'Islamic Empire' that stretches from the Sudan to Senegal."

The origins of those fears were orchestrated by the United States in the last days of the Carter administration:

> The White House agreed to suggestions from the Pentagon that African heads of state, including Tunisian Prime Minister Muham-

mad Mizali, be shown U.S. satellite photos of the Libyan movements in Chad and Libyan troop concentrations near their own
borders. This was done in the final days of October and the first few
days of November.[24]

The American effort brought about some results. The Tunisian foreign
minister declared: "You in the West won World War II in North Africa. If
you don't act promptly enough to end the threat from Qaddafi, you may
lose World War III here."[25] Senegal's president, reflecting on these
photos and on information he received from the French intelligence
SDECE, accused Libya of using Chad as a military base from which
other African countries could be attacked for the sake of building an
"Islamic empire." Senegal broke diplomatic relations with Libya, as did
Ghana, Gambia, and Niger.[26] In an interview with *Jeune Afrique*,
Niger's president accused Qaddafi "of attempting to subvert the trans-
Saharan tribes by telling them that Libya is their homeland."[27] Egypt and
Sudan helped to fuel the African fears, contending that Qaddafi's inter-
vention in Chad was in reality an advancement of Soviet influence in
Africa. By the end of 1981, Libya's troops withdrew from Chad in
compliance with the request of the Chadian government and the fears of
African heads of state were never realized.

Other accusations against Libya, which could not be substantiated,
were the claims that Libya had sponsored the Moslem uprising in Kano
Province in Nigeria, and the failed coup d'état in Gambia. In each case
Libya challenged the West to present any evidence to back its accusations.

On October 25, the *New York Times* reported that the U.S. ambassador to Italy had been called back to Washington to protect him from a
Libyan assassination attempt (as revenge for the August 19 air clash over
the Gulf of Sirte). And on November 12, the acting U.S. ambassador to
France was fired at in Paris. Secretary Haig, testifying before the House
Foreign Affairs Committee, stated that the attack "might have been
sponsored by the Libyan government."[28] In both incidents Libya's role
was never confirmed.

The episode that attracted the most media coverage in the West was the
official U.S. claim that Libya had sent an assassination squad to kill
President Reagan and top U.S. officials. Details of the alleged plot,
which led to very tight security measures for the president and other top

U.S. officials, were reportedly obtained by the CIA through ⌐
named, non-American informant with first-hand knowledge of L
plans."[29] Qaddafi responded to the U.S. allegations, "We haven't se
any people to kill Reagan or any other people in the world." Qaddafi
described Reagan as "silly" and "ignorant" because he believed these
charges and added, "America must get rid of this administration and fell it
down, as they did with Nixon, and elect another respectful president to get
respect for America."[30] Though both the president and the State Department claimed to have had evidence of the plot, a high-ranking FBI official
told CBS News on December 7, 1981, that he had real doubts about the
evidence of the Libyan conspiracy. And on December 14 the *New York
Post* reported, "Angry State Department officials said they strongly
suspect that Israeli intelligence is supplying reporters with the most
dramatic details of the plot." By the end of the month U.S. officials told
the news media, "The threat has disappeared." Once again, the allegations were never proven.

During the period 1981–1982, there were no hijackings or kidnapping
incidents that were related to Libya as in the early 1970s; however, by the
end of 1982 Qaddafi started talking again about the Libyan people's right
to liquidate Libyan dissidents abroad.

LIBYA'S POLICY TOWARD THE SUPERPOWERS

POLICY TOWARD THE SOVIET UNION

Libya's relations with the USSR during 1981–1982 became stronger than
they had been at any time in the past, to the degree that rumors were
circulating early in 1981 that Libya, like Syria, Iraq, and South Yemen,
might sign a friendship treaty with the Soviets. But Libyan officials
pointed out that Libya would sign only if faced with conditions similar to
those confronted by Syria prior to its signing of the treaty with the
USSR.[31]

The prospect of closer ties with the Soviets was nourished substantially
in April 1981, when Qaddafi paid an official visit to the USSR. Two
months later, Major Jallud concluded a visit to Moscow in which an
important protocol on economic cooperation was signed between the two
countries. *Le Monde* reported that "Jallud wanted the assurance of
Moscow's backing if Libya ever found itself in war with Egypt and

..r, the apparently strong Libyan-Soviet relations were
..ee of certain disagreements between the two countries
..cy issues. Soviet leaders were reportedly dissatisfied with
..vention in Chad, though the Libyan leader had pointed out in
visit to Moscow that the Soviet leadership had recalculated its
..a regarding Libyan intervention in Chad because, as he put it, "It
..ealized that Libya and Chad represent a serious threat to imperialist
..terests in the African continent."[33]

By the same token, Qaddafi stated that the Soviet Union was a major
power and his stances could not be completely identical to those of the
USSR.[34] The Soviet invasion of Afghanistan was heavily criticized and
so was the level of Soviet support to the Steadfastness Front. The Libyan
leader's open criticism of Soviet policy in Afghanistan embarrassed the
Soviet leadership. The *New York Times* reported that *Pravda* changed the
wording of a speech delivered by Qaddafi in Moscow against the Soviet
invasion of Afghanistan to reduce the level of potential embarrassment.

These points of disagreement were put aside, at least temporarily, and
Libya moved even closer to the Soviet Union as a consequence of the
Reagan administration's hard aggressive line against Libya. This aggres-
sive policy, which started in the early days of Reagan's assumption of
power and reached the level of military confrontation in August 1981, left
Libya with no option but to move even further toward the Soviets. As
Ronald Bruce St. John writes: "Ironically, the policies of the United
States government have fostered the Soviet-Libyan relationship by in-
creasing Qaddafi's sense of isolation, thus pushing him towards even
closer ties with the Soviet Union."[35]

Libya's closer relations with the Soviets became very obvious when
two Soviet warships paid a visit to the port of Tripoli in July 1981 (the first
ever by Soviet warships to Libyan ports). On August 19, 1981, the day
the United States downed two Libyan jets in the Gulf of Sirte, Qaddafi
signed a treaty of mutual defense with Ethiopia and South Yemen. And in
contrast with Libya's previous stand regarding the Soviet invasion of
Afghanistan, a representative of the Afghan government was welcomed
at the celebration of the twelfth anniversary of the revolution on September 1, 1981. In his speech, Qaddafi raised the possibility of his
country's formal accession to the Warsaw Pact if Libya were to be
attacked again by the United States, and vowed to turn the Gulf of Sirte
into a "red Gulf." He also warned Greece, Italy, and Turkey, for the first

time, that they might pay the price of any new American attacks on Libya: "We warn the peoples of Western Europe, and in particular the people of Sicily and Crete, the peoples of Greece and Turkey, that the U.S., which is playing with fire, will cause a disaster for these people."[36] Many observers believe that the Libyan threat to those countries in Southern Europe was based on the speculation that Libya had acquired some of the SS-12 Soviet missiles, with a 500-mile range, that are capable of carrying nuclear warheads that could reach NATO bases in southern Europe.

As a result of the American-Libyan military clash of August 1981, the speculations started to rise again about whether Libya would join the Warsaw Pact, and whether Libya would sign a treaty of friendship and cooperation with the Soviets. Citing Libyan and foreign sources, an article in *Le Monde* on September 8 said that "the highest levels of the Libyan government have secretly decided to propose a treaty of friendship and mutual defense to the U.S.S.R. Libya is prepared to grant 'facilities' and possibly bases to the Soviet Union."[37] In January 1982, Qaddafi urged Syria to establish a "strategic" cooperation with the USSR.[38] The fact that the speculations and the Libyan threats never materialized supports the argument that Libya's threats to sign a treaty or to join the Warsaw Pact were nothing but a bargaining tool with which to confront the mounting pressure of U.S. policy. In all official Libyan statements regarding this issue, Libya's enrollment in the Warsaw Pact or signing a treaty with the Soviets were always correlated with "Libya facing a new American attack" or "Libya facing an external threat." Qaddafi was more explicit when asked about the circumstances under which Libya would carry out its threat to join the Warsaw Pact:

> It would be a necessity when America constitutes a real threat against Libya. If Egypt, the Sudan and other neighboring countries were to put themselves in the service of the Atlantic Alliance, for example, then the necessity [of Libya's joining the Warsaw Pact] might arise.[39]

In July 1982, there was some change in the wording of the Libyan leader's statements regarding the same issue: "In the event of a direct U.S. attack on Libya, the Soviet Union would not stand by with its hands tied." But when asked whether the Libyan plan to join the Warsaw Pact was still topical, he replied "nothing is unchangeable in politics."[40] Thus, it is more likely that the Libyan-Soviet relationship will remain strong, but no formal alliance with the Soviets can be expected. Nonalignment had been a cardinal feature of the Libyan revolution since 1969, and joining any of the world alliances not only would violate a basic line of Libya's foreign policy, but also would violate the essence of Qaddafi's thought as presented in his "Third Universal Theory."

Thus, as one scholar puts it: "At present, the most that can be said is that both sides [Libya and the USSR] have benefited from the relationship in the past and are likely to maintain if not expand the present level of co-operation as long as it remains in their mutual interests."[41]

POLICY TOWARD THE UNITED STATES

When Ronald Reagan assumed the presidency in January 1981, Libyan officials expressed some hope that there might be a positive change in the American position toward the Arab-Israeli conflict. Qaddafi believed Republicans to be more sympathetic toward the Arabs than the Democrats. Qaddafi sent a letter to President Reagan on January 27, 1981, asking him for an "unbiased American stand" toward the conflict. "On this occasion we call on America, under your administration, to play a different role, respecting the will of peoples and ending oppressive U.S. intervention, both covert and overt, in the international affairs of other countries." Qaddafi asserted that "the Libyan Arab people look forward to sound and equitable relations based on mutual respect and interests."[42] But the new U.S. administration was under the conviction that Libya was a proxy of the Soviets. This conviction was heavily reinforced by Sadat in Egypt and Numeiry in Sudan who warned that Libya's role in Chad was to expand Soviet influence and destabilize other African regimes friendly to the West. So the Reagan administration started, from its early days, to follow an aggressive policy toward Libya. The Libyan officials' reaction was first to point out that those claims were untrue and that Libya was an independent nonaligned country. In January 1981, Qaddafi reaffirmed that argument:

> The Americans realize that the Libyan presence in Chad is purely Libyan and they know the reasons behind it. They also know that Libya is an independent and neutral state, neither Marxist nor Communist and it is not under the Soviet Union's influence, and that there are no Soviet bases on Libyan soil. . . . If As-Sadat raves day

and night that there are Soviet bases in Libya, the Americans would laugh at what he says because the Americans possess spy satellites and know what is going out of or into the Soviet Union.[43]

The aggressive U.S. approach toward Libya did not stop, and Libya was back to its militant anti-American policy, condemning the U.S. "imperial" policy in the region and attacking all the "reactionary" Arab regimes such as Egypt, Sudan, Somalia, and Saudi Arabia. By April, Libya was officially asking the Arab regimes to reconsider their oil supplies to the United States, which backed the aggression of its "spoiled foster child Israel" on Arab rights and territories.[44]

The expulsion of the members of the Libyan Bureau in Washington proved that the U.S. administration was determined to put more pressure on Libya. To Libyan officials, "The new U.S. administration has proven that it is more stupid than the Carter administration [and] has no idea what international politics is all about."[45] Consequently, Libya started to use the Soviet card as a measure that might further deter American pressure on Libya. This approach was clearly illustrated in Jallud's statement of May 1981, "Libya is a neutral country but . . . U.S. pressures do not help it to remain neutral and could force it to become completely pro-Soviet."[46] In addition to this tactical approach, Libya was still trying to show its readiness for dialogue and compromise. This readiness was reflected in a June 1981 visit by a high-level Libyan official to Washington to meet with U.S. officials and members of Congress to clarify what was believed to be a "misperceived Libyan policy." The visit did not bring about any concrete results. By July Qaddafi was again calling on the Arabs to reexamine their "alliance with the enemy of the Arab nation and the cheap and deep flowing supplies of oil which only meets the requirements of the enemy."[47]

Widely published reports during the summer of 1981 that the CIA had articulated a plan to get rid of the Libyan leader caused a more extreme reaction. The Free Unionist officers reacted by issuing a communiqué threatening that they would "hit at the U.S. interests anywhere and undertake the physical liquidation of anyone who permits himself merely to think of harming the life of the leader of the Great 1 September Revolution, beginning with Ronald Reagan and ending with the smallest agent, whether in the Jamahiriyah or abroad."[48] In August 1981, Libya sent a note to the Security Council charging that the United States was making preparations to attack Libya militarily. And on August 17 Libya signed a friendship treaty with Ethiopia and South Yemen pledging to combat the "imperial influence" in the area. This treaty was viewed by the United States as "a threat to American interests in East Africa and the Indian Ocean," and Libya was seen as attempting to "undermine Numeiry's regime in Sudan."[49] The downing of two Libyan jets on August 19 by the United States in the Gulf of Sirte and the joint American-Egyptian military maneuvers on the eastern Libyan borders, resulted in an unshakeable conviction by the Libyan leadership that Reagan and his "Arab agents" were undoubtedly determined to overthrow the revolutionary regime in Tripoli. Consequently, Libya resorted again to the use of the Soviet card, threatening that any new American attack on Libya could mean the beginning of World War III; Libya would not only retaliate by hitting the NATO bases in southern Europe but also that the USSR would come to Libya's help against the United States. By the end of the year Qaddafi said that he would also form his own rapid deployment force to counter American military intervention in any Arab country.[50]

Libya's basic stand was that normal diplomatic relations with the United States could and should be maintained to promote their mutual interests. This was despite the very basic contradictions between the two countries' foreign policies. Such was the essence of Qaddafi's statements of September 1981:

> We went to all states and asked them to mediate with the U.S. so that we might have normal relations with the U.S. We did not want to be enemies or friends with the U.S. We wanted to have diplomatic relations with the U.S. And if there was any room for mutual interests then we would welcome it. But the U.S. insists that there should be no relations as long as there is revolution in Libya.[51]

One of the main obstacles to normal relations, according to the Libyan view, was President Reagan himself, who was perceived as "a liar," "silly," and "ignorant." In one of his statements, Qaddafi characterized Reagan as follows: "He was born to be an insignificant and unsuccessful actor; all his acting dealt with the smuggling of funds outside America. How could he become the president of the greatest state on earth? What a comedy—the comedy of the 20th Century, the absurdity of the 20th Century, the triviality of the 20th Century."[52]

Throughout 1982, Libya's policy toward the United States continued to follow the same dual approach, reacting to the growing American squeeze on the one hand, and expressing willingness for dialogue to solve policy differences, on the other. Thus, we find that in February 1982, Libya was accusing the United States of perpetrating "an aggressive terrorist incident" against a Libyan civilian airplane as "part of its provocative aggressive designs against the Libyan people."[53] Before this incident, Libya had informed the chairman of the OAU that it had detected American troops in Chad, which constituted a "dangerous situation." Libya called for the prompt withdrawal of those troops. The U.S. economic blockade of Libya was viewed as another step of "American terrorism" against Libya to force the revolutionary regime to "surrender" and give up its "revolutionary principles." The "proxy regime of Saudi Arabia" was accused of taking part in this "plot" which was characterized as "a campaign of starvation" against Libya. Libya's position was that "the U.S. was wrong to imagine its measures will make the Libyans kneel after being starved."[54] On March 9, Tripoli radio announced that an American informant had told the Libyan security authorities that Israel would soon launch a military offensive on southern Lebanon, and that during the same time the United States would attack Libya.[55]

Libya's willingness for dialogue was said to be expressed first by Qaddafi during his visit to Austria in March 1982, when it was widely reported that he had asked Chancellor Kreisky to mediate between the two countries (the United States and Libya).[56] In June 1982, Qaddafi reasserted this readiness when he stated, in an interview with the Italian *La Reppublica:* "I believe dialogue is possible with the U.S. . . . . This is why we issue continual invitations, we are always willing to negotiate."[57] Qaddafi's assessment of Reagan also witnessed some change by 1982: "He has changed a little, no doubt. At first, he was a 100 percent ignoramus as far as international relations are concerned. Today, he grasps at least 25 percent of the world problems."[58]

Ronald Reagan's move to the White House in January 1981 marked a new outlook and a new U.S. frame of analysis for Third World problems and events. In contrast to the Carter administration which, to a large extent, had dealt with those problems as indigenous cases that "could not be laid at the door of the Soviet Union,"[1] the Reagan administration saw those problems as inseparable from the strategic contest between the two superpowers. As early as January 1981, Secretary of State Haig outlined this new outlook:

> In approaching the developing world we do not construct any false dichotomies between North-South and East-West issues, treating the former as economic and the latter as military. Rather we recognize that progress in our relations with many nations of the South is dependent in part on our success in dealing with East-West security problems.[2]

In the Middle Eastern context, the indigenous problems of the region were seen as secondary in importance compared to what was perceived to be the crucial issue, namely, confronting "Soviet expansionism" in the region. And under the conviction that the countries of the region shared the same U.S. concern about Soviet expansionism, the Reagan administration came up with what it called "the strategic consensus" to be the guide for its conduct in the Middle East through 1981–1982. The U.S. secretary of state explained his doctrine as follows:

> Soviet actions forged the strategic consensus, and what were they. Let's not kid ourselves about this. Angola, Ethiopia, South Yemen,

North Yemen, Afghanistan I, Afghanistan II, the fall of the Shah of Iran created a strategic consensus. I said we had to use it, constructively, to forge a better sense of protection against external aggression from the Soviet Union. And that this was intimately interrelated with the Peace Process.[3]

Based on this view, the Reagan administration dealt with the countries of the region as a collective system that should be used against "Soviet aggression," without paying much attention to the contradictions within this supposed system. And as one scholar argued, those countries' "internal problems and aspirations are by and large seen as irrelevant in Washington."[4] The military aspect of the U.S. policy was heavily emphasized as a way of bolstering "the strategic consensus" and strengthening the friendly regimes against the Soviet or Soviet proxies' "threat" to the stability of the region. For instance, the preliminary 1982 bilateral aid proposals inherited from the Carter administration were raised to $900 million on the security side,[5] and the Reagan administration's arms sales to Sudan, Morocco, Tunisia, Egypt, and Saudi Arabia received congressional approval, whereas Carter's proposal of increasing economic aid floundered helplessly.

The U.S. image of Libya during 1981–1982 was as follows. When Ronald Reagan was asked on March 4, 1981, about the prospect of an American-Soviet summit, he replied, "it would make it a lot easier if the imperialism of Soviet surrogates were to be moderated."[6] The example he gave was "Qaddafi in Chad." On March 18, Secretary Haig was more specific when he said that Washington "now sees Libya as a Soviet satellite."[7]

Both statements accurately represent the prevailing image of Libya held by most U.S. officials during the period under study (see figure 8). As the analysis of the publicly available official documents has indicated, this image was held by the president, Secretary Haig, and the policy planning staff of the State Department. The analysis also revealed a slightly different image of Libya held by a handful of State Department bureaucrats—those called "Africa specialists," headed by Chester Crocker, assistant secretary for African affairs. These area specialists saw Libya and its leadership as "a regional problem." Libyan policy was seen as "subversive," "terrorist," "destabilizing," and "obstructive" to the American interests in Africa and worldwide. This image deviated from the prevailing U.S. image in only one category, namely, its depiction of

156

Libya's relations with the Soviets, which were described as "a marriage of convenience."[8] Libya, according to this image, was seen as a country whose objectives may coincide with those of the Soviets, and whose policies may indirectly serve Soviet interests. But in all accounts Libya's distance from the Soviets was still intact (though the distance was shorter than it was during the Nixon and Carter administrations).

In accordance with the research design set forth in the first chapter, I turn now to the prevailing U.S. image of Libya during 1981–1982. For a systematic introduction of this image, I will use the ideal types of images as a framework.

The theory of cognitive consistency as developed by scholars such as Rosenberg, Abelson, and Tannenbaum, is very applicable to the prevailing U.S. image of Libya in 1981–1982. As described by the theory, relations among bad elements are positively valued (as bad), and relations

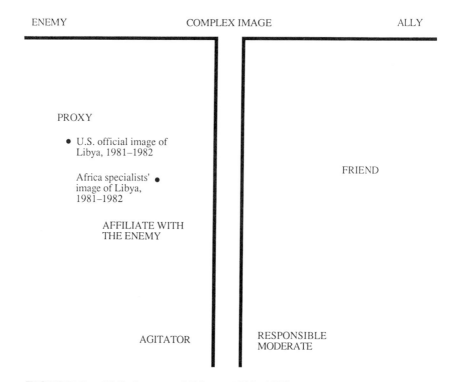

FIGURE 8.   U.S. Images of Libya, 1981–1982

among good elements are positively valued (as good) and relations between good and bad elements are negatively valued. In other words, we tend to like those associated with us and dislike those associated with our enemy. The Reagan administration viewed the Soviet Union as representing evil (the enemy image), and consistently, Libya was viewed as an extension of that evil because of its perceived intensive friendly relations with the Soviets, and its "misconduct," which was viewed as inseparable from the enemy's aggressive conduct. Libya is inferior in capability and culture to the United States, so it was perceived as a "proxy" of the enemy. The components of the prevailing U.S. image of Libya in 1981–1982 are as follows.

    1. *Motivation.* To the perceiver state, the proxy's motivations are, in essence, a reflection of the enemy's motivations, which are viewed as evil, immoral and unlawful. Thus Libya was seen as "subversive," "terrorist," and an aggressively destabilizing force in the region. Libya's intervention in Chad was seen as part of Soviet strategy to dominate Africa. The neighboring states of Tunisia, Egypt, and Sudan were viewed as exposed to an "imminent danger" stemming from Libya's perceived "subversive" conduct that could lead eventually to the expansion of Soviet influence in those "friendly" countries. Consequently, as one State Department official put it, "Libya is beginning to rival the Persian Gulf as the focus of strategic concern in the region."[9] Reagan went even further to consider Libya "a serious menace to world peace."[10] Another State Department official was so explicit as to describe Qaddafi "as Moscow's surrogate, sowing the seeds of disruption in a band from Morocco . . . to Saudi Arabia."[11] Both the Egyptian and the Sudanese regimes played a role in enhancing this U.S. image of Libya and in exploiting this image to get more American aid, especially military aid, to counter the alleged Soviet threat coming from Libya. U.S. State Department officials, who requested not to be identified, confirmed to me in an interview that Sudan, Egypt, and Tunisia have all played the Soviet-Libyan card to get more aid from the United States. For instance, Numeiry stated in March 1981, "We would see no danger in either Libya or its leadership if the matter concerned them alone. But we see danger in the fact that the Libyan leadership has become subject to a greater strategy and with long-term objectives in Africa."[12] In April, the Egyptian defense minister claimed that because of his alliance with the Soviet Union, Qaddafi represented a real threat to Egypt.[13] And in October

Sadat sent his top aide to Washington with a "very urgent message," asking for more arms to Sudan to counter the "Libyan-Soviet threat."

Central to the prevailing U.S. image of Libya, as the verbal evidence indicates, were Libya's perceived terrorist and subversive activities in Africa in general and Chad in particular. The basic question to be answered is why did the Reagan administration overemphasize its allegations of Libya's terrorist and subversive activities? The question becomes more compelling, since what were described as Libyan terrorist and subversive activities were much less in evidence in the 1981–1982 period than in 1970–1976.

Two important factors could serve as a basis for an answer. First, the U.S. campaign of overemphasizing Libya's alleged terrorist and subversive activities was a preplanned campaign directed against the Soviet Union by using what was seen as a Soviet proxy to attack the policies of the Soviet Union and its friends. Libya was a favorable choice for this campaign. This also served to punish Libya, whose policy was based on a revolutionary line that opposed Zionism (that is, Israel) and the U.S. policy in the Middle East, calling for revolution within regimes that were friendly to the United States. This Libyan policy was described by a high-ranking U.S. official as "unprecedented obstruction to our own interests and objectives."

This line of argument is supported not only by the United States' actions, but also by its official statements. In terms of policy, the selective application of U.S. policy against what was called international terrorism was well known to many observers. In Jeff McConnell's words,

> The recent murder by Taiwanese security forces of a Taiwanese dissident teaching at Carnegie Mellon [University], and the indifference shown to the case by the administration, is a controlled experiment verification of the insincerity of the "terrorism policy." The longstanding ties of terrorist Cubans to the CIA and other U.S. agencies, and the presence in the U.S. of Nicaraguan counterrevolutionary groups are further indications of U.S. insincerity.[14]

On November 22, 1981, the journalist Alan Cowel reported that the British also "tend to feel that if the U.S. is so keen to halt terrorism, why doesn't it also have a campaign against private American funding of the Irish Republican Army?"[15]

The U.S. policy toward Iraq is also a very informative example. The

1979 export act requires the State Department to compile a list of governments that have "repeatedly provided support for acts of international terrorism." The Carter administration named Iraq, Libya, South Yemen, and Syria. In 1981 the Reagan administration added Cuba to the list and took Iraq off. This was despite the fact that the State Department's 1981 human rights report cited incidents of human rights violations by the Iraqi government. The document stated that in 1981 "there were creditable reports of government directed assassinations of Iraqi dissidents in other countries."[16] A State Department official explained the Reagan administration's action in the Iraqi case by saying, "We felt that Iraq wasn't as bad as the other countries on the list."[17] But in March 1981, Secretary of State Haig offered the Congress a better explanation, based on what he called "some shift in the Iraqi attitude"; the administration's behavior toward Iraq reflected a "greater sense of concern about the behavior of Soviet imperialism in the area."[18] Thus, as Jeff McConnell argues:

> What the campaign against "international terrorism" in its not-so-public side is really about, are the longstanding American aims of propping up clients fighting the Soviet Union and progressive governments. Otherwise, why be concerned just with "international terrorism" and not also with the "domestic" terrorism of the kind the U.S. exports to El Salvador, Argentina, Guatemala, Thailand, Indonesia and many other nations?[19]

I asked one senior State Department official why the United States did not condemn Libya's revolutionary activities abroad when they were very noticeable in the early 1970s, and why it condemned them when they were not so noticeable later. The answer was, "We became more sophisticated and more aware of the effect that they may have on the international system." The most obvious verbal evidence that could be presented in support of this argument is Haig's statement of March 18, 1981, that "Libya is an integral part of a Soviet-run terrorist training network."[20]

The second factor was the deliberate leak, by various administration agencies (especially intelligence agencies), of information about alleged terrorist activities by Libya that were supported by the Soviet Union. Journalists with close ties to the intelligence agencies, such as William Safire, Jack Anderson, John Cooley, and others, started as early as March 1981 publishing reports about Libyan-Soviet connections and the terrorist activities conducted by the Soviet "surrogate" (Libya) in Africa and the

Middle East, pointing to the implications of these activities on Western influence in those areas. For example, on March 1, Drew Middleton, writing in *New Times*, emphasized what he called "a strong possibility that the Soviet Air Force would have use of Libyan bases in the event of a crisis in the Mediterranean."[21] William Safire repeated the same line, using the same words.[22] John Cooley, writing in the *Washington Post*, presented what he called "evidence of Soviet buildup in Libya"; following the State Department line, he pointed out the grave military consequences of that buildup.[23] By July 1981, U.S. officials alleged, without presenting any evidence, that the Soviets were involved in the Libyan military intervention in Chad.[24] This was despite Qaddafi's assertion that the Chad operation was 100 percent Libya's responsibility and that no Soviets were involved in it. Interestingly enough, it turned out to be American citizens who had been servicing the Libyan planes who took part in the Chad operation. The State Department called that "reprehensible."[25]

In accordance with the administration's aim of exposing the evil motives of the Soviet enemy and its proxies, manifested in "subversive," "terrorist," "destabilizing" and "immoral" activities, the CIA, after reviewing the old definition of terrorism, broadened the definition to include the conduct of internal liberation movements and to exclude acts transcending national boundaries. Alexander Cockburn, commenting on the new definition, argues that "in cases where the epithet might be attached to the United States, its allies, satellites or clients, Western journalists find it almost impossible to use the word terrorist." Thus, according to the new definition, Cockburn says: "It is not terrorism when the South African government dispatches its forces on a raid against the Namibian refugee camp of Kassinga, as it did on May 4, 1978, and wipes out 600 people, more than the combined victims of Carlos, the Baader Meinhof gang and the Red Brigades combined."[26]

Using the new definition, the CIA released its new report on terrorism in June 1981 (revised three times to be congruent with Haig's assessment of international terrorism) in which Libya was described as the "most prominent state sponsor of and participant in internal terrorism." "Right-wing terrorism" in which Libya was perceived to have played no part, was consequently removed into the category of domestic violence and was not dealt with in the report, because, as the report claimed, "It is difficult to categorize . . . because it is perpetuated anonymously by groups with few or no articulated goals."[27]

Not only by leaking information to the press and reformulating the definition of "terrorism," but also in order to give more circulation to its view that "the threat to the West comes from an international subversive network linked through Cuba and Libya to the Soviet Union,"[28] the Reagan administration actively assisted in the mass circulation of two books. The first was a novel called *The Spike*, written by Robert Moss and Arnaud de Borchgrave, two journalists reported to have close connections with the U.S. intelligence agencies. The novel portrays the administration's perspective on the threat posed by the Soviets and their "proxies" to the West. The second was Claire Sterling's *The Terror Network* in which she calls the Libyan leader "the Daddy Warbucks of international terrorism." In her book she attaches all "terrorist" groups and actions to the Soviet Union. The International Communication Agency "arranged for its centers around the world to make sure the book [was] promoted to local leaders."[29] Moreover, it was reported that Secretary Haig made a point of sending copies of Sterling's book to all the members of the Senate Foreign Relations Committee."[30] By late April both Sterling and de Borchgrave were the leading witnesses before the newly established Judiciary Subcommittee on Security and Terrorism. And by October 1981, the deputy U.S. representative to the United Nations was using Sterling's book to promote the Soviet-Libyan "terrorist" connection in the UN General Assembly.[31]

The story of the "Libyan hit squad" in November 1981, when the U.S. administration charged Libya with sending killers to the United States to assassinate the president and top U.S. officials, was the biggest official leak of them all. The press people themselves discovered the artificiality of the story, especially after Qaddafi's public challenge to Reagan to present any evidence to back the American charges and official U.S. refusal to present any evidence. Joseph Kraft wrote in the *Washington Post*, December 10, 1981, "Exactly what part of the community first began leaking what part of the Libyan hit squad story is not clear to me. But the earliest accounts . . . all bear fingerprints. The same fingerprints. The stories all appear to come from the intelligence-cum-law-enforcement community."[32]

Whether the story was true or not is hard to substantiate, since the

Libyan leadership denied it, and U.S. officials declined to present any evidence, but the fact of making it public (by leaking it to the press) was certainly consistent with the administration's campaign that was based on a stereotyped image of Libya as the most prominent terrorist state in the world, linked to the "international terrorist network" established by the Soviet Union to threaten the security and well-being of the West. Former President Carter told NBC News in December 1981 that he had received several similar reports of Libyan attempts on his life, but he never went public with these stories.

Thus it is safe to conclude that the evidence derived from both the U.S. official statements and behavior proves that what really mattered to the Reagan administration was not Libya's activities per se (terrorist or not), but instead using Libya and its leaders as the battleground for attacking the main enemy, the USSR. This approach was congruent with the administration's objective as illustrated by Secretary Haig, in late March 1982: "The administration's first priority is challenging the Soviet Union."[33] Because of this, many scholars and observers[34] concerned with U.S.-Libyan relations were inclined to see Libya as a scapegoat targeted by the Reagan administration to emphasize more general themes rather than for its own policies. In the final analysis, what really disturbed the U.S. administration about Libya was not its behavior in Africa or elsewhere but rather, as one observer put it, "The strategic partnership that Qaddafi has forged with the Soviet Union. [U.S. officials] fear that Libya with immense stockpiles of Soviet combat hardware and substantial contingent of Soviet bloc military advisers, is being converted into a Kremlin strong base for future aggression."[35] George Shadyac, a political activist, was more blunt in his remarks: "According to Haig, the principal perpetrator of terrorism in the world is Russia. If that is true, why don't we deal with the source rather than a few little countries like Libya and El Salvador?"[36]

So Libya's motives were seen as evil and immoral, and its leadership was described as motivated by lust for subversion, assassination, and terrorism. As one State Department official put it, Qaddafi was "the most dangerous man in the world."[37] But as argued above, the danger did not stem from Libya's actions per se, rather from its being perceived as a proxy to the Soviets and every action it took perceived as an integral part of a larger strategy. Hence the descriptive language used by U.S. officials to describe Libya and its policies was, in fact, the means of expressing what the Reagan administration's view of the USSR and its proxies was all about.

2. *Capability*. The proxy state's capabilities are thought to be derived from the enemy's capabilities, and other states' weakness and lack of determination to confront the proxy are seen as contributing factors in enhancing the perceived capabilities of the proxy. The Reagan administration's prevailing image of Libya's capabilities closely corresponded to this formula. By perceiving Libya as a proxy of the Soviet Union, U.S. officials saw Libyan capabilities as an integral part of Soviet capabilities, and Libyan policies and behavior were seen as constituting a serious threat not only to American interests in Africa, but also, as Reagan himself put it, constituting a "serious menace to world peace." This overestimation of Libyan power was further enhanced as a consequence of Libya's successful military operation in Chad. The Libyan-Chadian announcement of future merger between the two countries, January 6, 1981, was interpreted by U.S. officials as the first step in a Libyan strategy to absorb other African countries. Thus President Reagan started talking about "the imperialism of the Soviet surrogate—Libya," and the assistant secretary for African affairs warned that Qaddafi's goals "seem[ed] to be far-reaching, possibly to bring about the creation of an Arab-Islamic bloc including Moslems of Africa and the Middle East" and that the merger with Chad "was not mere hyperbole, it was a real expression of Qaddafi's expansionist goals to absorb his Arab and Muslim neighbors in a Libyan-dominant state."[38] One could easily notice the uneasy tension within the U.S. image of Libya whereby Libya was viewed as both proxy to the Soviets and as a builder of the Islamic empire. This tension did not bother the U.S. officials at all. One of them, who asked to be anonymous, described Qaddafi as "a Communist and a fanatic Moslem." The deputy assistant secretary for African affairs expressed the same view: "Qaddafi envisions . . . the creation of a super Libya, as it were, with Qaddafi as its spokesman."[39] A third U.S. official, Kenneth Adelman, asserted before the UN General Assembly, "The regional arms race in northern Africa has been spurred precisely by Libya."[40]

Central to this prevailing U.S. image of Libya's capability—which resembles to a large extent a U.S. image of a superpower, not a Third World country—is the perceived huge Libyan stockpile of sophisticated Soviet arms and Libya's financial ability to accumulate more Soviet military hardware. Responding to a question by one of the senators who asked how, with only 2.5 million people, Libya became able to threaten other countries, a high-level State Department official said: "Libya does have substantial economic financial resources which are discretionary and available on short notice. It has an enormous stockpile of weaponry of all kinds and aircraft to bring them into African airports, if desired, or through other means."[41]

Secretary Haig asserted that Libya's oil money was almost exclusively allocated for the purchase of Soviet arms to pursue the policies of subversion and destabilization. Despite their differences about the estimated cost of these military purchases, U.S. officials agreed that the "Libyan stockpiles of weaponry" far exceeded both Libya's defense requirements and its manpower's ability to absorb, given that the Soviets had purportedly stored those weapons in Libya solely for use in "future crisis situations." This view was clearly expressed in the House Foreign Affairs staff report of March 1981, which emphasized that the Soviet Union was using Middle Eastern countries to stockpile weapons for future contingencies, and that "many states [were] clearly worried over the pattern of Soviet arms deliveries to the region, especially to Libya and South Yemen."[42]

During 1981 and 1982, the United States' overestimation of Libya's capabilities was quite evident in its official accusation of Libya as being behind most subversive and terrorist activities around the world. In March 1981, Reagan mentioned Qaddafi by name in conjunction with communist bloc nations attempting to promote terrorism in El Salvador.[43] Haig and other high-level State Department officials accused Libya of being behind all coup d'état attempts and subversive activities in Africa. Referring to what he perceived as Qaddafi's destabilizing policies, Haig contended, on October 29, 1981, "Chad is a good example, with the destabilizing efforts that [Qaddafi] has manipulated against the Sudan, Somalia, some of the central African republics, and even farther south than that his fine hand is felt."[44] Several attempts made on the lives of American diplomats in Europe were also blamed on Libya, such as the assassination attempts on U.S. diplomats in France and Italy in 1981.

The bizarre story of the "Libyan hit squad" in late 1981, and all the security measures taken to protect President Reagan and some U.S. officials, signifies, in essence, an overestimation of Libya's capability. Worldwide activities of this scope cannot be carried out but by a superpower, and certainly Libya is not one. This is not to underestimate the fact that Libya has become one of the militarily powerful Middle Eastern countries. But to claim that Libya's power and policy constitutes "a menace to world peace," a role reserved for a superpower, undoubtedly represents an exaggeration of Libya's capability. After all, Libya is a Third World country and will remain so for some time to come.

3. *Decisional Style and Locus.* Despite the fact that Qaddafi did not hold any official post, and Libyan political institutions (people's congresses and the revolutionary committees) shared the decision-making responsibility, U.S. officials in 1981–1982 still viewed Qaddafi as central to the decision making process in Libya. Qaddafi's style of decision making was perceived as authoritarian, individualistic, and despotic. He was often referred to as the "Libyan dictator" who spends oil wealth to pursue conspiracies against his neighboring countries. The Libyan decisional structure was viewed as an extension of the Soviet one, the function of which was to initiate policies that served Soviet designs in Africa, the Middle East, and Latin America. Therefore, all U.S. official statements referred to Libya's policy and activities during this time as "Qaddafi's policy of subversion," "Qaddafi's activities," "Qaddafi's intentions," "Qaddafi's goals."[45] Haig referred to him as "the Qaddafi phenomenon."[46] These references indicate a U.S. official view that Libya's foreign policy is exclusively the domain of the Libyan leader and his sole responsibility. This view is to a large extent congruent with the perceiver state's image of the decisional style and locus of the perceived proxy: "The decisional style of these elites viewed as surrogates of the enemy will be described as 'despotic,' 'deceitful' and able to formulate and hatch the most devious conspiracies; . . . their decisional locus will be seen as monolithic and as part of the 'enemy's' decisional structure."

Other dimensions of Libyan foreign policy did not receive much attention in the publicly available official U.S. statements from the period under study. Therefore, the conclusion has been drawn that they did not play much of a role in affecting the official U.S. prevailing image of Libya in 1981–1982.

11 ⤳ U.S. POLICY TOWARD LIBYA, 1981–1982

When I discussed the ideal patterns of policy in the first chapter, I presented the policy of intervention as a behavioral pattern that reflects increased fear of a country perceived as inferior in capability and culture. The perceived threat seems to come from a country that is strongly affiliated with the perceiver's enemy to the degree that that country comes to be viewed as the enemy's proxy. This perception can lead to either overt intervention or covert intervention. Finally, intervention may be pursued to send a signal to a third power that is perceived as supporting the misconduct of the target country. The Reagan administration's behavioral pattern toward Libya during 1981–1982 conformed to its image of Libya during the same period: an intense perception of threat led to an intensely hostile policy. Thus, it was natural that the administration's policy should turn to intervention, though elements of that policy are also consistent with pressure policy (see figure 9).

What to do about Libya was the first issue discussed by the interdepartmental foreign policy study group ordered by Reagan only a few days after his inauguration. The result of the study were plans whose ultimate aim was to promote the downfall of the Libyan regime, or, as Don Oberdorfer reported, "to make life uncomfortable, at a minimum, for the leader of radical Libya."[1] Haig was said to have "rejected an early report from within the State Department setting forth the substantial risks to Americans and American policies of taking direct action against Libya."[2] The secretary "was slightly obsessed with knocking . . . Qaddafi from power"; he viewed Qaddafi as "a cancer that [had] to be removed."[3] Another State Department official was even more explicit: "Overthrow-

166

ing Col. Qaddafi would be the world's most popular crusade."[4] Reagan himself implied the same objective when he responded to a question as to whether he would like Qaddafi overthrown: "Diplomacy would have me not answer this question."[5] As the empirical evidence suggests, the administration's policy against Libya and its leaders took the form of a comprehensive campaign of intervention and pressure that covered all aspects of relations between the two countries.

POLITICAL FACTORS

Using the pretext of combating "international terrorism," under which Libya was labeled the most prominent supporter of such activity, the Reagan administration pursued an active campaign of pressure to isolate Libya internationally. Thus, on May 6, 1981 (only a week after Qaddafi's visit to the USSR), the Reagan administration expelled all the members of the Libyan People's Bureau in Washington, charging them with having

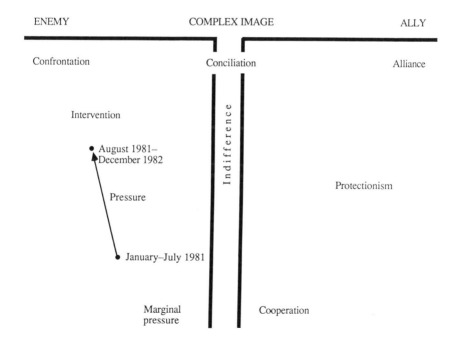

FIGURE 9.   U.S. Policy Toward Libya, 1981–1982

connections with the attempted assassination of a Libyan student in Colorado. State Department spokesmen justified the administration's action by declaring, "From the first days of the administration, both the president and Secretary Haig have made known their very real concern about a wide range of Libyan provocations and misconduct, including support for international terrorism."[6] Using the Libyan intervention in Chad as an example of what the administration termed unacceptable Libyan patterns of international behavior, the administration focused most of its pressure on African governments to get them to take hostile stands toward Libya. On June 12, the administration announced that "the U.S. would support all African nations that want to resist 'interventionism' from Libya."[7] Both Sudan and Egypt played an active role in this campaign to isolate Libya in the continent by using the same American claims that Libya's role in Chad and in Africa was to expand the Soviet influence, and that therefore more African states would be subjected to Libya's destabilizing policies. This was despite the fact, as presented by Andrew Young, that "a Libya-dominated Chad caused little alarm initially, because Africans saw [Libya's actions there] merely as an expulsion of French influence."[8] This statement is supported by the fact that the June 1981 meeting of the OAU had issued a resolution praising Libya for establishing peace in Chad and affirming the Chadian president's right to invite whom he wished to help maintain Chadian security.[9]

To change this situation and achieve the goal of isolating Libya, the United States, with the help of Egypt and Sudan, started putting pressure on the Chadian president to ask for the withdrawal of Libyan troops from Chad and to replace them with an OAU peacekeeping force. This action was clear in Chester Crocker's statement:

> Seriously concerned by Libyan presence, we and others encouraged the Chadians to ask for Libya's withdrawal and to seek OAU help in solving internal problems. . . . The United States moved directly to facilitate and support the peacekeeping effort. We allocated $12 million to support the Nigerian and Zairian contingents with nonlethal equipment and to aid transport of supplies to Chad.[10]

The Reagan administration's perception of Libyan conduct was quite evident in Crocker's statement: "African security is not served if Soviet arms, Cuban forces, and Libyan money and arms are combined to overthrow legitimate governments in the horn. . . . We cannot ignore the real security threats facing our African partners, especially when these are prompted or fueled by our global adversaries."[11]

Based on this perception, which was intensified by the conclusion of a treaty between Ethiopia, Libya, and South Yemen in August 1981, the United States airlifted several shipments of arms to Somalia, increased economic and military aid to the new military regime in Liberia, and initiated a foreign military sales and training program in Niger. Libya's withdrawal from Chad by the end of 1981 did not change the U.S. image of Libyan conduct or its policy of isolating Libya internationally. The intensive U.S. efforts to dissuade many African leaders from attending the 1982 OAU summit meeting in Tripoli, Libya—and consequently to deprive the Libyan leader of the opportunity to be the spokesman for the contintent—was a case in point. George Bush toured many African countries for this purpose, as did the U.S. ambassador to Morocco. Qaddafi claimed to have evidence that the United States bribed many African leaders—evidence that he stated would create a scandal if made public. Thus, as a result of American pressure, combined with that of Egypt and Sudan, the OAU summit meeting was moved to Ethiopia. In addition, most of the African countries subjected to U.S. pressure broke diplomatic relations with Libya.

Western Europe was another area in which the United States pursued its policy to isolate Libya. Claudia Wright reported that "NATO allies, Italy in particular, were asked not to permit state visits by Qaddafi."[12] The Italian government was also asked not to sell any military spare parts to Libya. Greece was the target of the same U.S. pressure to prevent an official visit by the Libyan leader to Greece. And in March 1982, the U.S. government informed Austria of its dissatisfaction with Qaddafi's visit to Vienna in March of that year. Though most European governments did not share Washington's view of, or its policy toward Libya, some of them, like Italy, reluctantly agreed to the U.S. request and canceled scheduled visits by the Libyan leader to their countries. (Austria and Greece were exceptions.)

ECONOMIC FACTORS

In conjunction with political pressure, the Reagan administration used economic pressure as another tool to put the squeeze on Libya. Under the conviction that Libya's oil revenues were "almost exclusively diverted to the purchase of armaments, the training of international terrorists and the conduct of direct interventionism in the neighboring states of North Africa,"[13] U.S. officials maintained that by putting pressure on the Libyan oil industry, the United States would make it difficult for Libya to finance terrorism. The United States would thereby also remove the perception that it indirectly financed "Qaddafi's antics." One U.S. official contended, "We are paying for his depredations." Another agreed that "an embargo 'of Libya's oil' would be very important politically."[14]

This general approach was encouraged by world economic conditions (the world oil glut), and by the enthusiastic attitude of Congress. On October 21, 1981, Gary Hart and Edward Kennedy sponsored an amendment declaring that: "Congress condemned the Libyan government for its support of international terrorism movements, its disruption of efforts to establish peace in the Middle East, and its attempts to control other North African nations," and calling on the president to "review steps the U.S. might take with its allies to force Libya to stop such activities including the possibility of prohibiting the importation of Libyan oil."[15] The administration in October 1981 ordered all American citizens in Libya to leave that country and invalidated U.S. passports for travel to Libya, because of what it called "the danger which the Libyan regime poses to American citizens."[16] This action was reportedly preceded by repeated warnings to the American oil companies working in Libya to remove their people and terminate their operations. The *Wall Street Journal* quoted a U.S. official on July 14, 1981, as saying: "The companies won't get another warning. We're playing confrontation politics, and we want them out, whether there is a coup in the works or not."

Despite some initial reluctance, by late 1981 most of the companies concerned began evacuating their American employees.[17] Claudia Wright reported that the oil companies had been replacing Americans with other nationals for more than eighteen months prior to the administration's decision and that most oil sales to American purchasers had stopped by mid-October 1981.[18]

The administration's decision was not well received in other circles. The 2,000 U.S. citizens in Libya were the most affected by the decision; most did not want to leave Libya. The *Wall Street Journal* published a letter of protest by an eleven-year-old American girl living in Libya to President Reagan, which stated: "I really would like to tell you what I think of your ordering Americans back to America; . . . if that's your idea of freedom, you belong in a Funny Farm. . . . The people here are very nice and wouldn't harm Americans for a million years." In March 1982, the Reagan administration further tightened its economic squeeze on Libya by ordering a ban on all future imports of Libyan oil. The decision also put expanded controls on most U.S. exports to Libya. Accordingly, licenses would be required for all exports to Libya, except food and agricultural and medical supplies. All licenses were to be denied for exports of oil and gas equipment, "sensitive" high-techology items, and weapons and military items.[19]

The U.S. economic embargo came at a time when U.S. oil imports from Libya were at their lowest level (less than 3 percent of U.S. oil imports came from Libya at the beginning of 1982, as compared with about 10 percent in 1980). This ban did not disturb U.S. consumption, since the United States could compensate for the loss of Libyan oil imports because of the oil glut. The economic embargo reduced U.S.-Libyan trade relations in 1982 to their lowest ebb since the Libyan revolution in September 1969 (see table 17).

The U.S. economic embargo did not bring any change in Libyan behavior, nor did it create any major economic problems for Libya. The only losers in this episode of the pressure campaign were the U.S. firms that had done business in Libya, while the net profit went to the West European countries to whom Libya moved its business. For instance, when the Reagan administration blocked the delivery of a dozen Boeing airliners (which caused the firm the loss of $600 million), Libya switched to Europe's airbus industries. The U.S. commerce journal reported in February 1983 that European countries were substantially profiting from Reagan's policies toward Libya. One official of a U.S. shipping firm that

TABLE 17.   U.S. Trade with Libya, 1981–1982
($U.S. thousands)

	Exports to Libya	Imports from Libya
1981	809,024	5,475,910
1982	300,946	533,215

Source: U.N. Statistical Papers, *Commodity Trade Statistics 1981–1982, ser. D, vol. 38, nos. 1–8.*

had done some business with Libya maintained, "Libya discovered it can
get most of the high technology products it needs from Germany, France,
Italy, and the U.K. Consequently, European-Libyan trade has increased."[20] Lisa Anderson, a Middle Eastern and North African scholar,
argues that severing economic ties and ordering the Americans home
from Libya was in reality an elimination from Libya of a potential source
of American influence. She contends: "Neither America nor Libya has
an interest in precipitating either the short-term economic dislocations or
the complete Libyan dependence on the Soviet bloc that would result from
a breaking of economic and educational ties [the U.S. had expelled 200
Libyan students studying nuclear physics]."[21]

America's West European allies who declined to take part in the U.S.
campaign of economic pressure on Libya held a view similar to that of
Lisa Anderson. The German foreign minister, Hans-Dietrich Genscher,
justified his government's refusal to go along with the U.S. policy on
Libya by saying that "the U.S. was wrong in trying to isolate Libya or
depict the Libyan leader as a Soviet pawn." Lord Carrington, the British
foreign secretary, indicated, "Our relations with Libya have gone
through a difficult period, but they're all right now."[22] Claude Cheysson,
the French foreign minister, was more assertive when he said, "The
Libyans [are] now following a more moderate course, as shown by their
withdrawal from Chad, and . . . they should be encouraged and not
isolated."[23] In December 1981, Secretary Haig was told by Italy's foreign
minister that "the 10 members of the EEC had already decided in
September not to break ties or take action against Libya despite American
pressure to do so."[24]

MILITARY FACTORS

In this light, the Reagan administration's policy toward Libya was more
aggressive and clearly reflected a more interventionist policy in 1981–
1982. This policy contained two kinds of intervention, namely, overt and
covert.

OVERT INTERVENTION

This type of intervention centered mainly on creating military provocations against Libya that could escalate into a larger U.S. military opera-

tion. Behind this policy approach was a threefold objective. First, to squeeze Libya militarily to deter it from pursuing what was perceived as more subversive and destabilizing activities against its neighboring countries. Second, to send a signal to a third power (the USSR), which was perceived as the mastermind behind the Libyan activities) that the new administration in Washington was determined to take a more confrontational line in world politics against the "lawless activities of the Soviet Union and its 'surrogates.' " Third, to prove to the friends and allies of the United States that it pays to be an American friend.

Thus, in May 1981, the United States sent two radar surveillance planes (AWACs) to monitor the Egyptian-Sudanese borders with Libya. Claudia Wright reports that "there was a coup d'état attempt planned for that time within Libya" and that the role of the AWACs was "to co-ordinate the military support that might have been sent by Egypt across the border to aid the rebels."[25]

On August 19, U.S. aircraft shot down two Libyan jets during military maneuvers in the Gulf of Sirte, claimed by Libya as an integral part of its territorial waters. The incident took place while the Egyptian forces were conducting maneuvers at the Libyan border. Despite official U.S. claims that the administration never intended to provoke any military confrontation with Libya, both verbal and behavioral evidence indicates that the military confrontation was planned "to test Qaddafi's reactions."[26] It was reported that Reagan himself took the decision of conducting naval maneuvers within the Gulf of Sirte, after an extensive discussion in the National Security Council in which many U.S. agencies took part.[27] Other evidence that the military provocation was preplanned was that the maneuvers were conducted below the 32° 30′ line, "which had been drawn by the Carter administration in talks with the Libyans as the southernmost boundary for American naval and air exercises."[28] Reagan's response to a question about his message about the Gulf of Sirte incident also suggests its preplanned nature: "We're determined that we are going to close that window of vulnerability that has existed for some time with regard to our defensive capability."[29]

Some U.S. officials claimed that the administration was surprised at Libya's reaction because the maneuvers were held in international waters.[30] But a statement by Caspar Weinberger on August 19, 1981, indicates clearly that a Libyan response was anticipated and that orders were given in advance to return fire in case of a Libyan attack.[31]

The other component of this policy of overt intervention was the Reagan administration's strategy of giving military support to third-party countries that were perceived to be vulnerable to the "Libyan threat." That was the essence of the Reagan administration's statement on June 2, 1981, that "the U.S. would support all African nations that want to resist 'interventionism' from Libya."[32] Consequently, the administration had decided to increase military assistance to Libya's neighbors. It was reported that Tunisia, which had received fifty-four M-604 tanks to counter what Pentagon officials called the threat of the Libyan tank, as well as $15 million in military credits in 1981, would be given $95 million in FY 1982. Sudan, which received $30 million in 1981, got $100 million in 1982. And Egypt would jump from $550 to $900 million in military credits, and from $846 for military training to $2 billion in 1982.[33] In June 1981, the deputy secretary of defense told officials in those countries neighboring Libya that "the U.S. is now willing to encourage actions against Libya although African nations would have to take the lead."[34]

The extent to which the Reagan administration was willing to support "an action" against Libya by neighboring states was quite evident in Reagan's reported assertion to Sadat in the summer of 1981, that the United States would back any Egyptian invasion of Libya and would "take care" of any attempt by the Soviets to rescue their "proxy."[35] This assertion, if true, reflects the administration's readiness for a regional confrontation with the Soviets over Libya, which was exactly what the Carter administration tried to avoid when it restrained Sadat from taking any military action against Libya in the summer of 1979. The report, however, is consistent with Claudia Wright's speculation:

> Part of current contingency plans for U.S. military operations in trouble areas of the Middle East and North Africa—areas like Libya —is the plan to supplement the main "triple squeeze" (as Haig calls it), consisting of three kinds of direct military operations—ships, Marines, emigre paramilitary operations—with a "fourth squeeze," to be prepared in tight secrecy and flashed at the Soviet Union to deter it from coming to its client's rescue.[36]

The U.S. militaristic option toward Libya continued through 1981 and 1982. For instance, immediately after Sadat's assassination in October 1981, the AWACs policy was again used: two of these planes were sent to monitor the Libyan-Egyptian border. And in November a large-scale military maneuver (Bright Star) took place on the border, with the participation of troops from the United States, Egypt, Sudan, Oman, and Somalia.

To close the circle on Libya, the United States also increased its military aid to Hissen Habre, the Chadian former defense minister, and with the assistance of Egypt and Sudan, Habre managed to assume power again in Chad (after the withdrawal of Libyan forces).

By mid-December press reports suggested that knocking out the Libyan oil fields with heavy B-52 bombing was another option considered by the Reagan security experts. A top U.S. official was quoted as saying: "If one of Qaddafi's terrorists fires a grenade into the Rose Garden, we aren't going to answer him simply by telling people not to buy his oil."[37]

In February 1982, Libya once again accused the United States of military provocation when two F-14 fighters from the aircraft carrier *J.F. Kennedy* buzzed a Libyan commercial plane in flight from Athens to Tripoli. U.S. officials denied the incident, but the Greek government protested the violation of Greek airspace by two American fighters.[38] The following month, U.S. Navy Secretary John Lehman announced that the Sixth Fleet would probably conduct more exercises in the disputed Gulf of Sirte within the next six months—this despite warnings from the Libyan leader that any more exercises in the Gulf would mean a war in which Libya might ask for the direct assistance of the Soviet Union.

COVERT INTERVENTION

The United States' covert attempts to overthrow the Libyan revolutionary regime were a central focus of Western press reports throughout 1981. There were some reports by respected journalists specializing in Libyan affairs that as early as in the first two months of Reagan's administration there was a CIA plan prepared by Max Hugel for the purpose of eliminating the Libyan leader.[39] This plan did not become known to the public until July 1981, when some of its details were leaked to the press. To assert the existence of such a plan, Claudia Wright, for instance, wrote in *International Affairs*, "Tunisian and Saudi officials confirm privately that they were told by officials of the Reagan administration that Qaddafi would be eliminated by the end of 1981."[40]

On July 25, Michael Getler of the *Washington Post* reported that in a letter to President Reagan members of the House Select Committee on

Intelligence had objected "to a CIA plan for a covert action operation in Africa." The committee members were "troubled by the plan itself, which they felt was not properly thought through, and the proposed secret action."

On August 3, 1981, *Newsweek* revealed that the covert action referred to in the intelligence committee's letter was "a large-scale, multiphase and costly scheme to overthrow the Libyan regime of Col. Qaddafi." The CIA's goal, it proclaimed, was Qaddafi's "ultimate removal from power." The plan was reported to have three phases: (1) "a disinformation campaign to embarrass Qaddafi and his government"; (2) the creation of a "counter government to challenge his claim to national leadership"; and (3) "an escalating paramilitary campaign, probably by disaffected Libyans, to blow up bridges, conduct small-scale guerrilla operations and demonstrate that Qaddafi was opposed by an indigenous political force."[41] The White House denied that the administration was involved in any "assassination attempt" against Qaddafi, though it did not deny that it was involved in a plot to overthrow the Libyan regime. Later official sources leaked to the press that there was a plan, but it was against Mauritania; then the story was again changed, and it was leaked that the covert action was planned against Mauritius. However, some press reports, including those of the *Baltimore Sun* and the London *Sunday Times,* claimed to have "independently confirmed that Libya was the country in question."[42]

What makes the *Newsweek* story more credible is that some of the elements said to have been in the plan corresponded closely to the administration's conduct vis-à-vis Libya. For instance, "disinformation" on what was called Libyan terrorism was regularly leaked to the Western press from Egyptian, Moroccan, Tunisian, Israeli, and the Lebanese Phalangist sources.[43] Jeff McConnell identified five themes in the misinformation and propaganda campaign against Libya: (1) that Qaddafi is the major source of terrorism in the world, (2) that Libya is a militaristic and imperialist country, (3) that Libya is a "Soviet proxy," (4) that Qaddafi is a "lunatic" and "the most dangerous man in the world," and (5) that Libya is repressive not meeting its people's needs, and that an opposition is growing that is worthy of support. The disinformation campaign's objective, McConnell argued, was to test the receptivity of both U.S. and world opinion to any action against Qaddafi. Furthermore, it tested Qaddafi himself and how he would react to the leaked suggested actions by the United States.[44]

Another element of the reported covert plot story that was consistent with Reagan's conduct toward Libya was the CIA's attempt to recruit and mobilize an active opposition to the Libyan revolutionary regime from among Libyan exiles abroad. This covert policy was confirmed by prominent publications like the *Wall Street Journal* and *Newsweek,* which quoted a senior U.S. official as stating, "I don't think anything is going to gear up from this side until there is a clear sense that there is something to work with."[45] Another official statement to this effect was cited by Jay Peterzell in March 1982, that political discontent with Qaddafi inside Libya "is emerging into an organized opposition."[46]

The CIA's connections with exiled Libyan dissidents were reportedly centered on individuals who had been officials of the royal government before the 1969 revolution. It became widely known that Omar Yahya (one of the monarch's advisers before the revolution now serving as an advisor to Sultan Qabus of Oman) had become one of the CIA's links with the Libyan opposition abroad. It was reported that Yahya frequently used the apartment of James Critchfield (a former chief of the CIA's Middle East Division) during his stay in Washington.[47] Another report stated, "Exiled Libyans, including the supporters of Al Huni, [who] now leads Libyan emigres in Egypt, say they have asked the U.S. what it would do, if anything, to help neutralize or overcome the Soviet bloc security forces supporting Qaddafi."[48]

In May 1984, Libya charged that the United States, in conjunction with Britain and Sudan, were behind a series of explosions and assassination attempts in Libya, including the attempt to attack Qaddafi's residence. Libya announced that "the plotters were from the Moslem brotherhood movement and that they were trained in the United States and Sudan. Thus in both word and deed the United States seems to have borne out the *Newsweek* reports of covert U.S. action against Libya and suggest that the objective of the covert CIA plan was and still is "the ultimate removal of Qaddafi."

The premises and the structure of the U.S. interventionist policy toward Libya have been analyzed in detail by many scholars, particularly those specializing in Middle Eastern and Libyan affairs. Roger Fisher, an expert on negotiations at Harvard University, contends, "We have a John Wayne image of the world; . . . you ride in with your six guns loaded. . . . But what you do is to push Qaddafi toward the Soviets. That's the same thing that we did with Castro."[49] Commenting on the "confrontational" approach of the Reagan administration toward Libya,

Claudia Wright argues that "it was almost unprecedented for the U.S. to settle its political differences with other countries by openly espousing military confrontation, economic embargo, subversion, sabotage and assassination. The means chosen," she adds, "were so plainly inadequate for the ends. If the new administration sought to demonstrate its power to punish Libya and thereby demonstrate that it pays to be an American friend, the 1981 campaign was a disastrous failure."[50]

On the same track, Lisa Anderson maintains: "If the administration's purposes are to strengthen U.S. influence in international affairs, discourage international violence, or undermine the Libyan government, these purposes—whatever their merits—are not being served by the current policy. American preoccupation with Col. Qaddafi serves only to increase his visibility throughout the world and strengthen his position at home."[51]

Reacting to the official U.S. conviction that Qaddafi is a Soviet "puppet," Michael Hudson, director of Georgetown University's Center for Contemporary Arab Studies, depicts the U.S. image of and confrontational policy against Libya as a Broadway show that is very amusing to the Russian theater-goers:

> Their special amusement stems no doubt from the fact that one of the main objectives of the American protagonist is to discipline or even remove Qaddafi because he is a Soviet client. Soviet foreign policy officials in particular appreciate the irony that the Libyan leader, apostle of an austere form of Islam and author of a theory that condemns communism as well as capitalism, is seen as their friend; . . . But what makes the play even funnier for the Soviets is that every move made by the Americans actually forces Qaddafi closer to them.[52]

In conclusion, it is useful to point out that the premises of the U.S. policy toward Libya continued to exist in 1983–1986 and that Libyan policies still "pose a threat to international peace and security." Thus, it is very likely that the hostile pattern of U.S. conduct vis-à-vis Libya will continue as long as the United States holds the same image of Libya that prevailed during the Reagan administration.

CONCLUSION

The overall findings of this study concerning the prevailing image of Libya on the part of the United States, 1969–1982, may be summarized under the following broad propositions.

Proposition 1:

> If the United States perceives an intense Soviet threat, and Libyan policy toward the USSR is very hostile, then the United States will attempt a rapprochement with Libya, despite its hostility toward other U.S. concerns—such as access to oil, relations with Israel— and despite its revolutionary activities against regimes friendly to the United States.

This proposition describes U.S. conduct between 1969 and 1974, when Libya's actions and statements were very antagonistic toward the USSR. Its behavior was satisfactory enough to U.S. decision makers to enable them to attempt a rapprochement toward the revolutionary regime, despite its hostility to other U.S. goals in the Middle East.

Proposition 2:

> If the United States perceives an intense Soviet threat and Libyan policy toward the USSR is moderate, then the United States will exert marginal pressure on Libya.

This proposition describes U.S. policy toward Libya between 1974 and 1976. Although Libya's conduct related to Western access to oil, relations with Israel, and its revolutionary activities abroad remained the same as in the earlier period (1969–1974), Libya changed from being highly hostile toward the Soviet Union to a more moderate policy, as reflected in the rapprochement of May 1974. One can only conclude that this caused the change in the U.S. image of and policy toward Libya, 1974–1976.

Proposition 3:

> If the United States perceives little threat from the Soviet Union and Libya is friendly toward the USSR, then the United States will attempt a rapprochement toward Libya, if other variables are kept constant.

The third proposition clearly reflects the Carter administration's image of and policy toward Libya. Because the administration perceived little threat from the USSR, as reflected in the October 1977 Declaration, SALT II, and its attitude toward the presence of Soviet military personnel in Cuba, the prevailing U.S. image of Libya was not much affected by Libya's relations with the Soviet Union. A preestablished stereotype of Libya as a country sponsoring terrorism determined U.S. conduct toward Libya. When U.S. officials came to grips with the reality of Libyan conduct as regards terrorism, they followed a less hostile policy, and relations between the two countries began to flourish in 1978–1979, despite Libya's friendship with the Soviets.

In late 1979 and 1980, the picture was a little different. The USSR's conduct in Afghanistan, the increased influence of the Brzezinski group (with its strategic frame of analysis) on U.S. decision making, in addition to Libya's annoying interference in American politics (the Billy Carter affair)—all these circumstances led to a tougher approach toward Libya. Thus, regarding Libya's revolutionary activities as a variable, if that variable is controlled, the effect of Libya's relations with the Soviets on Libya's image in U.S. eyes was nil in 1977–1979.

Proposition 4:

> If the United States perceives an intense Soviet threat and if Libyan relations with the USSR are very friendly, then the United States will adopt an aggressive policy of pressure and intervention toward Libya.

Obviously, the fourth proposition reflects the prevailing image of Libya held by the Reagan administration during 1981–1982, when the Soviet threat was felt to be greater than at any other period covered by this inquiry. This affected the Reagan administration's entire analysis of world politics. Libya was viewed as a proxy of the Soviet Union and as part of a Soviet-run "terrorist network"; consequently, Libya was used by the U.S. government as a battleground on which to display its confrontational approach toward the USSR. And the U.S. policy of intervention and pressure against Libya was not only to punish Libya for "lawless" activities, but also to demonstrate to the Soviet Union that the new administration was determined to close down the "window of vulnerability that has existed in the past." (See figures 10 and 11.)

Comparatively speaking, the Nixon, Ford, and Carter administrations

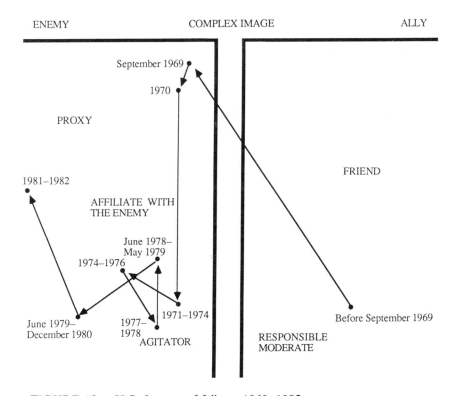

FIGURE 10.   U.S. Images of Libya, 1969–1982

182

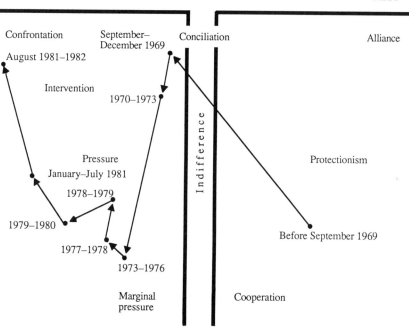

ENEMY   COMPLEX IMAGE   ALLY

FIGURE 11.   U.S. Policy Toward Libya, 1969–1982

all adopted different approaches to Libya, and all differed from the
Reagan administration's approach. The first three administrations used a
dual-track policy, consisting of "carrots" and "sticks"—on the one
hand, hostile rhetoric mixed with some marginal pressure, political and
military; on the other hand, growing trade relations because of pragmatic
economic considerations. Although this dual approach was congruent
with the dual image of Libya held during these periods, it has caused
misunderstanding and misperception in U.S.-Libyan relations. In Lisa
Anderson's words:

> Although from both sides of the U.S.-Libyan relationship the "car-
> rots" were viewed as no more than incentives to modify what each
> deemed as the other's reprehensible behavior in international rela-
> tions, they were received—again on both sides—as indications of
> more flexibility than probably existed. . . . Both the Libyan and the

American policy-makers interpreted the mixed signals as suggesting that each government was more amenable to pressure than was the case.[1]

From a theoretical point of view, this misunderstanding is logically predictable because, as Jervis argues:

> The propensity for an actor to perceive the messages and behavior of another in terms of his own evoked set is usually reinforced by the belief that the other shares his concerns and information. So if messages are sent from a background that differs from that of the receiver, misunderstanding will result.[2]

Because the Reagan administration regarded the Libyan threat as intense, it rejected the dual-track approach as "financing Libya's adventurism." Consequently, it pursued a highly aggressive policy of pressure and intervention that was congruent with its prevailing image of Libya. Therefore, with the exception of the Carter years, the prevailing U.S. official image of Libya has been substantially affected by Libya's conduct toward the Soviet Union.

This emerging congruence between the verbal and behavioral aspects of the U.S. approach toward Libya has methodological implications. That is because in most studies dealing with image, words and actions are used as operational indicators of one nation's image of another. In this study, by contrast, I have elected to use words as the sole indicator of image; foreign policy behavior was used as a control device to explore the degree of congruence between image and actual policy. But, as the findings of this study indicate, the general pattern indicates a substantial agreement between the two that validates the procedures used in other studies dealing with image. Nevertheless, I repeat the caution that congruence between verbal constructs (image) and policy should never be taken as axiomatic, but as a hypothesis that must be empirically confirmed or disconfirmed. The lack of congruence between the Carter administration's image of Libya and its policy in 1979–1980 is a case in point.

This study's finding, that the East-West contest was the predominant factor affecting the U.S. image of Libya in this period, conforms substantially to the U.S. image of and policy toward Libya during the 1950s. For instance, the Draper Committee report, submitted to President Eisenhower in 1959, emphasized:

The West, should it lose completely its strategic position in North Africa, would find its control over the Mediterranean seriously threatened. North Africa, moreover, flanks the routes which the Soviets would follow in their efforts to penetrate Africa. . . . Libya . . . serves as a buffer between the Middle East and the Maghreb and at least partially shields the latter from the full force of Arab nationalism. . . . So long as Libya remains friendly to the West, the West can control the Southern Shore and part of the East Mediterranean.[3]

The report recommended Libya as one of the countries in which the United States should prepare the military officers' corps to be future leaders for the country. It also called for strengthening the friendly Tunisian regime to take over Tripoli in case of an Egyptian- or Soviet-sponsored coup in Libya. A CIA study made during the same time had confirmed "the effectiveness of using military assistance for these purposes." Both reports were consistent with and supportive of the joint chiefs' report in 1957:

The best interests of the United States will be served by taking steps to insure the continuation of a political atmosphere in the Libyan government which will be amenable to the continuance of the present base rights agreement. . . . The U.S. should encourage the orientation of the Libyan government toward the West, and away from Egyptian and Soviet influence.[4]

Jeff McConnell reported that a State Department document from the Kennedy administration revealed how the United States would achieve the above U.S. objectives in Libya: "The U.S. was to finance 50% increases in the size of the Libyan armed forces in the mid-1950s, then again in the mid-1960s, accompanied by expanded training, at least in part, to Westernize the officer corps."[5]

Accordingly, the Libyan revolution of September 1, 1969, was a significant setback to the American image of Libya and what U.S. policies toward that country should be. Despite its cool if not antagonistic attitude toward the United States, Libya was strongly anti-Soviet during the early years of the revolution, which made U.S. officials see it as a force they could live with. But when Libya turned into a friend of the Soviet Union, it became, to official U.S. eyes, "a strategic risk" that could affect the strategic balance of influence in the region. This study has largely confirmed the above analysis, although U.S. perceptions were moderated during the Carter years. The Reagan administration, in particular, provides an extreme illustration of this pattern; most of its officials saw Libya as a proxy for the Soviet Union. However, it may appear that a contradiction was embedded in the administration's logic. That is because one of the cardinal features of the proxy images is its derivative nature, in the sense that the perceiver should view the proxy's capabilities and motivations as an extension of the enemy's. Thus, strong capabilities and evil motives are to be assigned to the proxy, whose conduct is to serve the enemy's evil designs. While the administration's image corresponded generally to this pattern, it underestimated Libya's capabilities and their relevance to the Arab-Israeli balance of power. Libya's role was seen as marginal and its potential effect on US. projects for peace in the region was never adequately perceived. Hence, we are left with two pictures of Libya: first, a strong proxy for the Soviets that is trying to build an empire in Africa and to expand Soviet designs of influence through its "destabilizing," "disruptive," and "terrorist" activities in Africa; second, a weak nation that could not affect the course of events in the Arab-Israeli conflict.

This paradox could have two possible explanations. Reagan administration officials could have strongly associated Libya with the Soviets in Africa and viewed it independently from the Middle Eastern context. But this explanation is not viable, because it enhances the contradiction instead of solving it. The alternate explanation centers on declining Soviet influence in the Arab-Israeli conflict during 1981–1982, and its effect on U.S. officials' view of Libya. In other words, since Libya was perceived by the United States as inseparable from a Soviet network of proxies, the relevance of its capabilities and role to the Arab-Israeli conflict was substantially minimized because of the perceived diminished influence of the Soviet Union itself in the conflict. This explanation not only solves what could be seen as a contradiction in the Reagan administration's image of Libya, but also restores a more coherent picture, one dependent on the strategic frame of analysis. But because the U.S. stereotype of Libya as a proxy was associated with the U.S. perception of a threat, and since active Soviet policy in the Middle East was at its lowest ebb in 1981–1982, Libya's policies in the Arab-Israeli conflict were substantially ignored. All official U.S. statements regarding Libya during this period clearly testify to this fact.

To summarize, the objectives of U.S. policy toward Libya between 1969 and 1982 may be arranged in this order of importance: (1) to reduce Soviet influence in the Middle East (although this was less salient to the Carter administration), and (2) to eliminate Libya's threat to peace in the Arab-Israeli conflict.

Libya's revolutionary activities abroad were the major concern for the Carter administration, as was the potential effect of these activities on the Arab-Israeli war. Though Libya's revolutionary activities were very intense between 1969 and 1976, they did not affect the prevailing U.S. image of or policy toward Libya during the Nixon and Ford administrations. To Reagan officials, those activities were a major concern, but the concern stemmed from the perception that Libya's revolutionary activities were part of a Soviet-run network of terrorism.

Libya's policies toward the Arab-Israeli conflict in the 1969–1976 period were called "militant," "radical," "extreme," and constituting an obstacle to closer relations between the two sides. To the Carter administration, U.S.-sponsored peace efforts were seen as a potential target for Libya's revolutionary activities against moderate Arab regimes involved in peace negotiations. Libya's use of oil as a political weapon did not affect the U.S. image of Libya or its policy toward that nation during the entire period under study.

It is safe to conclude that the core concern for U.S. policy during the 1969–1982 period centered on combating the Soviet Union. Tensions in U.S.-Libyan relations will continue so long as the dominant concern for the United States is the strategic contest with the Soviets and as Libya's relations with the Soviet Union grow stronger.

EPILOGUE

Between 1983 and 1985, official U.S. rhetoric and policy toward Libya continued to be intensely hostile. By 1986 relations seem to have reached a new climax of hostility that caught the attention of the whole world. On January 7, 1986, President Reagan accused Libya of fomenting the December 1985 terrorist attacks at the Rome and Vienna airports: the Libyan regime had "engaged in armed aggression against the United States." He called for swift retribution and demanded the world to "act decisively and in concert to exact from Qaddafi a high price."[1] A set of economic sanctions against Libya were announced by the president, including severing all economic ties, freezing several hundred million dollars in Libyan government assets held by U.S. banks, and taking legal measures to force about 1,500 U.S. citizens working in Libya to leave that country immediately. In the meantime, U.S. intelligence personnel were voicing their concern about Libya's deployment of new Soviet surface-to-air missiles (SAMs), including SA-5s which were seen as a potential threat to the Sixth Fleet operations in the Mediterranean Sea.[2]

To Qaddafi, the U.S. economic sanctions were "tantamount to a declaration of war"; in response, he asserted that Libya would shoulder the responsibility "for ridding the region of U.S. military bases [and] that more co-operation between Libya and the Soviet Union will be pursued."[3]

The war of words between the two countries started to have more substance when U.S. navy forces began a new series of maneuvers in front of the Libyan Gulf of Sirte. Qaddafi branded the maneuvers "aggressive provocation," ordered his army on "total alert," and promised to defend "Libya's territorial waters" if the U.S. naval forces crossed what he called "the line of death—the 32nd parallel." To U.S. officials, the navy exercise was meant to exert more pressure on Qaddafi, hoping it might ‑provoke him into a military confrontation, or, as one Pentagon official put it, "If they don't react, we've exposed them as a paper tiger."[4]

The U.S. decision to proceed with the maneuvers reflected the new official conviction "that if we want to settle the account with Qaddafi we will have to do it ourselves."[5] This conviction was the result of the reluctance of the United States' allies to take part in U.S. economic and military plans against Libya. Therefore, the maneuvers were part of a plan aimed at provoking Qaddafi into a military confrontation.

However, the plan was called off and revised to provide "the optimum margin of safety." The revised plan, named "Prairie Fire," was approved by Reagan at a National Security Council meeting on March 14, 1986. On March 24, U.S. navy vessels sailed into the Gulf of Sirte, challenging Qaddafi to respond—and he did. By the time the Gulf confrontation ended on March 17, the United States reported sinking two Libyan vessels and temporarily shutting down an SA-5 missile base. U.S. officials hailed the operation as a victory and claimed that it diminished the Soviets' prestige "both by revealing the inferiority of the weapons [the Soviets] had supplied to Libya and by exposing their reluctance to do anything other than light up their ships and head for safety when fighting broke out." For his part, Reagan proclaimed the operation "a message to the whole world that the United States has the will and . . . the ability to defend the free world's interest."[6]

On March 5, an explosion occurred at a West Berlin night club. U.S. officials blamed the incident on Libya and used it as a pretext to accelerate the speed and broaden the scope of its military plans against Libya. Early on the morning of April 15, U.S. and naval forces launched a series of strikes against five Libyan targets, including the military compound where Qaddafi's residence was located. The main result of this attack was extensive civilian damage and casualties that reportedly included members of Qaddafi's family. With the exception of Canada, Israel, and Britain, which approved the attack and assisted in its execution, voices of criticism were raised all over the world against the United States and its military aggression against Libya.

In view of such escalating hostility, strategic factors continue to be of primary importance in the U.S. image of and policy toward Libya. This is true despite the offficial U.S. claim that the reason for the United States' hostility is Libya's support of terrorism. In other words, the perception of Libya as a proxy of the Soviet Union is the most important variable in understanding U.S. policy. The following evidence supports this claim.

First, official U.S. statements preceding and following the United States' attacks on Libya in 1986 reflect to a large extent the real purpose behind those actions. In 1985, some months before U.S. hostility reached its climax, President Reagan was pointing to the same old network of terrorism sponsored and supported by the Soviets. He named Libya, Iran, North Korea, Cuba, and Nicaragua as members of this network. With the exception of Iran, all of these states were seen as surrogates of the Soviet Union: ''The strategic purpose behind the terrorism sponsored by these outlaw states is clear: to disrupt or alter our foreign policy . . . and, finally, to remove American influence from those areas of the world where we're working to bring stable and democratic government. [7]

Assistant Secretary for African Affairs Chester Crocker emphasized in late 1985 the same destructive role played by this ''terrorist network'': ''I can say, without exaggeration, that the Soviets, their Cuban allies, and their Libyan associates have systematically exploited internal divisions, civil strife, and historical cleavages to promote discord and dissension.''[8] On the basis of this view, U.S. officials naturally saw U.S. military actions against Libya in a broader context, asserting that those actions resulted in diminishing Soviet prestige and influence in the region; they also claimed that Soviet weapons did not compare well to U.S. weapons.[9]

Second, analysts should not isolate the United States' policy toward Libya from the general pattern of U.S. conduct toward other world problems and events. The backbone of this pattern of conduct is what U.S. officials call a ''roll-back'' strategy—one premised on the belief that ''the Soviets have long made it their business to probe the Third World, seeking to add satellites to their orbit,'' and that ''the U.S. can no longer afford to watch passively as the Soviets consolidate their power.''[10] Consequently, U.S. foreign policy efforts should be directed at rolling back communism, or at least making ''Soviet expansionism'' more costly.

It was quite consistent with this foreign policy line that in the same week of March 1986 when U.S. navy forces were attacking Libya, Reagan asked the Congress for $100 million in aid to the Nicaraguan contras, warning the nation that Nicaragua's president Daniel Ortega was an agent of the Kremlin and that Nicaragua would become a "second Cuba"—worse, a "second Libya, right on the doorstep of the United States."[11] In the same period also, the United States was reported to have supplied stinger missiles to the rebels in Angola, while back home the administration expelled a number of Soviet diplomats from the Soviet UN mission.[12] Therefore, U.S. hostility toward Libya is an indispensable part of a general pattern of conduct aimed at rolling back what are perceived to be spots of Soviet influence all over the world. However, U.S. policy toward Libya seems to be more aggressive and provocative than policies toward other nations in the alleged Soviet network. Reasons for this additional intensity might be Qaddafi's open hostility toward the United States, his perceived isolation in the Arab world, and finally, the absence of domestic opposition in the United States such as may be seen against military interference in other nations friendly to the USSR such as Nicaragua. Both the American public and the Congress favored taking some action against Qaddafi; thus Libya was a convenient target for an escalation of military action.

The restrained Soviet reaction to U.S. aggression against regimes associated with the USSR (Libya, Nicaragua, Angola, Afghanistan) have encouraged U.S. officials to intensify and accelerate the execution of their policy toward the Soviet Union and its perceived proxies. For instance, Soviet reactions to the U.S. military strikes against Libya amounted to nothing more than ritual statements condemning the strikes and pledges of support for Libya. In addition to responding half-heartedly, the Soviets at that time also seemed to be making one concession after another regarding arms control and certain regional problems. Some of these concessions came only days after the U.S. attacks on Libya and Nicaragua. This might have convinced U.S. officials that "it pays to be tough" toward the USSR and its proxies.

A third and most important argument for seeing U.S. hostility against Libya as resulting from a perception that Libya is a proxy of the Soviet Union may be seen by comparing U.S. policy toward Libya with its policy toward Iran.

In 1984 Iran was classified by U.S. officials as one of the most active supporters of international terrorism. On July 8, 1985, President Reagan placed Iran at the top of the list of terrorist states. He charged, "In 1983 alone, the Central Intelligence Agency either confirmed or found strong evidence of Iranian involvement in 47 terrorist attacks; . . . . since

September 1984, Iranian-backed terrorist groups have been responsible for almost 30 attacks."[13]

Because of its declared policy of combating terrorism, the Reagan administration announced various legal measures to prohibit any arms transfer, direct or indirect, to Iran, and went to great lengths to organize a worldwide embargo against such arms sales. European allies, in particular, were the subject of continuous U.S. pressure to avoid any negotiation with terrorists and their sponsors. Yet the news came out that at the same time that Reagan was encouraging an escalation of hostility toward Libya and sending U.S. aircraft to bomb Libyan cities under the pretext of fighting terrorism, his agents had, since May 1985, been secretly supplying arms to Iran and supplying it with information in its war against Iraq. Anyone who wishes to believe the United States' declared opposition to terrorism must reconcile such declarations with the contradictions in U.S. policy toward Iran in 1985 and 1986.

It is clear that the Reagan administration is not concerned with terrorism per se. The terrorism that most concerns the administration is that attributed to Soviet proxies and surrogates; thus fighting terrorism essentially means combating worldwide Soviet influence. Hence, the Reagan administration's secret dealings with Iran should be understood in the context of Iran's strategic viability to the United States in the superpower competition. Consider the following factors:

(1) The United States cannot afford to ignore Iran's strategic geographical position. In addition to being one of the world's principal oil producers, Iran is strategically situated on the Persian Gulf, where most of the world's oil reserves are located and through which most oil shipments flow. In addition, it borders on the Soviet Union. Obviously, Iran represents a glittering geopolitical prize.

(2) Iran's strategic importance becomes more crucial considering the projected Soviet demand for oil in the near future. For instance, a 1978 study done by the CIA (updated in 1981) concluded that in view of the deterioration in Soviet oil production, access to Persian Gulf oil would become a first priority for the USSR. The CIA study predicted that the Soviets would try to destabilize the Gulf area regimes and to install radical ones, with the result that the United States and Western nations in general would be deprived of a crucial energy source.[14] The same conclusion was reached in 1980 by the House Committee on Foreign Affairs, which reported that over the next decade Gulf oil would be under the direct or

indirect control of the Soviets. It argued that the Soviet military presence in South Yemen, Ethiopia, and Afghanistan, in addition to about fifty Soviet battalions on the borders of Turkey and Iran, indicated Soviet preparations to extend their control over the Gulf region. The report called this a great danger to Western security.[15] Such speculations about the Soviet threat not only strengthen U.S. fears of Soviet "expansionism," but also can be used to legitimize any course of action that would defend U.S. national interests in the Middle East.

(3) A better understanding of Iran's attitude and policy toward the Soviet Union might have given the United States a clearer view of Iran's potential role in future U.S. strategies toward the USSR. Verbal attacks by Iranian officials against the Soviet Union, the crackdown on internal communist movements in Iran, and Iran's continuous support to the Mujahadeen in Afghanistan—all are indicators of hostility toward the USSR. In addition, the Israelis convinced U.S. officials that some "moderate" elements in the Iranian regime were prowestern and should be cultivated. In this light, Iran's hostility to the United States and its alleged terrorist activities might have been of less concern to U.S. officials. Thus a secret rapprochement was attempted with Iran. It is significant to compare these overtures with U.S. policy toward Libya just after its revolution; the resemblance is striking, because Iran's current policy toward the USSR is similar to Libya's at that time.

(4) The U.S.-Israeli contacts through which Iran was approached might shed some light on the U.S. motives for attempting to restore relations. In a memo of January 17, 1986, Reagan's NSC adviser John M. Poindexter referred to a potential increase in communist influence and radicalization in the Gulf region if relations between Iran and Iraq deteriorated further. Poindexter agreed with the Israelis that the United States should approach "moderate" elements in Iran as a means of preventing future Soviet expanionism, and endorsed the Israelis' suggestion of providing weapons to Iranian moderates.[16] President Reagan authorized this supply of arms in a document that referred to the operation as vital to U.S. national security and as a defense "against Iraq and Soviet intervention."[17]

To the same end, the CIA (as reported in the *New York Times* of January 12, 1987) deliberately provided Iran with inaccurate information about Soviet threats to its territory, including falsified pictures exaggerating the number of Soviet forces stationed on the Iranian border and inaccurate reports about the infiltration of some Soviet agents into Iranian communist organizations. The *Times* reported that this action was designed to serve U.S. strategic objectives in the region.[18]

In view of these arguments, one may safely conclude that rolling back what is perceived to be Soviet expanionism continues to be the most important variable affecting the United States' image of and policy toward Libya. (The latest U.S. military assistance to Chad, to confront what was called "Libyan occupation" of that country, is a case in point.) One may expect that U.S. behavior toward Libya will continue to be provocative and confrontational as long as this image prevails.

NOTES AND INDEX

NOTES

INTRODUCTION

1 Quoted in R. Pfaltzgraff and J. Dougherty, *Contending Theories of International Relations: A Comparative Survey*, 2d ed. (New York: Harper & Row, 1981), pp. 483–84.

2 Quoted in G. Hopple, "Elite Values and Foreign Policy Analysis: Preliminary Findings," in *Psychological Models in International Politics*, ed. L. Falkowski (Boulder, Colo.: Westview Press, 1979), p. 213.

3 *Image* will be defined in the next chapter.

4 See Ole J. Holsti, "Foreign Policy Decision-Making Viewed Psychologically: Cognitive Process Approaches," in *Thought and Action in Foreign Policy*, ed. Matthew Bonham and Michael Shapiro (Basel and Stuttgart: Birkhauser Verlag, 1977).

5 Quoted in M. Rokeach, *Beliefs, Attitudes and Values: A Theory of Organization and Change* (New York: Jossey-Bass, 1968), p. 12.

6 Alexander L. George, "The Causal Nexus between Cognitive Beliefs and Decision-Making Behavior: The 'Operational Code' Belief System," in *Psychological Models in International Politics*, ed. Falkowski.

7 Milton Rokeach, *The Open and Closed Mind: Investigation into the Nature of Belief Systems and Personality Systems* (New York: Basic Books, 1960).

8 See ibid.; George, "Cognitive Beliefs"; and Charles Osgood, "Cognitive Dynamics in the Conduct of Human Affairs," *Public Opinion Quarterly* 24, no. 2 (Summer 1960).

9 Robert Jervis, *Perception and Misperception in International Politics* (Princeton, N.J.; Princeton University Press, 1976).

10 Eunice Cooper and Marie Johada, "The Evasion of Propaganda," quoted in ibid.

11 Rokeach, *The Open and Closed Mind*, p. 50.

12 Jervis, *Perception and Misperception*, p. 291; see also Osgood, "Cognitive Dynamics."

13 Jervis, *Perception and Misperception*, p. 117.

14   Robert Abelson and Milton Rosenberg, "Symbolic Psycho-Logic," *Behavioral Science* 3 (January 1968), quoted in ibid.

15   T. M. Newcomb, "An Approach to the Study of Communication Acts," *Psychological Review* 60 (1953).

16   Leon Festinger, *A Theory of Cognitive Dissonance* (New York: Row, Peterson, 1957), p. 155.

17   Charles Osgood and P. Tannenbaum, "The Principle of Congruity in the Prediction of Attitude Change," *Psychological Review* 67 (1955): 42–55; see also Robert B. Zajonc, "The Concepts of Balance, Congruity, and Dissonance," *Public Opinion Quarterly* 24, no. 2 (Summer 1960).

18   S. Miller, *The Unwelcome Immigrant* (Berkeley and Los Angeles: University of California Press, 1969), quoted in Jervis, *Perception and Misperception*, p. 292.

19   Planck is quoted in Warren Hagstrom, *The Scientific Community* (New York: Basic Books, 1965), p. 283.

20   See, for instance, Kenneth Boulding, *The Image: Knowledge in Life and Society* (Ann Arbor: University of Michigan Press, 1956); Harold and Margaret Sproul, *Man-Milieu Relationship Hypotheses in the Context of International Politics* (Princeton, N.J.: Princeton University Press, 1956).

21   Ole Holsti, "Cognitive Processes Approaches to Decision Making: Foreign Policy Actors Viewed Psychologically," *American Behavior Scientist* 20 (1976), 11–32.

22   George, "The Causal Nexus."

23   Hopple, "Elite Values and Foreign Policy Analysis," p. 213.

24   George, "The Causal Nexus," p. 106.

25   See ibid., pp. 104–13.

26   Quoted in ibid.

27   Morton Halperin, quoted in Holsti, "Cognitive Processes Approaches to Decision Making," p. 30.

28   Holsti, "Cognitive Processes Approaches to Decision Making," p. 30.

29   Jervis, *Perception and Misperception,* p. 204.

CHAPTER 1   METHODOLOGY

1   See Walter Lippman's definition, in William Buchanan and Hadley Cantrib, *How Nations See Each Other* (Urbana: University of Illinois Press, 1953).

2   Ole R. Holsti, "The Belief System and National Images: A Case Study," *Journal of Conflict Resolution* 4 (1962).

3   Richard K. Herrman, *Perceptions and Behavior in Soviet Foreign Policy* (Pittsburgh, Pa.: University of Pittsburgh Press, 1985).

4   Albert E. Eldridge, *Images of Conflict* (New York: St. Martin's Press, 1979).

5   Holsti, "The Belief System and National Images."

6   Ibid.

7   Richard W. Cottam, *Foreign Policy Motivation: A General Theory and a Case Study* (Pittsburgh, Pa.: University of Pittsburgh Press, 1977).

8   David J. Finlay et al., *Enemies in Politics* (Chicago: Rand McNally, 1967), p. 1.

9   Cottam, *Foreign Policy Motivation*, p. 65.
10 Ibid.
11 Herrmann, *Perceptions and Behavior*, p. 63.
12 Cottam, *Foreign Policy Motivation*, pp. 65–66.
13 Ibid.
14 Ibid.
15 Ibid.
16 Ibid.
17 Robert Abelson and Milton Rosenberg, "Symbolic Psycho-Logic," *Behavioral Science* 3 (January 1968), quoted in *Perception and Misperception in International Politics*, ed. Robert Jervis (Princeton, N.J.: Princeton University Press, 1976), p. 117.
18 Fritz Heider, *The Psychology of Interpersonal Relations* (New York: John Wiley, 1958), p. 183.
19 Cottam, *Foreign Policy Motivation*.

CHAPTER 2   THE UNITED STATES' OBJECTIVES IN THE MIDDLE EAST

1   CIA program, quoted in *U.S. News and World Report*, May 2, 1977.
2   Ibid.
3   "The Middle East: U.S. Policy, Israel, Oil and the Arabs," *Congressional Quarterly*, September 1977, p. 84.
4   Ibid.
5   Ibid.
6   Ibid.
7   From a statement made by State Department spokesman William Dyess, February 23, 1981. Alexander Haig, Jr., said essentially the same thing the next day. See *Congressional Quarterly*, October 17, 1981.
8   William Quandt, *Congressional Quarterly*, September 1981, p. 64.
9   Richard Cottam, *Foreign Policy Motivation: A General Theory and a Case Study* (Pittsburgh, Pa.: University of Pitsburgh Press, 1977).

CHAPTER 3   LIBYA'S FOREIGN POLICY, 1969–1976

1   Mohammad H. Heikal, *The Road to Ramadan* (London: Collins, 1975), p. 185.
2   Raymond A. Hinnebusch, ed., *Political Elites in Arab North Africa: Morocco, Algeria, Tunisia, Libya, and Egypt* (New York: Longman, 1982), p. 182.
3   Ibid., p. 183.
4   Ruth First, *Libya: The Elusive Revolution* (New York: Africa Publishing Co., 1974), p. 17.
5   Henri Habib, *Libya: Past and Present* (Malta: Aedam Publishing House, 1979), p. 103.
6   John K. Cooley, *Libyan Sandstorm: The Complete Account of Qaddafi's Revolution* (New York: Holt, Rinehart & Winston, 1982), p. 101.

7   Heikal, *The Road to Ramadan*, p. 185.
8   Colin Legum, ed., *Africa Contemporary Record: Annual Survey and Documents* (New York: Africa Publishing Co., Holmes and Meier, 1969–82), vol. 2 (1969–70), p. B-23.
9   Ibid., p. B-24.
10 Habib, *Libya*.
11 Marius Deeb and Mary Jane Deeb, *Libya Since the Revolution: Aspects of Social and Political Development* (New York: Praeger Special Studies, 1982).
12 Legum, ed., *Africa Contemporary Record*, vol. 9 (1976–77).
13 Ibid., vol. 5 (1972–73).
14 Ibid., vol. 5 (1972–73).
15 Ibid.
16 Ibid.
17 Cecil Blake and Saleh Abu-Osba, eds., *Libya Terrorist or Terrorized: An Inquiry into Politics, Ideology and Communication* (Canada: Jerusalem International Publishing House, 1982), p. 260.
18 Ibid.
19 Heikal, *The Road to Ramadan*, p. 197.
20 Legum, ed., *Africa Contemporary Record*, vol. 7 (1974–75), p. B-59.
21 Cooley, *Libyan Sandstorm*, p. 112.
22 Legum, ed., *Africa Contemporary Record*, vol. 7 (1974–75), p. B-53.
23 *Time*, October 19, 1981.
24 John Wright, *Libya: A Modern History* (Baltimore: Johns Hopkins University Press, 1982), p. 203.
25 Gwynne Dyer, "Libya," *World Armies*, 1979, quoted in ibid., p. 203.
26 BBC, "Summary of World Broadcasts," ME/5637/A/4, quoted in ibid., p. 203.
27 First, *Libya*.
28 Wright, *Libya*.
29 Cooley, *Libyan Sandstorm*, p. 59–60.
30 Henry Kissinger, *Years of Upheaval* (Boston: Little, Brown, 1982).
31 John M. Blair, *The Control of Oil* (New York: Pantheon Books, 1976), p. 221.
32 Wright, *Libya*, p. 239.
33 Congressional Research Service, Foreign Affairs Division, *Chronology of the Libyan Oil Negotiations 1970–1971* (Washington, D.C.: Library of Congress, January 25, 1974), p. 4.
34 Wright, *Libya*, p. 237.
35 Ibid.
36 Ibid.
37 Congressional Research Service, *Chronology . . . 1970–1971*, p. 12.
38 Quoted in Cooley, *Libyan Sandstorm*, p. 66.
39 Ibid., p. 68.
40 Wright, *Libya*, p. 244.
41 The British Petroleum Company (BP) markets gasoline in the United States under its name and those of Sohio and Boron.
42 Quoted in Wright, *Libya*, pp. 244–45.

43 Cooley, *Libyan Sandstorm*, p. 74.
44 Ibid., p. 72.
45 Charles F. Doran, *Myth, Oil, and Politics: Introduction to the Political Economy of Petroleum* (New York: Free Press, 1977), p. 59.
46 Cooley, *Libyan Sandstorm*, p. 82.
47 First, *Libya*, p. 241.
48 Habib, *Libya*, pp. 297–98.
49 Heikal, *The Road to Ramadan*, p. 187.
50 Legum, ed., *Africa Contemporary Record*, vol. 4 (1971–72), p. B-42.
51 *New York Times*, August 18, 1973.
52 Heikal, *The Road to Ramadan*.
53 Legum, ed., *Africa Contemporary Record*, vol. 5 (1972–73), p. B-58.
54 Cooley, *Libyan Sandstorm*, p. 246.
55 Legum, ed., *African Contemporary Record*, vol. 5 (1972–73), p. B-59.
56 *New York Times*, June 11, 1978.
57 *Washington Post*, June 13, 1975.
58 Roger F. Pajak, "Arms and Oil: The Soviet-Libyan Arms Supply Relationship," *Middle East Review* 13 (Winter 1980–81), 54–55.
59 David Newsom, statement before the Subcommittee on U.S. Security Agreements and Commitments Abroad, Committee on Foreign Relations, U.S. Senate, 91st Cong., 2d sess., July 20, 1970 (Washington, D.C.: GPO).
60 Quoted in First, *Libya*, p. 242.
61 First, *Libya*, p. 242.
62 Quoted in ibid.
63 James O'Toole, *Energy and Social Change* (Cambridge, Mass.: MIT Press, 1976).
64 This view was expressed by such writers as Cooley, Wright, and Legum.
65 *New York Times*, September 28, 1976.
66 Legum, ed., *African Contemporary Record*, vol. 9 (1976–77).
67 Ibid.
68 First, *Libya*, p. 17.
69 Legum, ed., *African Contemporary Record*, vol. 4 (1971–72), p. B-43.
70 Ibid., p. B-42.
71 Ibid., vol. 5 (1972–73), p. B-62.
72 Ibid., p. B-136.
73 Ibid., vol. 7 (1974–75), p. B-61.
74 Ibid., vol. 9 (1976–77), p. B-69.
75 Ibid., p. B-70.
76 Ibid., p. B-73.
77 Ibid., pp. B-73–B-74.
78 Ibid., vol. 5 (1972–73), p. C-100.
79 Nathan Alexander, "The Foreign Policy of Libya: Inflexibility and Change," *Orbis* 24 (Winter 1981), 831.
80 Legum, ed., *Africa Contemporary Record*, vol. 5 (1972–73), p. B-54.
81 Ibid., vol. 9 (1976–77), p. B-73.

82 Ibid., p. B-74.
83 Cited in Blake and Osba, ed., *Libya Terrorist or Terrorized*, pp. 100–01.

CHAPTER 4 THE U.S. IMAGE OF LIBYA, 1969–1976

1 Ruth First, *Libya: The Elusive Revolution* (New York: Africa Publishing Co.), p. 87.
2 Anthony Cave Brown, ed., *Dropshot: The American Plan for World War III against Russia in 1957* (New York: Dial Press/James Wade, 1978), p. 45.
3 First, *Libya*, p. 87.
4 Quoted in ibid., p. 88.
5 First, *Libya*.
6 Report of the Special Study Mission to Africa, South and East of the Sahara, U.S. House of Representatives, Committee on Foreign Affairs, 84th Cong., 2d sess., July 27, 1956 (Washington, D.C.: GPO, 1956), pp. 12–13.
7 David Newsom, statement before the Senate Foreign Relations Committee, July 20, 1970.
8 John K. Cooley, *Libyan Sandstorm: The Complete Account of Qaddafi's Revolution* (New York: Holt, Rinehart & Winston, 1982), p. 14.
9 Ibid., p. 13.
10 *Department of State Bulletin*, September 29, 1969.
11 Newsom, statement before Senate Foreign Relations Committee, July 20, 1970.
12 David Newsom, interview, Washington, D.C., July 19, 1983.
13 David Newsom, statement before a Joint Hearing of the Subcommittee on Africa and the Near East, Committee on Foreign Affairs, U.S. House of Representatives, July 19, 1971, *Department of State Bulletin*, August 14, 1971.
14 Officials interviewed were: Mansur Kikhia, former Libyan foreign minister and former Libyan representative at the UN; Harold Sandres, former NSC member and former deputy assistant secretary of state for the New East; David D. Newsom, former assistant secretary for African affairs and former U.S. ambassador to Libya; and Harold Josif, former U.S. chargé d'affaires in Tripoli.
15 Harold Sandres, interview, Washington, D.C., August 10, 1983.
16 Newsom, statement before Senate Foreign Relations Committee, July 20, 1970.
17 Cooley, *Libyan Sandstorm*, p. 106.
18 *Department of State Bulletin*, March 2, 1970.
19 *New York Times*, January 25, 1970.
20 Cited in Henry Kissinger, *Years of Upheaval* (Boston: Little, Brown, 1982), p. 860.
21 John M. Blair, *The Control of Oil* (New York: Pantheon, 1976), p. 118.
22 Newsom, statement before Senate Foreign Relations Committee, July 20, 1970.
23 Hearings before the Subcommittee on Multinational Corporations, Committee on Foreign Relations, U.S. Senate, 93rd Cong., 2d sess., August 30, 1974, pt. 6 (Washington, D.C: GPO, 1974), p. 317.
24 Newsom, interview.
25 Mansur Kikhia, interview, Washington, D.C., June 23, 1983.

26 Sandres, interview.
27 Harold Josif, interview, Washington, D.C., August 10, 1983.
28 John Wright, *Libya: A Modern History* (Baltimore: Johns Hopkins University Press, 1982), p. 252.
29 Newsom, statement before the House Foreign Affairs Committee, July 19, 1971.
30 Kikhia, interview.
31 Newsom, interview.
32 *Weekly Compilation of Presidential Documents*, vol. 12, no. 30 (1976).
33 Newsom, interview.

CHAPTER 5 U.S. POLICY TOWARD LIBYA, SEPTEMBER 1969-1976

1   Henry Kissinger, *Years of Upheavel* (Boston: Little, Brown, 1982), pp. 859-60.
2   David Newsom, interview, Washington, D.C., July 19, 1983.
3   Kissinger, *Years of Upheaval,* p. 120.
4   Quoted in ibid.
5   Newsom, statement before Senate Foreign Relations Committee, July 20, 1970.
6   Newsom, interview.
7   See John K. Cooley, *Libyan Sandstorm: The Complete Account of Qaddaffi's Revolution* (New York: Holt, Rinehart & Winston, 1982), p. 87.
8   Ibid., p. 98.
9   Ibid., pp. 99-100.
10 Mansur Kikhia, interview, Washington, D.C., June 23, 1983.
11 Newsom, interview.
12 Colin Legum, ed., *Africa Contemporary Record: Annual Survey and Documents* (New York: Africa Publishing Co., Holmes and Meier, 1969-82), vol. 5 (1972-73), p. B-54; vol. 10 (1977-78), p. A-78.
13 Harold Sandres, interview, Washington, D.C., August 10, 1983.
14 David Newsom, statement before the Subcommittee to Investigate Individuals Representing Interests of Foreign Governments, Judiciary Committee, U.S. Senate, August 4, 1980, *Department of State Bulletin,* October 1980.
15 Kikhia, interview.
16 Newsom, interview.
17 John M. Blair, *The Control of Oil* (New York: Pantheon, 1976), p. 232.
18 Hearings before the Subcommittee on Multinational Corporations, Committee on Foreign Relations, U.S. Senate, August 30, 1974.
19 *Department of State Bulletin,* September 24, 1972.
20 Ibid., September 24, 1975.

CHAPTER 6 LIBYA'S FOREIGN POLICY, 1977-1980

1   *Facts on File: Weekly World News Digest with Cumulative Index, 1977* (New York; Facts on File, Inc., 1977), p. 569.
2   Colin Legum, ed., *Africa Contemporary Record: Annual Survey and Documents*

(New York: Africa Publishing Co., Holmes and Meier, 1969–82), vol. 11 (1977–78), p. B-73.

3   Ibid., p. B-70.
4   Ibid., p. B-71.
5   *Facts on File, 1977*, p. 874.
6   Ibid., p. 930.
7   Marius Deeb and Mary Jane Deeb, *Libya Since the Revolution: Aspects of Social and Political Development* (New York: Praeger Special Studies, 1982), p. 136.
8   Tripoli Radio, March 19, 1978; quoted in Legum, ed., *Africa Contemporary Record,* vol. 12 (1979–80), p. B-73.
9   Legum, ed., *Africa Contemporary Record,* vol. 12 (1979–80), p. B-63.
10 Ibid., vol. 10 (1977–78), p. B-83.
11 Ibid.
12 Ibid., vol. 13 (1980–81), p. B-71.
13 John Wright, *Libya: A Modern History* (Baltimore, Md.: Johns Hopkins University Press, 1982), p. 217.
14 See, for instance, Ronald Bruce St. John, "The Soviet Penetration of Libya," *World Today* 38 (April 1982); also John C. Campbell, "Communist Strategies in the Mediterranean," *Problems of Communism* 28 (May–June 1979).
15 Campbell, "Communist Strategies," p. 5.
16 St. John, "The Soviet Penetration of Libya."
17 See Roger Pajak, "Arms and Oil: The Soviet-Libyan Arms Supply Relationship," *Middle East Review* 13 (Winter 1980–81), 82. See also the *New York Times,* May 23, 1975.
18 Legum, ed., *Africa Contemporary Record,* vol. 12 (1979–80), p. B-72.
19 Ibid.
20 St. John, "The Soviet Penetration of Libya," p. 137.
21 Legum, ed., *Africa Contemporary Record,* vol. 12 (1979–80), p. B-72.
22 Ronald Bruce St. John, "Libya's Foreign and Domestic Policies," *Current History,* December 1981.
23 Ibid., p. 427.
24 *The Current Digest of the Soviet Press,* January 5, 1977, p. 14.
25 *New York Times,* June 13, 1977.
26 Legum, ed., *Africa Contemporary Record,* vol. 10 (1977–78), p. B-78.
27 Cecil B. Blake and Saleh Abu-Osba, eds., *Libya: Terrorist or Terrorized: An Inquiry into Politics, Ideology and Communication* (Canada: Jerusalem International House, 1982), p. 104.
28 John Cooley, *Libyan Sandstorm: The Complete Account of Qaddafi's Revolution* (New York: Holt, Rinehart & Winston, 1982).
29 *New York Times,* February 15, 1979.
30 *Moment,* December 1979, p. 21.
31 *Impact International* 8 (8–21 December 1978), 8.
32 David Newsom, statement before the Subcommittee to Investigate Individuals Representing Interests of Foreign Governments, Judiciary Committee, U.S. Senate, August 4, 1980, *Department of State Bulletin,* October 1980, p. 61.

33 Legum, ed., *Africa Contemporary Record,* vol. 13 (1980–81), p. B-66.
34 Ibid., vol. 12 (1979–80), p. B-64.
35 Ibid., vol. 10 (1977–78), p. B-77.
36 Ibid., vol. 11 (1978–79).
37 Ibid., p. B-71.

CHAPTER 7 THE U.S. IMAGE OF LIBYA, 1977–1980

1   K. Oye, D. Rothchild, and R. Lieber, *Eagle Entangled: U.S. Foreign Policy in a Complex World* (New York: Longman, 1977), p. 304.
2   In listing those assumptions, I rely heavily on Steven Spiegel, "The Philosophy Behind Recent American Policy in the Middle East," *Middle Eastern Review* 13 (Winter 1980–81).
3   Ibid., p. 5.
4   Oye, Rothchild, and Lieber, *Eagle Entangled,* p. 304.
5   *Facts on File, 1977,* p. 380.
6   Hearing before the Subcommittee on International Terrorism, Committee on Foreign Affairs, U.S. Senate, 95th Cong., 1st sess., September 14, 1977 (Washington, D.C.: GPO).
7   Ibid., pp. 83–84.
8   *Facts on File, 1977: Weekly World News Digest with Cumulative Index, 1977* (New York: Facts on File, Inc., 1977), p. 380.
9   John Cooley, *Libyan Sandstorm: The Complete Account of Qaddafi's Revolution* (New York: Holt, Rinehart & Winston, 1982).
10 David Newsom, statement before the Subcommittee to Investigate Individuals Representing Interests of Foreign Governments, Judiciary Committee, U.S. Senate, August 4, 1980, *Department of State Bulletin,* October 1980, p. 61.
11 Alfred L. Atherton, Jr., statement before the Subcommittee on Europe and the Middle East, Committee on International Relations, U.S. House of Representatives, 95th Cong., 1st sess., June 8, 1977 (Washington, D.C.: GPO).
12 Ibid., p. 121.
13 Cyrus Vance, *Department of State Bulletin,* February 1979.
14 Jimmy Carter, *Keeping Faith: Memoirs of a President* (New York: Bantam Books, 1982), p. 414.
15 *Facts on File, 1978: Weekly World News Digest with Cumulative Index, 1978* (New York: Facts on File, Inc., 1978), p. 245.
16 Atherton, statement before House International Relations Committee, June 8, 1977, p. 120.
17 "Review of Developments in the Middle East, 1978," hearing before the Subcommittee on Europe and the Middle East, Committee on International Relations, U.S. House of Representatives, 95th Cong., 2d sess., June 12, 1978 (Washington, D.C.: GPO).
18 Atherton, statement before House International Relations Committee, June 8, 1977, p. 120.
19 Newsom, statement before Senate Judiciary Committee, August 4, 1980.

20 Ibid., p. 61.
21 Jimmy Carter, report to the Senate Judiciary Committee investigating Billy Carter's relationship with Libya, August 5, 1980, *Congressional Quarterly Weekly Report*, August 9, 1980, p. 2305.
22 Larry McDonald, statement before the House of Representatives, February 28, 1979, *Congressional Record*, February 28, 1979, p. E804.
23 Atherton, statement before House International Relations Committee, June 8, 1977.
24 "Review of Developments in the Middle East."

CHAPTER 8 U.S. POLICY TOWARD LIBYA, 1977–1980

 1 Johnny Rizq and Robin Allen, "Libya Presses for Decision on Boeings," *Middle Eastern Economic Digest* 23 (December 14, 1979), 15.
 2 Robert Samuelson, "Truck Deal Could Fire Back," *National Journal* 10 (July 8, 1978), 1095.
 3 David Newsom, statement before the Subcommittee to Investigate Individuals Representing Interests of Foreign Governments, Judiciary Committee, U.S. Senate, August 4, 1980, *Department of State Bulletin*, October 1980, p. 61.
 4 *Science* 202 (December 1978).
 5 Newsom, statement before Senate Judiciary Committee, August 4, 1980, p. 62.
 6 *Middle-East Intelligence Survey*, February 16–29, 1980, p. 7.
 7 *Science* 202 (December 1978).
 8 Newsom, statement before Senate Judiciary Committee, August 4, 1980, p. 62.
 9 Robin Allen, "Libya: Politics Do Not Intrude in Day to Day Business," *Middle Eastern Economic Digest* 23 (December 7, 1979), 46.
10 Jeff McConnell, "Libya: Propaganda and Covert Operations," *Counterspy*, November 1981–January 1982, p. 29.
11 Newsom, statement before Senate Judiciary Committee, August 4, 1980, p. 63.
12 Muammar el Qaddafi, interview with *Newsweek*, quoted in John Cooley, *Libyan Sandstorm: The Complete Account of Qaddafi's Revolution* (New York: Holt, Rinehart & Winston, 1982), p. 282.
13 See, for instance, McConnell, "Libya"; Claudia Wright, "Libya and the West: Headlong into Confrontation," *International Affairs*, Winter 1981–82.
14 *New York Times*, May 9, 1980.
15 McConnell, "Libya."
16 Jimmy Carter, *Keeping Faith: Memoirs of a President* (New York: Bantam Books, 1982), p. 548.
17 Quoted in Cooley, *Libyan Sandstorm*, p. 255.
18 *New York Times*, January 21, 1979.
19 Carter, *Keeping Faith*, p. 548.
20 Allen, "Libya," p. 46.
21 Quoted in ibid.
22 Newsom, statement before Senate Judiciary Committee, August 4, 1980, p. 61.
23 "Foreign Economic Trends and Their Implications for the U.S. and Libya,"

report prepared by the U.S. Embassy, Tripoli, January 1979, U.S. Department of
Commerce, pp. 9   11.
24   Carter, *Keeping Faith*, p. 546.

CHAPTER 9   LIBYA'S FOREIGN POLICY, 1981–1982

1   Foreign Broadcast Information Service (FBIS), daily report, Middle East and
    Africa, April 13, 1981.
2   Colin Legum, ed., *Africa Contemporary Record: Annual Survey and Documents*
    (New York: Africa Publishing Co., Holmes and Meier, 1969–82), vol. 14
    (1981–82), p. B-56.
3   FBIS, May 26, 1981.
4   FBIS, April 27, 1981.
5   Quoted in Legum, ed., *Africa Contemporary Record*, vol. 14 (1981–82) p. B-56.
6   Ibid., p. B-57.
7   Muammar el Qaddafi, speech in Algiers, FBIS, January 19, 1982.
8   FBIS, April 23, 1982.
9   Qaddafi, cable to the Arab heads of state, FBIS, July 1, 1982.
10 Ibid., p. Q-1.
11 Qaddafi, speech, September 1, 1982, FBIS, September 2, 1982, p. Q-1.
12 Ibid., p. Q-2.
13 Qaddafi, interview with *La Reppublica* (Rome), July 14, 1982, FBIS, July 20,
    1982.
14 Qaddafi, speech, third regular session of the Basic People's Congress, October 10,
    1982, FBIS, October 12, 1982, p. Q-2.
15 Legum, ed., *Africa Contemporary Record*, vol. 14 (1981–82), p. B-70.
16 Qaddafi, address to the People's Congress, March 2, 1982, FBIS, March 5, 1982,
    p. Q-2.
17 Az-Zaglar, speech at the G.P.C., January 3, 1982, FBIS, January 4, 1982, p. Q-1.
18 Qaddafi, speech, March 2, 1982, p. Q-3.
19 Qaddafi, speech at rally celebrating the Jamahiriya system, Tripoli Conference
    Center, March 2, 1982, FBIS, March 4, 1982, p. Q-5.
20 Qaddafi, speech, March 2, 1982.
21 This distinction was made clear by Qaddafi in an interview with the second TV
    channel in Rome in March 1981, FBIS, March 10, 1981.
22 Qaddafi, speech, September 1, 1981.
23 Legum, ed., *Africa Contemporary Record*, vol. 14 (1981–82), p. B-67.
24 John K. Cooley, *Libyan Sandstorm: The Complete Account of Qaddafi's Revolu-
    tion* (New York: Holt, Rinehart & Winston, 1981), p. 200.
25 Ibid.
26 Ibid.
27 Quoted in ibid., p. 203.
28 Raymond W. Copson, *Libya: U.S. Relations*, issue brief no. IB81152, Foreign
    Affairs and National Defense Division (Washington, D.C.: Congressional Re-
    search Service, 1982).

29 Ibid., p. 18.
30 Qaddafi, interview with ABC news, December 6, 1981.
31 Libyan justice secretary, statement to Agence France Presse, FBIS, February 22, 1981.
32 Legum, ed., *Africa Contemporary Record,* vol. 14 (1981–82), p. B-64.
33 Qaddafi, interview with *Al-Watan* (Kuwait), April 29, 1981, FBIS, May 4, 1981, p. Q-4.
34 Ibid.
35 Ronald Bruce St. John, "The Soviet Penetration of Libya." *World Today* 38 (April 1982), 127.
36 Qaddafi, speech, September 1, 1981.
37 *Le Monde,* September 8, 1981, FBIS, September 10, 1981.
38 FBIS, January 19, 1982.
39 Qaddafi, interview with *Time,* June 8, 1981, p. 31.
40 Qaddafi, interview with *La Reppublica,* p. Q-6.
41 St. John, "The Soviet Penetration of Libya," p. 138.
42 Qaddafi, letter to Ronald Reagan, FBIS, January 27, 1981.
43 Qaddafi, speech, FBIS, January 21, 1981.
44 FBIS, April 20, 1981.
45 Qaddafi, statement in FBIS, May 14, 1981.
46 Abdulsalam Jallud, interview in *Al-Qabas* (Kuwait), FBIS, May 7, 1981.
47 Qaddafi, message to Arab heads of state, July 19, 1981, FBIS, July 20, 1981.
48 *Jana* (Tripoli), FBIS, August 14, 1981, p. Q-1.
49 Legum, ed., *Africa Contemporary Record,* vol. 14 (1981–82), p. B-62.
50 Ibid., p. B-63.
51 Qaddafi, speech, September 1, 1981, p. Q-9.
52 Ibid., p. Q-8.
53 *Jana* (Tripoli), February 3, 1981, FBIS, February 4, 1982.
54 FBIS, March 12, 1982.
55 FBIS, March 10, 1982.
56 FBIS, March 19, 1982.
57 Qaddafi, interview with *La Reppublica.*
58 Qaddafi, interview with a delegation of Austrian political scientists, Tripoli, FBIS, June 23, 1982, p. Q-3.

CHAPTER 10   THE U.S. IMAGE OF LIBYA, 1981–1982

1 Christopher Coker, "Reagan and Africa," *World Today* 38 (April 1982), 123.
2 *New York Times,* January 18, 1981.
3 Alexander Haig, interview with *Newsweek,* October 29, 1981, *Department of State Bulletin,* December 1981.
4 Aaron Segal, "The United States and North Africa," *Current History* 80 (December 1981), 401.
5 Coker, "Reagan and Africa," p. 126.
6 *New York Times,* March 5, 1981.

7   H.M.L. Beri, "Libya-U.S. Relations," *Strategic Analysis*, January 1981, p. 554.
8   Chester Crocker, statement before the Subcommittee on African Affairs and the Subcommittee on Near Eastern and South Asian Affairs, Committee on Foreign Relations, U.S. Senate, 97th Cong., 1st sess., July 8, 1981, *Department of State Bulletin* (October 1981).
9   *Time*, October 19, 1981, p. 28.
10 *New York Daily News*, December 12, 1981.
11 *Washington Post*, March 21, 1981, p. A-3.
12 FBIS, March 31, 1981.
13 Kamal Hasan Ali, Egyptian minister of defense, interview with *Al-Majallah*, April 24, 1981.
14 Jeff McConnell, "Libya: Propaganda and Covert Operations," *Counterspy*, November 1981–January 1982, p. 32.
15 *New York Times*, November 28, 1981.
16 *Congressional Quarterly Weekly Report*, March 13, 1982.
17 Ibid.
18 McConnell, "Libya," p. 32.
19 Ibid.
20 Quoted in Beri, "Libya-U.S. Relations," p. 553.
21 Quoted in Louis Eaks, "America's Plan to Destabilize Libya," in *Libya: Terrorist or Terrorized*, ed. Cecil Blake and Saleh Abu-Osba (Canada: Jerusalem International Publishing House, 1982).
22 *New York Times*, May 23, 1981.
23 Quoted in Eaks, "America's Plan."
24 Crocker, statement before Senate Foreign Relations Committee, July 8, 1981.
25 *New York Times*, November 3, 1981.
26 "Libya: What Kind of Target," *Africa News*, May 25, 1981, p. 7.
27 "Pattern of International Terrorism 1980," CIA National Foreign Assessment Center, quoted in Claudia Wright, "Libya and the West: Headlong into Confrontation," *International Affairs*, Winter 1981–82.
28 *Africa News*, May 25, 1981, p. 8.
29 *New Statesman*, August 21, 1981, p. 16, quoted in McConnell, "Libya," p. 33.
30 *Africa News*, May 15, 1981, p. 11.
31 *Department of State Bulletin* 82 (January 1982), 62.
32 Quoted in Blake and Abu-Osba, eds., *Libya Terrorist or Terrorized*, p. 66.
33 *Congressional Quarterly Weekly Report*, April 3, 1982.
34 This view is held by such scholars as Lisa Anderson and M. Hudson, and observers such as Jeff McConnell, Y. Shadyac, Ned Temko, and Claudia Wright.
35 *U.S. News and World Report*, May 18, 1981.
36 *Africa News*, May 25, 1981.
37 *New York Times*, November 28, 1981.
38 Crocker, statement before Senate Foreign Relations Committee, July 8, 1981.
39 Chester Crocker, statement before the Subcommittee on Africa, Foreign Affairs Committee, U.S. House of Representatives, November 4, 1981, *Department of State Bulletin*, January 1981.

40 Kenneth Adelman, speech before the UN General Assembly, October 9, 1981, *Department of State Bulletin,* January 1982.
41 Crocker, statement before Senate Foreign Relations Committee, July 8, 1981.
42 *Congressional Quarterly Weekly Report,* April 3, 1981.
43 Beri, "Libya-U.S. Relations," p. 533.
44 Haig, interview with *Newsweek,* p. 28.
45 This usage is also used by the press, which indicates a general American consensus that Libya's foreign policy is the sole responsibility of the Libyan leader.
46 Haig, interview with *Newsweek.*

CHAPTER 11   U.S. POLICY TOWARD LIBYA, 1981-1982

1 *Washington Post,* August 20, 1981.
2 Ibid.
3 Jeff McConnell, "Libya: Propaganda and Covert Operations," *Counterspy,* November 1981–January 1982, p. 313; *New York Daily News,* May 17, 1981; also quoted in John Wright, *Libya: A Modern History* (Baltimore, Md.: Johns Hopkins University Press, 1981), p. 17.
4 *Wall Street Journal,* July 14, 1981.
5 *New York Times,* December 16, 1981.
6 *Department of State Bulletin,* June 1981.
7 *New York Times,* June 13, 1981.
8 Andrew Young, statement in *Foreign Affairs* 59 (1981), 664, quoted in McConnell, "Libya," p. 32.
9 William D. Brewer, "The Libyan-Sudanese 'Crisis' of 1981: Danger for Daifur and Dilemma for the U.S.," *Middle East Journal,* Spring 1982, p. 212.
10 Chester Crocker, statement before the Baltimore Council on Foreign Relations, October 28, 1982, *Department of State Bulletin,* December 1982.
11 Ibid.
12 Wright, *Libya,* p. 13.
13 Alexander Haig, *New York Times,* June 12, 1981.
14 *Newsweek,* November 30, 1981.
15 Wright, *Libya,* p. 14.
16 The administration's statement was made on December 10, 1981, by William Clark, acting secretary of state, *Department of State Bulletin,* January 1982, p. 46.
17 Exxon announced that it had terminated all its operations in Libya as early as November 1981, while others such as Mobil did not terminate its contracts until summer 1982.
18 Wright, *Libya,* p. 14.
19 *Congressional Quarterly Weekly Report* 40 (March 13, 1982).
20 FBIS, May 11, 1983.
21 Lisa Anderson, "Ignore Qaddafi," *New York Times,* December 17, 1981.
22 *New York Times,* December 12, 1981.
23 Ibid.
24 Ibid.

25 Wright, *Libya*, p. 15.
26 John Cooley, "Qaddafi's Nervous Neighbor," *Middle East International*, September 4, 1981.
27 *Washington Post*, August 20, 1981.
28 Wright, *Libya*, p. 15.
29 Ronald Reagan, question and answer session on the downing of two Libyan jets, August 20, 1981.
30 Alexander Haig, interview with CBS News, August 19, 1981.
31 Caspar Weinberger, news briefing, August 19, 1981, *Department of State Bulletin*, October 1981, p. 57.
32 *New York Times*, June 3, 1981.
33 Ibid.
34 Jay Peterzell, "Reagan's Covert Action Policy (III)," *First Principles*, Center for National Security Studies, March 1982.
35 *Washington Post*, August 20, 1981.
36 Claudia Wright, *New Statesman*, August 10, 1982, quoted in McConnell, "Libya," p. 32.
37 *New York Post*, December 14, 1981.
38 *New York Times*, February 5, 1982.
39 Wright, *Libya*, p. 16.
40 Quoted in ibid.
41 *Newsweek*, August 3, 1981.
42 See Peterzell, "Reagan's Covert Action Policy," p. 2; Mcconnell, "Libya."
43 Phile Kelly, *The Middle East*, August 1981, quoted in McConnell, "Libya," p. 34.
44 McConnell, "Libya," p. 34.
45 Quoted in ibid., p. 35.
46 Peterzell, "Reagan's Covert Action Policy," p. 4.
47 *Newsweek*, July 27, 1981.
48 McConnell, "Libya," p. 36.
49 *Christian Science Monitor*, December 10, 1981.
50 Wright, *Libya*, p. 18.
51 *New York Times*, December 17, 1981.
52 Michael Hudson, "The Politics: Middle East 'Western,' " *Washington Post*, December 13, 1981.

CONCLUSION

1 Lisa Anderson, "Libya and American Foreign Policy," *Middle East Journal* 36 (Autumn 1982), 521.
2 Robert Jervis, *Perception and Misperception in International Politics* (Princeton, N.J.: Princeton University Press, 1976), p. 205.
3 Quoted in Jeff McConnell, "Libya: Propaganda and Covert Operations," *Counterspy*, November 1981–January 1982, p. 26.
4 Ibid., p. 25.

5 State Department, "North Africa in the Mediterranean Littoral," August 9, 1963, quoted in ibid., p. 28.

EPILOGUE

1 *Department of State Bulletin,* March 1986, p. 36.
2 *Time,* January 13, 1986.
3 Qaddafi, press conference with Western news media, *Time,* January 20, 1986, p. 27.
4 *Time,* February 3, 1986, p. 24.
5 Statement by CIA official, quoted in *Time,* April 7, 1986.
6 Ibid., p. 13.
7 Ronald Reagan, address before the American Bar Association, July 8, 1985, *Department of State Bulletin,* August 1985, p. 8.
8 Chester Crocker, address before the World Affairs Council, November 1985, *Department of State Bulletin,* January 1986, p. 29.
9 See, for example, the statement made by Secretary of State George Shulz on "Face the Nation," April 17, 1986, *Department of State Bulletin,* June 1986, p. 17.
10 *Time,* March 31, 1986, p. 7.
11 Ibid., p. 4.
12 *Department of State Bulletin,* June 1986.
13 Reagan, address before the ABA, p. 7.
14 U.S. Central Intelligence Agency, *International Energy Situation,* U.S. Office of Economic Research, Development Analysis Center, 1978.
15 U.S. Congress, House Committee on Foreign Affairs, "U.S. Security Interest in the Persian Gulf," report of a staff study mission to the Middle East and Horn of Africa, Oct. 21–Nov. 13, 1980 (Washington, D.C.: GPO, 1981).
16 John M. Poindexter, Memorandum for the President, January 17, 1986; quoted in *Al-Ahram,* January 11, 1987.
17 Ibid.

INDEX

Abelson, Robert, 3, 5, 21, 156
Adelman, Kenneth, 163
Affiliate with the enemy: definition of, 16–17; as image pattern, 14, 22; as U.S. image of Libya, 83, 84
Afghanistan, 104, 121, 123, 148, 155, 180, 192
Agitator: definition of, 17–18; as image pattern, 22, 25; as U.S. image of Libya, 83, 84, 125, 132
Alexander, Nathan, 69
Al-Fatah, 46, 47, 59
Al-Gamassi, General, 49
Algeria, 54, 79, 139
Al-Huni, 177
Ali, Mohammed, 109
Al-Jihad fund, 47
Alliance, as policy pattern, 29–30
Ally: and alliance policy pattern, 29–30; definition of, 18–19; as image pattern, 22
Al-Sanussi, Abdullah Abid, 87–88
Al-Shalhi, Omar, 87
Amerada Oil Company, 53, 54, 56
American Jewish Congress, 131
American Overseas Petroleum Company, 57
Amin, Idi, 70
Amoseas Oil Company, 54
Anderson, Jack, 159
Anderson, Lisa, 172, 178, 182
Angola, 145, 154, 190

Antagonism: as policy pattern, 25–27; as U.S. policy toward Libya, 107
Anticommunism, Libyan, 75–77
Arab-American People-to-People Dialogue Conference, Tripoli, 1978, 72, 107–08, 109–10
Arab-Israeli conflict: as central to Libya's foreign policy, 45–51, 78, 97–101, 139–42, 150; as factor in U.S. image of Libya, 77, 79, 82, 117–18, 122, 123, 185; as factor in U.S. policy toward Libya, 89, 129; and U.S.-Soviet relations, 115, 120. *See also* Camp David Accords
Arab Joint Defense Council, 141
Arab League, 99, 140
Arab Socialist Union (ASU), 60; First National Congress of, 1972, 69
Arab Summit meeting: in Algiers, 1973, 58; in Baghdad, 1978, 100; in Fez, 1982, 142
Arab unity, 44, 45, 67–68, 139–40, 145
Arafat, Yasir, 47, 101, 142
Atherton, Alfred L., Jr., 118
Atkins, James E., 80
Austria, 169
Axelrod, Robert, 4

Baader-Meinhof gang, 71
Baghdad Pact, 74
Begin, Menachem, 120

PITT SERIES IN POLICY AND INSTITUTIONAL STUDIES

Bert A. Rockman, Editor